Woodworker's Essential Shop Aids & Jigs

Original Devices You Can Make

Jeff Jammer 93

Woodworker's Essential Shop Aids & Jigs

Original Devices You Can Make

ROBERT WEARING

Sterling Publishing Company, Inc.   New York

Library of Congress Cataloging-in-Publication Data

Wearing, Robert.
  [Resourceful woodworker]
  Woodworker's essential shop aids & jigs : original devices you can
make / Robert Wearing.
     p.   cm.
  Originally published: The resourceful woodworker. Great Britain :
B. T. Batsford, 1991.
  Includes index.
  ISBN 0–8069–8584–4
  1. Woodworking tools. 2. Woodworker – Equipment and supplies – Design
and construction. I. Title.
TT186.W43   1992
684′.08′028—dc20

                                91–35985
                                 CIP

10 9 8 7 6 5 4 3

Published in 1992 by Sterling Publishing Company, Inc.
387 Park Avenue South, New York, N.Y. 10016
Originally published in Great Britain by B. T. Batsford, Ltd
as *The Resourceful Woodworker: Tools, techniques and tricks of the trade*
© 1991 by Robert Wearing
Distributed in Canada by Sterling Publishing
c/o Canadian Manda Group, P.O.Box 920, Station U
Toronto, Ontario, Canada M8Z 5P9
Printed and Bound in Great Britain
All rights reserved.

Sterling ISBN 0–8069–8584–4

Contents

Contents

Introduction

Jigs, tools, aids, devices, fixtures, gadgets

These are all terms for ways and means of doing things other than by straightforward tool use. A jig is a technical term to an engineer. Gadget is a rather belittling term. Here the terms will be used indiscriminately and non-specifically.

The ideas presented have been developed for a number of reasons. Often they guarantee more accuracy than does general handwork, so are particularly useful to workers who have not yet acquired the higher skills. Some will speed up production by eliminating slow, high skill handwork. Others are useful when a number of identical items is required. Some traditional handmade joints have been mechanized and some completely machine-made joints have been introduced. All can be produced with devices which are quite simple when compared with the expensive machinery designed solely for that purpose.

In the minds of some workers there is the belief that 'the old men' preferred to do all their work entirely by hand and that the artist craftsmen of the Arts and Crafts Movement were machine haters. These ideas are proved to be quite untrue when it is considered what power sources, other than muscles, were available to them. These were either the water-wheel or the steam-engine, both suited only to a large scale operation. Had the fractional horsepower electric motor existed, there is no doubt that they would have used it. The availability of light and portable woodworking machinery plus the increasing provision of home garages and workshops have totally transformed the working methods of the keen amateur and the small professional. I have considered as normal, there-fore, the use of such machinery, though it is by no means essential for every example given.

As far as tool-making is concerned, it is not the intention that the reader be encouraged to make most of the tools in the standard kit. Many are quite beyond the hand worker and others are economically not worth while. Those which are featured are either original tools, improvements on commercially available tools or re-creations of useful tools now no longer manufactured. The distinction between tool, appliance equipment etc is a fine one, so the reader should expect what he considers a tool to be in another section. The comprehensive index should clarify the position.

It cannot be claimed that all these devices are original. Over the years, many craftsmen must have produced similar solutions to the same problem and no doubt many readers will carry some of these ideas a stage further or modify them for additional purposes.

Exact species of timber are not required unless specifically stated. Similarly many of the sizes are merely suggestions. If a particular size is important, this is mentioned. Imperial/metric conversions are made to the nearest round number. Where it is important, exact conversions are given.

Where there is a slight difference between a photograph and a drawing, the latter can be taken to be an improvement.

Many of these ideas were originally published in an edited form in the magazine *Woodworker*, whose editor has kindly agreed to their re-use.

Drawings and photographs are by the author.

SECTION 1 Holding and Cramping

The Workbench

There can be few topics on which woodworkers will disagree more strongly than the design of the workbench. However for the worker who has not yet come to a strongly held opinion, Fig. 1 shows a design which well fulfils the needs of most serious amateurs and also professional craftsmen. It is designed primarily for cabinet making, hence there is no front apron, a feature which, though beloved of carpenters and joiners, makes the cramping of the workpiece to the bench virtually impossible.

The construction is simple yet robust, so the beginner should find no difficulty in making it or having it made. The vice is fitted for a right-handed worker. Left-handers will need the mirror image of the drawing. While giving ample working space, the bench can, with the vice removed, pass comfortably through the average doorway. Sizes are in the main, suggestions. Height however is an individual decision. A low bench will cause the backache some readers may have experienced when working at an evening class on a school-sized bench. On the other hand, a high bench restricts planing by making it difficult to apply strong downward pressure on the plane. Experiment on an existing bench, packing up the legs or standing on a raised plank, until the most comfortable situation has been achieved.

The underframing is best made in a good hardwood but where expense must be considered, good quality softwood will probably outlast the reader. Mortice and tenon joints have been used throughout. The mortices are chopped through, an easier process than chopping stopped mortices, and the tenons are wedged, Figs 2 &

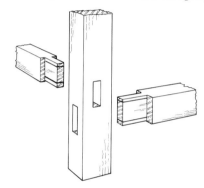

Fig. 2 Details of lower joint

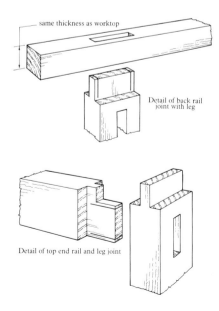

same thickness as worktop

Detail of back rail joint with leg

Detail of top end rail and leg joint

Fig. 3

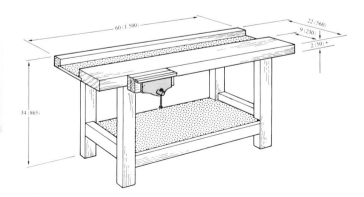

60 (1.500)

22 (560)
9 (230)
2 (50) +

34 (865)

Fig. 1 Suggested workbench

9

3. This gives a very rigid structure. The tenons through the bench top are stopped short and a long-grain filler piece is inserted, Fig. 4. This prevents the tenon standing proud as the top shrinks. The top is further fixed to the top cross rail by a coach bolt with washer. This operates through a slot in the rail in order to cope with possible shrinkage of the top, Fig. 5.

Ideally the top should be made from well seasoned hardwood. Alternatively hardwood strips of say 2 in (50 mm) width may be glued together, (assuming that sufficient sash cramps can be collected) then the assemble top can be cleaned up prior to letting out for machine facing and thicknessing. Softwood is rather a poor substitute. Another possibility is to glue together layers of plywood, blockboard, chipboard or MDF (medium density fibreboard). Glue up on a really flat

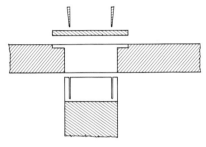

Fig. 4   Section of leg joint into worktop showing wedges and filler piece

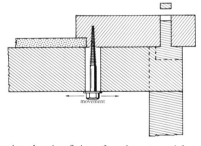

Fig. 5   Section showing fixing of worktop to end frame

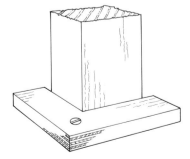

Fig. 6   Floor blocks to prevent movement of bench

surface weighing down with buckets of water or any other available heavy weights. Where such a built up top is used, surface it with a sheet of hardboard which can be renewed and add thin, solid wood edges.

It is not essential to chop a hole for the traditional planing stop. Better methods of holding for planing are described later.

Fit the shelf from any of the man-made materials. This provides convenient storage, the weight of which adds to the stability of the bench. Do not make the well board from softwood. Over a number of years the surface of this flakes giving the risk of splinters under the finger nails when picking out tools from the well. Ply, blockboard or chipboard are preferable.

Movement of the bench when working, can be prevented if necessary, by screwing to the floor two L-shaped pieces of thick ply. Fit these to the inside faces of two diametrically opposite legs, Fig. 6.

A Planing Grip System
Figs 7 to 10

New systems to hold work for planing appear at intervals though most do not last long. This is a version of a well tried system that holds most work firmly and is easy to install.

Start by grooving the edges of the bench top to take $\frac{3}{4} \times \frac{1}{8}$ or $\frac{3}{16}$ in (20×5 or 6 mm) drilled mild steel strips. This is most easily done by plough plane or by machinery before the top has been fitted. When a top is already fixed, a router with a slotting cutter will do the job.

Prepare the metal strip by marking out and centre punching for the holes at 2 in (50 mm) intervals and for the screw holes at 6 in (150 mm) intervals. Drill the hole at each end and bolt the two strips together. Now drill all the other holes and countersink the screw holes. At first screw in only the strip on the far side. On the front side cut out a portion the width of the wooden vice jaws. Do not screw on the front strips until the planing stop has been made. This is fitted in place then tested for square with the bench edge. Only then are the front strips screwed permanently in place.

For the planing stop, prepare a piece of $1 \times \frac{1}{4}$ in (25×6 mm) bright mild steel a little over the bench top width plus 1 in (25 mm). Drill two $\frac{3}{16}$ in (5 mm) holes for the rivets and two for woodscrews. Well countersink the latter on the underside and lightly countersink the rivet holes on the top surface. Cut the two side arms to length and braze or silver solder on the two pegs of $\frac{1}{4}$ in (6 mm) dia. rod. Be sure to make a left- and a right-handed version. Drill, countersink then rivet on the side arms. Note that the inside arm is riveted tightly

Fig. 7 Workbench holding method showing vice peg and stop bar

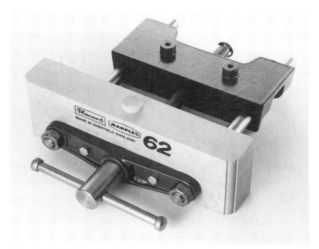

Fig. 8 The Record tail vice

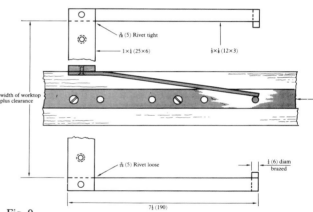

Fig. 9

while the outer one is left free to move stiffly. Grip each end in turn in the vice and tap the side arms into a bend which will allow the planing stop to sit snugly on the bench top when the pegs are in their holes.

The moving end of the grip is provided by an end vice. Here there are two possibilities. One is to buy the recently designed end tail vice by Record Tools, Fig. 8. The second is to modify a normal vice for that purpose. Quite a modest, inexpensive vice will serve for this purpose.

Fit the vice to the bench end in the normal way then prepare an extra thick wood jaw. Cut the housing centrally in the jaw then screw in place. If preferred, extra wood strips may be glued on to come up to the thickness of the metal jaw. A normal, thinner wood jaw is fitted to the fixed jaw of the vice and filler strips glued in to fill any gaps.

Make the little pressure plate from a scrap of $\frac{1}{16}$ in (1.5 mm) mild steel or brass then plane the gripping 'dog' from dense hardwood to be a sliding fit when the pressure plate is in position. The purpose of this plate is simply to prevent the screw from chewing up the dog.

Obtain a $\frac{1}{4}$ in (6 mm) thumb screw or solder a wing nut onto a piece of screwed rod. Drill and tap the

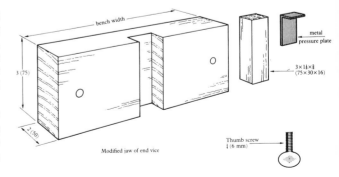

Fig. 10

11

movable jaw of the vice to take this screw. A 5 mm drill is suitable for both these threads.

In use, keep the dog slightly below the surface of the wood being planed. To hold circular or shaped work, screw a similarly shaped wood block to the metal planing stop using the screw holes provided.

NB. Make sure that the vice with its wood jaws in place will open a greater distance than the hole spacing on the metal edge strip.

Vice Jaws

The common bench vice can be rendered much more versatile when adapted to accept extra removable jaws.

First consider the basic wooden jaws themselves. If the fixed jaw is let in flush with the bench edge, it is argued that panels, ply sheets and long boards can be more conveniently gripped. This is partly true. When worn however, replacing it perfectly in line with the bench edge is a very precise and time-consuming operation. Such a flush jaw cannot hold any removable jaw.

A standing out fixed jaw is easy to fit, can still cope with gripping long boards etc (see page 14), and can grip a sash cramp which, in its turn, grips tapered, cylindrical or shaped work by the ends. More importantly, it will accept any number of removable jaws, which, unlike packing pieces, open and close with the vice.

The basic wooden jaws will need minor modification. Cut a small rebate at each end. It is convenient at this stage to add to the moving jaw a routing strip, which is just wider than the thickness of the metal jaw. Glue on a strip a little wider than is required, then with the jaw screwed in place, run the router along it with its fence against the inside of the jaw, thus making the outer edge of the strip truly parallel with the inside face of the jaw, Fig. 12.

All the removable jaws are built on the same foundation of $\frac{1}{2}$ in (13 mm) plywood having a rebated (or built up) strip at each end, making an easy sliding fit over the rebated ends of the jaws, Fig. 13.

The reader will obviously devise jaws for his own particular purposes, but amongst the more common, the following are suggested as being particularly useful:

Carpet lined jaws for gripping finished or polished work, Fig. 14. Do not use foam backed carpet. The foam is difficult to glue and also perishes.

Taper jaws (one only) to hold items like tapered chair legs for planing and finishing, Fig. 15.

Vee groove jaws. For holding cylinders one of these jaws is enough. Two are required to hold square stock as when chamfering or planing octagons, Fig. 16.

Round work jaws. Turners and workers with rounders will find these jaws useful to hold work vertical. The two strips can be cramped together for boring, producing a precise grip. Two vee cuts will grip a range of sizes though perhaps with some risk of bruising. The cut-outs in these jaws should be sited clear of the vice slide bars so that long components may be gripped, see Fig. 17.

Fig. 12 Fixed vice jaw with routing strip

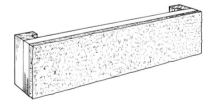

Fig. 14 Carpet faced jaw for polished work

Fig. 16 Vee groove jaws for cylinders etc

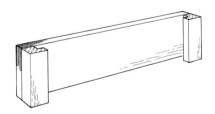

Fig. 13 Basic auxiliary jaw

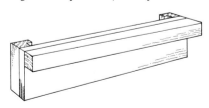

Fig. 15 Jaw to grip tapers

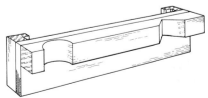

Fig. 17 Round work jaws

A Planing Stop

The old fashioned bench planing stop, consisting of a square block rising in a mortice, is not the most effective. Plywood permits a more successful model.

A solid wood block of say $8 \times 3 \times \frac{7}{8}$ in $(200 \times 75 \times 22$ mm) is held in the vice. A plywood strip, long enough to span the workboard of the bench, is glued (and screwed if preferred) to this. Make several such stops of different thicknesses, Fig. 18.

Before jointing, angle the top of the vice piece very, very slightly, Fig. 19. Now when the vice is tightened, the plywood strip is forced very firmly down onto the bench face.

Fig. 20

Fig. 18

Fig. 19

Fig. 21

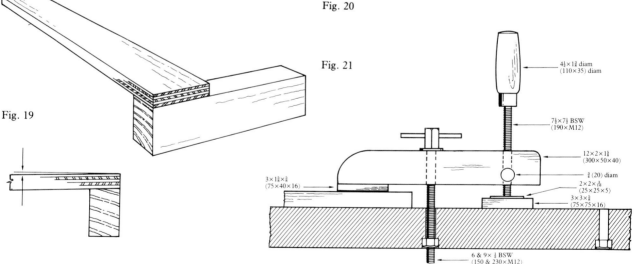

The Bench Holdfast

This highly successful holdfast, economical and easy to make, requires neither the large holes of the continental type bench nor the large metal inserts of the commercial holdfast. Fig. 20.

Prepare the hardwood block to the suggested sizes. While still parallel drill a $\frac{3}{4}$ in (20 mm) hole for the cylindrical nut. Note that this is not drilled centrally. Drill holes for the two screws slightly bigger than the nominal size to give a sloppy fit. Glue on the foot then shape the ends. The foot can be given a rubber facing (made from a piece of car inner tube) stuck on with a contact adhesive, Fig. 21.

The small amount of metalwork is quite straightforward. Saw out then file up or turn the cylindrical nut, in length a little less than the block thickness. Drill this centrally, preferably in a machine, using a drilling vice. First put through a small pilot hole, then increase, finishing with the appropriate tapping drill. For $\frac{1}{2}$ in BSW this is 10·5 mm, for 12 mm it is 10 mm.

Cut the screwed rods to length; $1\frac{1}{2}$ in (40 mm) goes into the handle. The end of the pressure screw is drilled at $\frac{1}{8}$ in (3 mm) then turned or filed down to $\frac{5}{16}$ in (8 mm). Make the metal plate for the pressure foot. Drill it centrally at $\frac{5}{16}$ in (8 mm) and countersink the under side. Drill four small screw holes and countersink on the upper side. The plate is loose riveted to the pressure screw. Spread the end to secure by driving a large centre punch into the hole. Drill a suitable cavity in the wooden pressure foot then screw the parts together (see page 156).

Turn the handle, fit the ferrule and before parting off, drill and tap. A bench-made handle, say octagonal, is equally suitable. Screw through the nut and attach the handle.

The head of the clamping screw can be made from either hexagon or round bar. Tap the bar, screw together then drill for a $\frac{1}{4}$ in (6 mm) tommy bar. Insert the bar then silver solder or braze the three pieces together. Clean off the scale and thread on an appropriate washer.

Now prepare the bench top. Mark several hole positions underneath and drill cavities for the hexagon nuts. A $\frac{1}{2}$ in nut requires a hole of $\frac{13}{16}$ in, a 12 mm nut, $\frac{3}{4}$ in (20 mm). Wood bits in these large metric sizes are still rare. Continue the holes through at $\frac{1}{2}$ in. With a long bolt and washer, pull the nuts tightly up into their cavities. Fit each hole with a piece of dowelling. The nut stops it from falling through. A pencil from below easily removes it when required.

Make a test cramping on some scrap wood. Aim to keep the block horizontal. In this position the handle can be forced on until it can no longer be turned. There is no pressure when unscrewing so the handle will not come loose. A second, longer clamping screw enables thicker jobs to be handled. Several coats of varnish will keep the holdfast looking smart.

A simpler but less perfect method for the pressure nut screw is described on page 155.

Long Board Holder

The holding in the vice of a long board for edge planing presents a problem, particularly so in the case of a thin board. Several solutions have been put forward, generally the work being supported by a peg into holes drilled in the leg. This method is a considerable improvement, Fig. 22.

There are two models, according to whether the fixed jaw of the vice is outstanding, see page 12, or flush. Preference has already been stated for the former. Prepare the two jaws from hardwood. In the case of the former the fixed jaw must be of the same thickness as the fixed jaw of the bench vice, Fig. 23.

Cramp both jaws together and drill through using the tapping size drill. Separate then tap the fixed jaw. On the moving jaw the hole is enlarged and extended in length to accept the screw with an easy fit. Now glue on a small tapered block of about 1 in (25 mm) at its thickest. This should cope with most of the work expected. Let in and fix a strong steel butt hinge. Screw into the fixed jaw either a piece of screwed rod or a roofing bolt. The latter should be threaded for its entire length.

Prepare and glue on the cramping piece, overhanging, say, 2 in (50 mm) at the hinge end for the G cramp which will hold the job to the bench.

A wing nut will do for the gripping, at a pinch, but it is better to drill a piece of steel bar and braze in a tommy bar. Then drill and tap for the screw. Naturally a lathe helps but the job can be done successfully without.

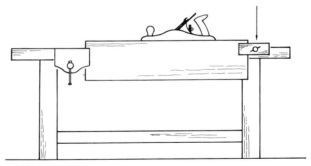

Fig. 22   The long board holder in use

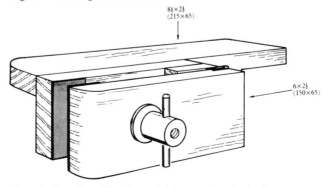

Fig. 23   Long board holder model for use with vice having outstanding jaw

Fit this nut and a large washer. Line the jaws with rubber, such as a piece from a car inner tube. Stick this on with an impact glue.

A refinement is to very slightly curve the gripping face of the moving jaw. This avoids gripping thin wood with the very tip of the jaw.

When the vice has a flush jaw the design is modified to suit, Fig. 24. Note that it is not merely a matter of turning the job over. The cramping piece is now fixed to the bottom of the fixed jaw. The G cramp then holds the fixed jaw flush with the bench edge.

The method of use, of course, is obvious.

Fig. 24 Long board holder model for use with vice having flush jaw

Boomerang Planing Grip

This planing grip device can quickly and easily be fitted to any bench at no cost.

About level with the corner of the vice, drill a series of very shallow $\frac{1}{4}$ in (6 mm) holes, say $1\frac{1}{2}$ in (40 mm) apart. Drill into these with a $\frac{1}{8}$ in (3 mm) drill, forming the pilot holes for 12 gauge screws. The larger holes keep the top free from any raised burrs after screws have been withdrawn.

Prepare several 'boomerangs' from plywood of various thicknesses. An arm length of $4\frac{1}{2}$ in (100 mm) is suggested but this is by no means critical. Drill at $\frac{1}{4}$ in (6 mm) and countersink.

Now grip a short board in the vice, protruding just less than the thickness of the workpiece.

Position the workpiece against this and screw the boomerang in place using a 12 gauge countersunk woodscrew into the most convenient of the prepared screw holes as Fig. 25 shows.

On commencing planing, the work is forced against the boomerang which turns and grips the work firmly. A light tap on the far end releases the work.

Planing and Gripping Tapers

Tapers are in most cases planed from the thick end to the thin. Planing one taper presents no problem since the work can be held in the vice. But more commonly, as in the case of legs, the taper is to be planed on two or four sides.

When a number of tapers is to be planed, it is worth making a special vice jaw, see page 12, where an identical taper has been fitted to the jaw.

The planing grip described on page 11 is another excellent method of holding tapers of all sizes.

This device, Figs 26 & 27, was produced originally to hold tapered chair legs for planing on the bench top.

First prepare a $\frac{1}{2}$ in (12 mm) plywood strip to be gripped in the vice. Plane the two top pieces of hardwood to thickness, about $\frac{3}{4}$ in (20 mm). Cut and clean up the shape on one, then glue together and plane off flush. Finally glue this component to the plywood strip.

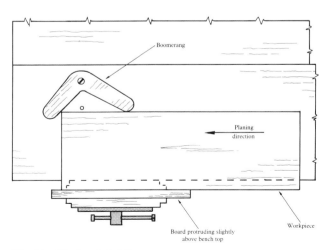

Fig. 25 The bench holdfast

Fig. 26 Gripping and planing a taper in the jig

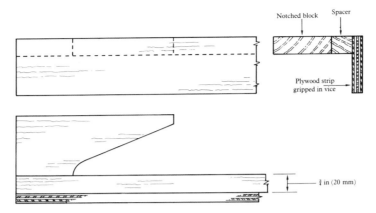

Fig. 27

The act of planing grips the piece quite firmly in the notch. In cases where the inner jaw of the vice stands out from the benchtop, make sure that the straight hardwood strip is a little wider than the jaw thickness, in order that the workpiece is settled on a good base.

A Holding Device to Plane Small and Thin Components

Fig. 28

Small components are a gripping problem merely because of their size.

Thin strips will buckle when planed against a stop, so it makes sense to grip them at the starting end so that they are in tension throughout the stroke.

Sizes are quite unimportant. Use what material is to hand. A $\frac{3}{8}$ in or $\frac{5}{16}$ in (8 or 10 mm) thread is most convenient and is readily available, Fig. 29.

Prepare two hardwood blocks to size and carefully mark out the hole centres. In the fixed jaw, counterbore the central hole $\frac{5}{8}$ in (16 mm) and draw in a nut. Appendix 4. Drill the end hole for tapping, $\frac{5}{16}$ in (8 mm). Drill the moving jaw for the screws to be an easy fit.

Turn and fit a handle, planing two flats to improve the grip. Cut the two screwed rods to size, clean up the ends and fit in place with nuts and washers. Close the jaws and skim the sides level if necessary. Now separate the jaws and take just a few shavings from the moving jaw. This is so that when the fixed jaw is gripped in the vice, the moving jaw is just free to move.

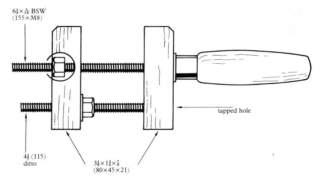

Fig. 29

Fig. 28   Holding small components for planing. The appliance

Fig. 30   Holding small components
Short thin piece held in the bench vice

Grip the workpiece just clear of the top surface and tighten well. Drop the device into the vice and grip it firmly, Fig. 30. A tail vice is handy for longer pieces, Fig. 31, but if this is not available work across the bench, the work being supported on a piece of ply or chipboard.

Fig. 32a   Traditional all wood handscrew

Fig. 31   Holding small components
Gripping a thin strip with an end vice

Cramps

There can be few readers who enjoy buying cramps. Unlike some other tools they do not make anything. Nevertheless, they are essential. Generally they are bought and used as four of a size. The major disadvantage is that good iron G cramps are very expensive for what they do, and since four are required, that cost is multiplied four-fold. Apart from the cost, iron G cramps have another disadvantage. They can easily damage the work; consequently wood blocks must be used to prevent this. Juggling these while the glue sets can be a problem for the single-handed worker. The G cramp with its swivelling foot cannot give that light nip at the very tip as can many of the cramps illustrated later. Though obviously G cramps have very great strength, it should be remembered that good joints require only to be pulled, not crushed together.

The simple handscrew

This derives directly from the traditional wooden handscrew, Fig. 32, and from the metalworkers' 'Toolmakers' clamp'. In addition to the advantages already

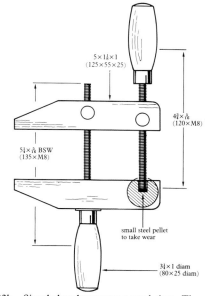

Fig. 32b   Simple handscrew suggested sizes. These may be increased using larger diam screwed rod

stated, the handscrew can grip in a depression or confined space, particularly useful in repair work. A variety of sizes is possible using threads of $\frac{5}{16}$ in (8 mm) or $\frac{3}{8}$ in (10 mm). The positions of the screw holes in relation to the sizes of block is shown in Fig. 33A&B.

Prepare a piece of dense hardwood for the jaws. This should be just over twice the jaw length and planed to the finished width and thickness. Saw to produce the two jaws and square one end of each by shooting board or disc sander. Cramp together and mark the centre lines for the holes. Separate and square the lines onto all four faces. On one jaw gauge the centres for the cylindrical nuts. Note the positions of these centres. They are not central in the jaws. Drill these holes using a sawtooth, dowel or lip and spur bit. The engineers'

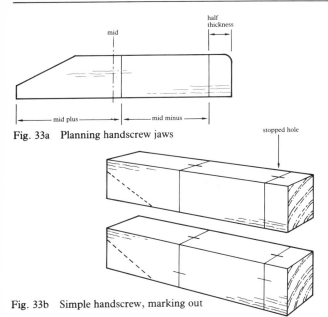

Fig. 33a   Planning handscrew jaws

Fig. 33b   Simple handscrew, marking out

twist drill will not start accurately enough. If this is the only tool available, put through a small pilot drill first. If working entirely by hand, bore from both sides to ensure squareness and avoid later twist when the tool is assembled.

The holes for the screws are marked centrally on the other (top) face and then drilled. Note that one hole does not go through. Saw and plane the tapered jaws and round-off the back corner slightly. The wood jaws, now complete, can be treated with linseed oil or given several coats of shellac or polyurethane varnish.

Turn or file up two cylindrical nuts slightly shorter than the jaw thickness. Drill centrally then tap for the selected thread. Cut the screws to length and clean up the ends. Clear any burr here by running on an ordinary nut. Make a small metal pellet and drive this into the blind hole.

The handles may be turned or benchmade to a hexagonal form. They are best drilled in the lathe. Grip the handles in the vice and cut the internal thread using the taper tap only. Force in the screwed rod, using two locked nuts. Turned handles can now have two flats planed on them. See Appendix 1. Assembly is quite straightforward. Finally, close the jaws and trim off any projecting end.

In use try to keep the jaws parallel. First tighten the centre or clamping screw. Then apply pressure with the outer or pressure screw. With a little experience, the operation is quite quick. Grip the centre handle with the left hand and the outer one with the right. Now clockwise rotation of the right hand tightens the jaws.

The improved handscrew
Fig. 34

This tool is in commercial production, and is particularly popular in North America. Nevertheless it is very straightforward to make, Fig. 35. Threads may be imperial or metric. Imperial has a faster action. Before starting make sure that the appropriate tap and die are available as well as round mild steel of the appropriate size. The metal should be what is termed *free cutting* for easy working and a good finish. Right- and left-hand taps and dies are needed. The latter can generally be ordered by a reputable tool dealer. Only the *Taper* or *first* tap is needed.

Make the hardwood jaws in the normal way and drill,

Fig. 34   Improved fast acting handscrew

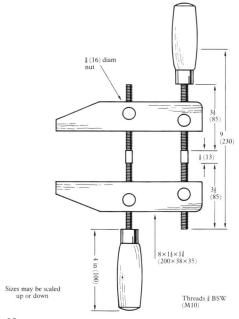

Fig. 35

off centre, for the cylindrical nuts. The holes for the screwed rod should be elongated to about three times their diameter. Either drill two holes and join up, or use the router, see page 62. Ideally do all the drilling in a drilling machine or drill stand. This obviates a twist in the assembled handscrew. Complete the shaping then finish with oil or varnish.

Prepare the nuts with a length just less than the jaw thickness. Drill these carefully, again using a machine. For sizes of tapping drills see Appendix 4. Tap two right-handed and two left-handed.

Now prepare the screws. Cut the material to length and mark the dead spot in the middle with felt marker or masking tape, Fig. 36. First cut the right-hand threads, one long and one short. Test that the cylindrical nuts run smoothly on them. Put on two hexagon lock nuts up to the dead spots, thoroughly tighten and grip them in the vice when cutting the two left-hand threads. Again, test with the appropriate nut.

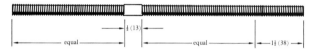

Fig. 36   Screw proportions

Assembling the improved handscrew

This is nothing like as difficult as it appears when the following routine is used, Fig 37.

1 Screw in the long threads
2 Bring the jaws together and just engage the short threads for half a turn.
3 Check that A = a and that B = b
4 Grip the dead spot with a Mole wrench or Combination pliers

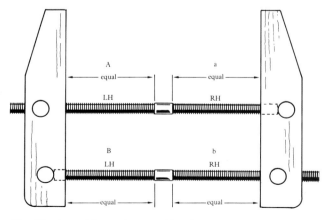

Fig. 37   Assembling an improved handscrew
the start

5 Screw together, working each screw a little at a time.
6 Still gripping the dead spot, screw on the handles forcing them up to the 1½ in (40 mm) mark. A flattened handle, Appendix 1, gives a good grip in the vice for this final tightening.
7 The handle with the right hand thread seldom works loose. The left hand handle needs a pin, not through the ferrule but through a more substantial part of the handle.

Grip the centre handle with the left hand then rotate the end handle clockwise to tighten. Try to keep the jaws parallel, unless of course tapered work is being gripped, a facility which only this handscrew provides.

The Table below shows the alternative sizes of components for the improved hand screw.

Jaw length		Opening capacity		Thread	
in	*mm*	*in*	*mm*	*in*	*mm*
4	100	2	50	$\frac{5}{16}$	M8
5	125	2½	65	$\frac{5}{16}$	M8
6	150	3	75	$\frac{5}{16}$	M8
8	200	4½	115	$\frac{3}{8}$	M10
10	250	6	150	$\frac{3}{8}$	M10
12	300	8½	215	$\frac{3}{8}$	M10
14	350	10	255	$\frac{7}{16}$	M12
16	400	12	300	$\frac{7}{16}$	M12

Widths and thicknesses are in proportion. In Imperial sizes use BSW or similar coarse thread

Two easy cramps

The following two cramps are both easy and cheap to make yet are really useful cramps to have about the workshop. Furthermore, they need neither special equipment nor skill in metalworking. All the requirements can be bought from a good hardware or DIY store. The reader is recommended to make these cramps four at a time.

The materials to be purchased for these cramps are lengths of screwed rod, $\frac{3}{8}$ in BSW or M10, hexagon nuts and washers to suit and 4 in file handles.

The handscrew

Figs 38 & 39, closely follows the simple handscrew described on page 17. Produce the jaws, accurately square and to size. Having cramped them together, mark the hole centres. First complete the top jaw of the drawing. Preferably using a sawtooth bit or a flatbit, bore the two holes for the nuts. These are $\frac{5}{8}$ in (16 mm) which is the size across the flats of the nut. The depth is slightly more than the nut thickness. On the same centre drill through with a $\frac{3}{8}$ in wood drill. Enlarge

Fig. 38   Two easy cramps
The handscrew

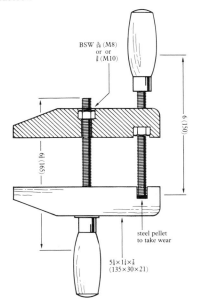

Fig. 39

It is unlikely that the nuts will work loose. If this does happen, thoroughly de-grease and return with a dab of epoxy resin glue. In use, aim to keep the jaws parallel for the most effective grip.

An adjustable cramp
Figs 40 & 41
This can be made in a variety of sizes. The model illustrated uses the same materials as the preceding handscrew.

Fig. 40   Two easy cramps
An adjustable cramp

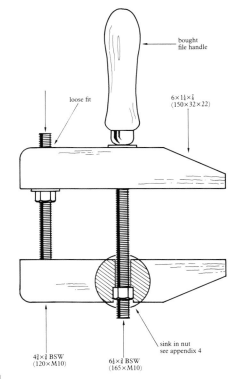

these through holes to give a loose fit either with a large twist drill or with a round file. Using a piece of the screwed rod, a hexagon nut and a large diameter washer, force a nut into each hole.

The lower jaw has one over-size through hole and one blind hole into which a small $\frac{3}{8}$ in steel pellet is forced.

The file handles are best bored in the lathe. Tap them $\frac{3}{8}$ in (M10) to a depth of $1\frac{1}{2}$ in (40 mm). A tap suitable for a limited use in wood can be made by filing four tapered flats on a piece of screwed rod and then fitting two lock-nuts, very firmly tightened, Appendix 4. With two lock-nuts temporarily on each screwed rod, the handles can be forced on. Assembly is straightforward. Remember that the cramp screw needs a washer under the ferrule.

Fig. 41

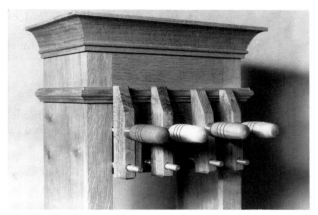

Fig. 42 Simple adjustable cramps being used in gluing on a small moulding

Prepare the jaws to size and mark out the centres. In the lower jaw on the drawing, counterbore for the nut, then drill through and slightly enlarge. This is only for the centre hole. For the end hole, drill through at $\frac{5}{16}$ in (8 mm) then tap from the inside with the workshop made tap described. Using two lock-nuts, the fixed screw can be forced into this hole. Add the nut and washer.

In the top jaw drill two $\frac{3}{8}$ in (10 mm) holes and enlarge to an easy fit.

Now drill the file handle at $\frac{5}{16}$ in (8 mm), tap and force in the screw.

Assemble the cramp with a washer under the ferrule.

In use, aim to keep the jaws parallel by adjusting the hexagon nut to the job thickness.

Fig. 42 shows a typical application of this type of cramp, the gluing on of a small moulding. Metal G cramps with swivelling feet would not grip so well, would be very much heavier and be liable to damage the moulding.

Larger fixed size cramp
Figs 43 & 44

These are worth making for regular repetitive jobs. An assortment of wood spacers will eventually build up. The model illustrated was specifically planned to grip $\frac{7}{8}$ in material to the bench. If desired the hexagon nut can be retained, lightly fitted on the outside of the moving jaw.

The spacers can be turned or bench made. Either drill in the lathe or from both ends, as a loose fit. The construction is exactly the same as for the adjustable cramp, page 20.

Most of the cramps described can be given a pair of lips or small jaws. These permit cramping on a very precise spot or over obstacles such as a lipping, Fig. 45.

Fig. 43 Larger fixed size cramp

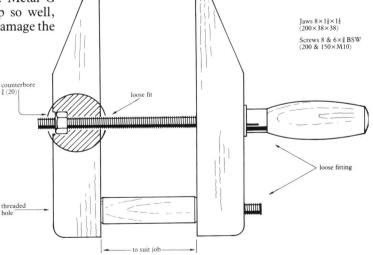

Jaws 8 × 1½ × 1½
(200×38×38)

Screws 8 & 6 × ⅜ BSW
(200 & 150×M10)

counterbore
¾ (20)

loose fit

threaded
hole

loose fitting

to suit job

Fig. 44

Fig. 45   Cramp with lips added

A longer reach cramp

Several of the cramps and handscrews described can be modified to give a longer reach but in doing so it should be remembered that by increasing the reach, some cramping strength is lost, so there is a limit. Such cramps are generally used for somewhat lighter work. To apply the pressure more accurately it is advisable to glue on two small jaw blocks. These may be faced with cork or rubber. Where weight is a consideration the screw diameter may be reduced.

Small fixed size cramps
Figs 46 & 47

Cramps of this type are particularly useful for dealing with repeated routine tasks. The specimen illustrated, made in sets of six, was designed as part of the process of making laminated, circular mirrors.

Prepare to size an adequate length of hardwood strip. Cut into lengths, making the jaws. From the remain-

Fig. 46   A small fixed capacity cramp

der, make the small spacing blocks to the size of the job in hand. Glue these in place, skim flush then slightly round the top surface.

Drill the lower jaw through at $\frac{1}{4}$ in (18 mm) and drill a similar shallow hole in the spacing block. Glue into this a short $\frac{3}{4}$ in (18 mm) dowel. Tap at $\frac{5}{16}$ in (8 mm) with the taper tap. Using lock-nuts fit the length of screwed rod. As an alternative a *roofing bolt* may be screwed in.

The top jaw requires a central hole of $\frac{5}{16}$ in (8 mm), slightly enlarged and a blind hole to take the dowel. Both jaws can now be shaped, finished and possibly varnished. Assemble and add a wing-nut and washer. Cheaper cast wing-nuts are larger, giving a better grip than the smaller, more elegant forged variety.

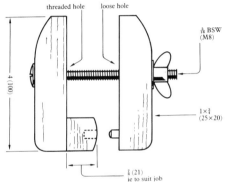

Fig. 47

In glue-up situations, the end of the jaws can be protected by covering with adhesive plastic sheet or tape.

Small semi-adjustable cramp
Figs 48 & 49

This is very suitable for small glue-up jobs and can be made in a variety of sizes according to demand and material available. The model illustrated has a capacity from about $\frac{3}{8}$ in (10 mm) to $1\frac{1}{2}$ in (40 mm). Black coach bolts or bright roofing bolts may be used though lengths of screwed rod are very much cheaper. Make four or six at a time.

Prepare a suitable strip to size and cut up, just over-long. Mark the hole positions. Dividers set to the distance between the screw centres speeds the process and guarantees accuracy. Alternatively a simple jig can be made for the drilling machine.

Use the tapping drill, $\frac{1}{4}$ in or 6 mm, for this, then later enlarge the holes in the moving jaw to give a sloppy fit. Shape the jaws, add the screws, washers and wing-nut.

The jaws can be covered with plastic sheet or tape if there is a chance of glue sticking.

Fig. 48   Small semi-detached cramp

Fig. 50a   Drawer slip cramps

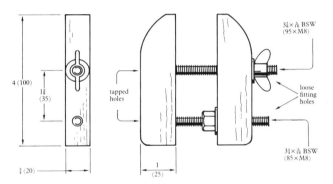

Fig. 49

Fig. 50b   Small light cramps
Securing a lipping – replacing many expensive iron G cramps and of very considerably less weight

Drawer slip cramp
Figs 50 & 51

This cramp is very similar to the previous one. The jaws have been made wider specifically for drawer work. Eight or even ten cramps can be needed for drawer work. On fine, light drawers the weight of many metal cramps is unacceptable. Additionally, few readers will want to buy so many so small G cramps. Generally they will prefer to buy bigger sizes.

These cramps make up as already described. Smaller sizes will use $\frac{1}{4}$ in (6 mm) screws, larger will take $\frac{3}{8}$ in (10 mm). Do not make bigger sizes still as they are not required for drawer slips and the wing-nuts will not give sufficient pressure.

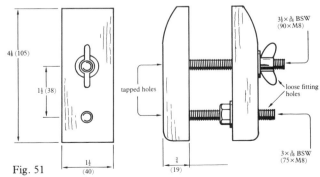

Fig. 51

Fig. 52   Lever cam cramp

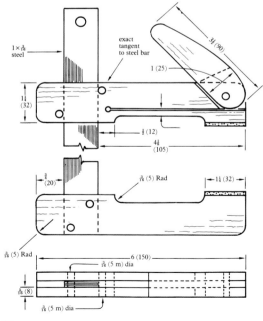

Fig. 53

Lever cam cramp
Figs 52 & 53

Cramps of this type have long been popular with makers of stringed instruments where a cramp is wanted which is not only light but has a fairly long reach. Only comparatively recently have they come onto the market. Previously craftsmen made their own.

Any good dense hardwood can be used. Manufacturers use beech and hornbeam. Fruit woods, oak and ash are equally successful. Brittle timbers are to be avoided as they tend to split in continuation of the sawcut in the moving arm.

Obtain the metal bar first: 25×5 mm bright drawn mild steel. Avoid black bar or any bright bar having rounded edges. Metric sizes are given because of the virtual disappearance in Britain of imperial sizes.

If made from the solid, the two wooden arms present problems. As yet there are no 5 mm hand or machine mortice chisels. If it is hoped to cut the mortices by router, there may not be sufficient depth of cut. It is considerably easier therefore to laminate the arms with the mortices in them.

First thickness a length of material to exactly the same thickness as the metal bar. Then thickness some more, somewhat thicker, say 7 mm. From this, cut up components as illustrated for the fixed bar, Fig. 54, the moving bar and the lever. Gluing can take place over a period as a number of five minute operations. Onto an outer layer glue a large inner piece. Next, when dry, hold an offcut of the metal bar in the mortice position and cramp on the short inner piece. This gives a very accurate mortice. Then add the top layer, cleaning up where necessary.

Try the bar and if the fit is too tight, lightly hammer the end of the bar, forming tiny hook like teeth, then pull out the bar which should cut away sufficient wood for a free fit. To remove the cut-out, cramp the two arms together, drill two $\frac{3}{8}$ in (10 mm) holes then remove the waste by sawing, planing or routing. In the moving

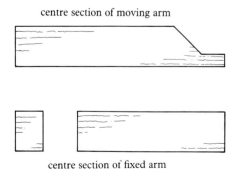

centre section of moving arm

centre section of fixed arm

Fig. 54

arm, drill a small terminal hole and make the sawcut. Shape the ends then drill for the 5 mm steel dowels. Those in the moving arm must be very accurately positioned.

The lever can now be glued together. Remove surplus glue and shape the cam. Draw the cam full size on paper, page 156, and stick this on the wood for shaping.

Drive in the metal dowels. Those in the fixed jaw can be lightly riveted before filing flush. When fitting, check that the jaw is square with the metal bar. Check that the moving jaw slides easily. Position the lever, drill through and tap in the dowel.

Glue on cork jaws, cut from a thin cork tile, then test out the cramp. Varnish or oil the tool and drill a small hanging hole in the bar.

Remember that this is a light duty cramp designed mainly to hold components together while gluing. It is not intended to crush up badly fitting joints.

One such cramp is not a lot of use on its own, so while set up, make a pair or better still, four.

Fig. 55   Carcase cramping system. Gluing up a small cabinet

A carcase cramping system
Figs 55 & 56

Sash cramps are undoubtedly essential tools for serious woodworking. They are generally bought four of a size. A set of four 48 in sash cramps is, however, extremely expensive. When setting up a workshop this is the smallest size that most workers will buy, on the assumption that what holds a lot, holds a little. This alternative system copes with most sash cramping situations with the added advantage that small constructions are not crushed under the weight of four large sash cramps. The capacity is from a few inches up to anything of which the workshop is capable of producing.

First the metal parts, Fig. 57. Easily available screwed rod is required in the sizes $\frac{1}{2}$ in BSW or M12. The suggested basic kit consists of 4 @ 6 in (150 mm) and 8 @ 12 in (300 mm). A possible addition to that is 4 @ 36 in (1 m). Cut to length and file or turn the ends cleanly so that nuts run on smoothly. Preferably build a wall storage rack. Beware of dropping onto a concrete floor which damages the ends. It is no time to discover that the nuts will not go on as the glue is setting.

Next make eight connecting nuts $1\frac{1}{2}$ in (40 mm) long, Fig. 58. Occasionally it may be possible to buy these, threaded M12 and 35 mm long. In North

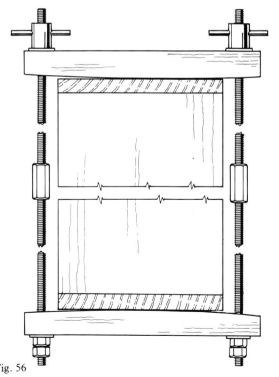

Fig. 56

Fig. 57   Carcase cramping system. The metal components

Fig. 58

America they are freely available in hardware stores as long threaded connectors. These can be sawn to make two. Otherwise, make from mild steel hexagon bar $\frac{5}{8}$ in (15 mm) across the flats, or even round stock. Saw, file up or turn then bore, preferably in the lathe. Use successively large drills finishing with the tapping size, 10·5 (10) mm. Tap at $\frac{1}{2}$ BSW or M12, a strenuous but not difficult job, made easier if a large tap wrench is available. The eight washers and eight hexagon nuts are freely available.

The four heavier spinner nuts can be made from round bar, 1 in (25 mm) dia. First drill and braze in $\frac{1}{4}$ in (6 mm) tommy bars. Then drill and tap the main hole. Fig. 59A.

Four wooden cramp bars are required for each job. Drill three holes at the end of each bar, $\frac{9}{16}$ in (13 mm) for a sloppy fit. These will then adapt for several sizes of job and eventually a useful stock of bars will be built up. Plane one face slightly curved and clearly mark it so.

Fig. 59A

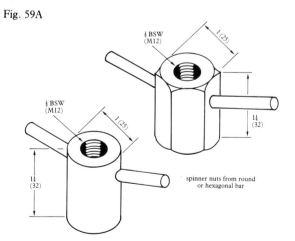

Fig. 59B (right)   Carcase cramping system
A lighter version for small carcases. These blocks are grooved to span protruding tenons or dowels.

To cramp up a carcase choose four cramp bars of a suitable size and join together sufficient lengths of screwed rod with the connecting nuts to span the job plus two bars and a bit to spare. Stand the carcase on stools, a Workmate or similar. Assemble the blocks, screwed rods, spinner nuts and washers, with two lock-nuts on the bottom of each rod. The assembled units can be slid into each end of the carcase then lightly tightened. This is a great convenience for the single handed worker when compared with assembling four sash cramps and blocks. The use of the slightly curved surfaces ensures that there is pressure at the centre of the carcase. Adjust the carcase for squareness and twist then fully tighten.

These components are useful for other applications. In a communal workshop do not permit parts to be borrowed in this way. Screwed rod is cheap enough. A kit reduced to 3 @ 6 in or 7 @ 12 in rods can easily be useless.

Traditional panel cramp
Figs 60 & 61

These are occasionally found hanging on the wall in old cabinet shops and appear in Victorian books on cabinet making. One of their main uses must have been for the gluing up of solid wood drawer bottoms. They invari-

Fig. 60   Traditional type of panel cramp in ash

ably had a wooden screw. This problem is easily circumvented by the use of $\frac{1}{2}$ in BSW (M12) screwed rod. Very accurate mortices can be achieved by routing then laminating, Figs 62A & B.

The construction is quite straightforward and should present no problems. Through tenons, wedged but without shoulders, are used. Housings can be cut to an even depth and with a fine finish by an electric or hand router. First saw carefully across the grain. If a radial arm saw is available, these cuts can be made with ease and precision.

The upper layer, slightly over-wide, is glued on then cleaned flush. The housings in the fixed member can be widened to take wedges.

The arms require to be made from well seasoned old hardwood since any warping may be transferred to the job. Small shoulders are cut on the edges, then the two arms are cramped together and the peg holes drilled. The arms can then be glued and wedged into the fixed member with the two moving members in place. Check that the diagonals are equal and that there is no twist.

For the screw, a piece of $\frac{1}{2}$ in BSW (M12) screwed

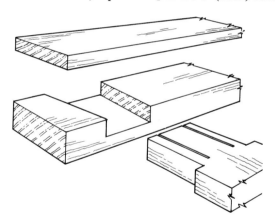

Fig. 62A   Mortice obtained by laminating. Fixed arm

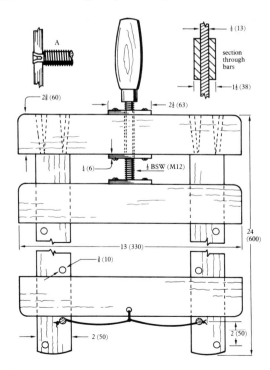

Fig. 61

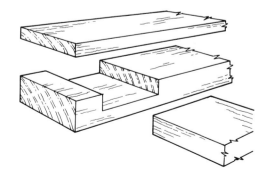

Fig. 62B   laminated moving arm

rod operates in a steel plate, Fig. 61A. This is drilled and fitted as described on page 156. This is a quite satisfactory arrangement since there is no strain when releasing the screw. The fixed member is fitted with two steel plates, one threaded and one clear. A $\frac{9}{16}$ in (13 mm) hole in the wood avoids the screw binding here.

The handle is turned from a dense hardwood, then drilled and tapped. All the screw components are now fitted to the cramp and secured with woodscrews. An over-large hole in the fixed member makes it possible to line up the screw precisely. When the screw has been positioned the handle is firmly fixed. To do this, the thread is gripped between two half nuts while the handle is twisted on. It may be pinned but this has not generally been found necessary.

When cramping up a joint, protect the arms from glue with paper or polythene. For thin wood, a weight on top may be helpful. The tendency for the work to rise may also be resisted by slightly angling the two gripping surfaces, but bearing in mind that minimum pressure needs to be exerted, readers may feel that this refinement is not worth while.

The tool is completed by tying two dowel pegs to the sliding member.

An oil or varnish finish is recommended.

Light panel cramp
Figs 63 & 64

This is an altogether lighter and smaller tool than the traditional panel cramp, though of course the design could be scaled up.

Prepare the three blocks to size, very accurately square. Mark the centres and drill the holes, using a pillar drill or a drill stand. In the fixed jaws counterbore first to let in the nuts, see page 155. All the through holes should be an easy fit on the metal rods. Those in the centre can be quite loose. Note that the holes for the

Fig. 63   Gluing up in a light panel cramp

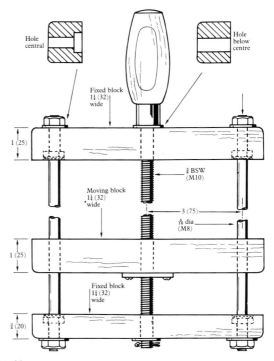

Fig. 64

screwed rod are slightly below centre, making sure that the screw remains clear of the work.

In making the threaded plate, both drill and tap in the drilling machine, turning the tap by hand. It is essential, to avoid binding, that the tap goes in truly vertical. Drill the screw for the split pin, then fit a suitably turned handle.

Assemble the three blocks on their metal slide bars, standing on a flat surface to obviate any twist, then fully tighten the nuts. Insert the screw into the assembly but with the threaded plate unsecured. By screwing or unscrewing the handle obtain a good working fit between the washers. For this, grip the screw in two half nuts. Lay in a widish parallel board and tighten well. In this position, screw on the threaded plate. Test for free movement. Unlike most cramps, this one works with its screw under tension not pressure.

Complete with an oil or varnish finish.

A very light cramp
Figs 65 & 66

The problem of cramping crossgrained walnut mouldings to a small clock case led to the production of several of these cramps. A reasonable span was required with

Fig. 65   A very light cramp

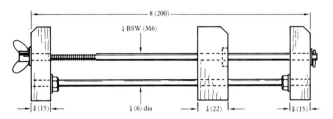

Fig. 66

the very minimum of weight. A firm, but not particularly heavy pressure was wanted.

The hardwood blocks were mass produced, all to exactly the same length. The simple drilling machine jig, Fig. 67, makes sure that all the holes are identically spaced, regardless of the size of drill used. The moving

jaw is made thicker because it is tapped. The drawing shows that a square nut could be let into this, though a thread merely cut in the wood will have a very long life. The fixed blocks are tapped in the lower holes, the upper holes being kept clear. For the plain rod, use $\frac{1}{4}$ in dia. steel though 6 or even 5 mm will suffice and be lighter. The main thread used is $\frac{1}{4}$ in BSW, a fairly fast thread. As this thread works under tension not pressure, there is virtually no limit to how thin it can be. However, as a fine thread will require a great deal of turning, it is wise to make 5 mm the lower limit.

The lower bar is threaded at both ends, screwed into the blocks and secured with a lock-nut and washer. Alternatively, if the bar is thick enough, it can be drilled and locked with a fine pin.

The threaded bar is fitted with a wing-nut. For neatness this is soldered or brazed, or even pinned. A lock-nut here is rather bulky but may be preferred to avoid heating and the subsequent cleaning. A complete alternative is to cast on a knob in fibreglass resin, page 151. A still further option is a hardwood knob, page 150. The screw is secured at its far end by means of a split pin and washer. By varying the washer thickness or turning the end block, excessive slack or tightness can be removed.

A rub of linseed oil gives an acceptable finish.

Test the cramp out and when satisfied, shape the blocks and polish. Oil or varnish is suggested. The jaws must be heavily chamfered or rounded on the outsides. This prevents misuse by making the screw push the sliding block instead of pulling it.

The drawing shows two possible widths for the blocks. Choice will be governed by the anticipated use.

Light aluminium bar is an alternative to wood.

Length can be varied but must not be made too great. Four nine-inch screws can be cut from a three-foot length of imperial bar. Slightly longer pieces come out of a metre length of metric bar.

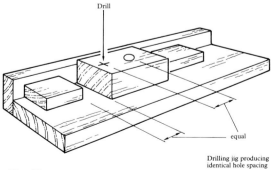

Drill

equal

Drilling jig producing identical hole spacing

Fig. 67

A larger light cramp
Figs 68 & 69

Cramps such as this can easily be put together, without finesse and using readily available materials, to cope with a particular problem requiring modest pressure, low weight and no risk of damage to the job.

Fig. 68 shows a small moulding being held while gluing. In such circumstances a heavy iron sash cramp would be unthinkable. The pressure required merely to support its own weight would certainly bruise the moulding.

For extra protection, cork jaws may be added.

A wire cramp
Figs 70 & 71

This is quite a powerful cramp, made from mild steel sheet of a thickness of about 16 SWG or 1·5 mm. Make a cardboard pattern first, then black the metal with a thick felt marker and scratch the outline clearly. Mark the hole centres with a heavy centre punch mark then drill all the holes. Saw out and file to shape. Fig. 72.

The easiest way to bend the sheet is to obtain a short length of $\frac{3}{4}$ in (20 mm) bar and drill it at $\frac{5}{16}$ in (8 mm).

Fig. 68 A longer light cramp
A greater span, with light weight, giving moderate pressure

Fig. 70 A wire cramp

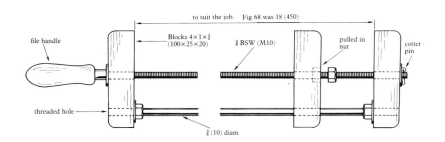

Fig. 69

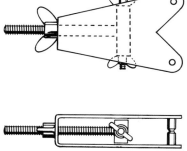

Fig. 71

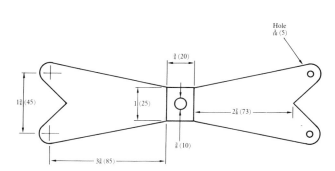

Fig. 72

The sheet can be bolted to this, checked for squareness, then hammered to shape, using a hardwood block to prevent hammer marks.

The two pins can have their spigots turned or filed, Fig. 73 & Appendix 2, or else they can be fabricated from a piece of rod and a piece of tube. File a small central groove to guide the wire.

The moving component consists of the end block and the screw. The former is drilled for the screw then drilled and tapped for the clamping screws. The tensioning screw also has a spigot formed on one end. The two are simply riveted together. Tension is applied by a wing-nut. The wire is clamped by wing-nuts and two washers. If small wing-nuts are not obtainable, the threaded block can be fitted with round-headed screws and washers.

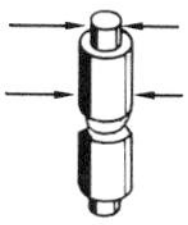

Fig. 73

Corner blocks for use with wire cramps
Figs 74 & 75

Make these from light angle iron. Old bed irons are light, thin and accurately rolled so make a good source of supply for a number of workshop projects. Cut to size, file up then file a very smooth, rounded notch for the wire to run through.

Cut the cork jaws from a thin cork tile and glue into place using an impact glue. Two sets of four can most usefully be made. Make sure that the width of the blocks is compatible with the size of the wire cramp.

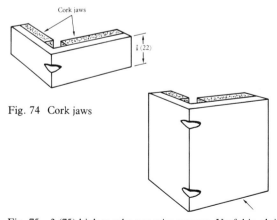

Fig. 74   Cork jaws

Fig. 75   3 (75) high to take two wire cramps. Useful in gluing up small boxes

A light wire cramp
Figs 76 & 77

This cramp, of virtually no weight, is ideal for small and slender picture frames, small boxes and circular laminations.

The vital part is a guitar or mandolin tuning key. These are available from most music stores. They can be bought as single keys or can be sawn from a strip of

Fig. 76   Wire cramp made from guitar tuning key
Also showing strip of mandoline keys and a single guitar key

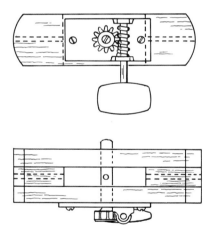

Fig. 77

Fig 78   The light 'guitar' cramp pulling up a lamination of a circular mirror frame. A fixed size cramp holds the joint flat on the assembly board

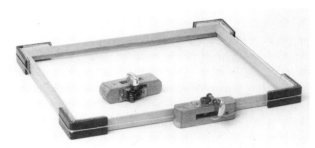

Fig. 79   The light 'guitar' cramp on a small picture frame, showing cork lined metal corner pieces

three or four. Note that the roller should be of metal, not the more expensive bone or plastic.

Rather than chop out a mortice in such a tiny component, build up the block as shown in Fig. 77. Then shape, clean up and sand the outside. Drill a hole to accept the key and then make two lengthwise holes. The tuning key can now be screwed in place.

An ideal material for the wire is the plastic covered type used on parallel motion drawing boards and available from drawing office suppliers. A more easily obtained alternative is twisted brass wire sold for picture hanging.

One end of the wire is secured with a guitar knot. The other end passes round the job then onto the key. As the key will not contain a great length of wire, several lengths will soon be stored up.

Small box constructions can be cramped up with two of these cramps and the corner blocks as in Fig. 75.

Jointing cramps
Figs 80 & 81

These cramps were designed primarily for the edge jointing of boards. The general decline in the use of hot scotch glue has meant that the traditional *rubbed* joint is

Fig. 80a   Jointing cramps pulling up an edge joint

Fig. 80b   A jointing cramp used to hold a chamfered block to prevent end grain from breaking out

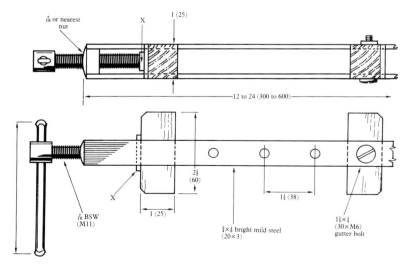

Fig. 81

no longer possible, so that all joints have to be cramped. For the small workshop, apart from cost, disadvantages of using sash cramps are their weight and length, particularly when gluing smallish components.

These cramps are light in weight, since they work in tension. The materials are very cheap and freely available. Neither special skill nor equipment is required, apart from brazing, which many small garages will undertake. Sizes range from 12 in (300 mm) to 24 in (600 mm).

The original models used $\frac{3}{4} \times \frac{1}{8}$ in (20×3 mm) bright (not black) mild steel strip and a $\frac{7}{16}$ in BSW thread. This was because a supply was available of square $\frac{7}{16}$ in nuts. This size of nut accommodates $\frac{3}{4}$ in boards. If these nuts are not available, saw up $\frac{3}{4} \times \frac{3}{8}$ in (20×10 mm) bar. True up the ends carefully, mark the centres then drill and tap. Use a machine or drill stand and, of course, a drilling vice to make sure that the hole is perfectly perpendicular.

Cut the strips to length plus 1 in (25 mm). Carefully mark the centres for the end holes and drill them. Bolt the pair together, mark the remaining holes and drill them all. With a countersink drill remove any burr from the drilling. Make an end spacer from tubing, or drill from the solid, Fig. 82. Now make the brazing aid from a tapped square block and a length of screwed rod. This makes sure that after brazing the screw is correctly lined up. Assemble as in Fig. 83, and braze. Saw off the two projecting lugs and file up the ends neatly. Clean off the scale from the brazing.

Next prepare the screw. Thread a small boss from round bar, thoroughly clean and de-grease, then braze it onto the screw. Clean up and drill for a tommy bar.

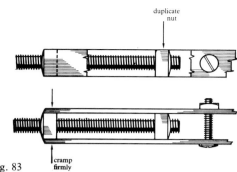

Fig. 83

This will later be kept in place by crimping the ends, either by nipping in a strong engineering vice or by a few careful hammer blows. Turn or file a spigot and attach the small drilled plate, x, see page 156. The spigot is spread out by using a large centre punch and a piece of heavy bar between the strips as a hammer.

Make the jaws from any dense hardwood and drill the fixed one for the retaining bolt. Attach the moving jaw with two $\frac{3}{8}$ or $\frac{1}{2}$ in countersunk screws. Slide on the fixed jaw and close the end with a gutter bolt, nut and spacer tube.

For edge jointing, glue the components then thread them through the cramps, a comfortable method for the single handed worker.

Fig. 84 shows how two jointing cramps may be linked together to cramp a lipping onto a triangular component as, for example, when making a corner cupboard.

Do not increase the lengths much beyond those given. If longer models are considered, use $1 \times \frac{1}{8}$ in (25×3 mm) strip and a $\frac{1}{2}$ in (12 mm) thread. The cramp can then be made to accept 1 in (25 mm) boards.

Fig. 82

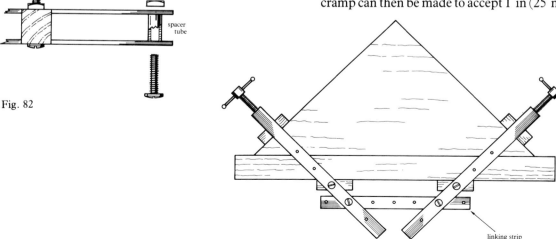

Fig. 84

Jointing thin boards

Few workshops, particularly amateur ones, are able to invest in several sets of short sash cramps; 36 in capacity seems to be the shortest most people are prepared to buy. This poses gluing problems with thin pieces like drawer bottoms, small panels and musical instrument components. The sheer weight of hardware is overpowering. Here are several solutions to the problem.

Fig. 85 shows the light jointing cramp described on page 32. Make up a support board of either thin chipboard or substantial plywood, truly flat and slightly less than the finished width of the jointed board. If it is to be frequently used, it is worth covering one face with adhesive plastic such as Fablon, to prevent the joint from sticking to it. Thin polythene sheet or even paper could be used.

The workpiece, with its support board, is threaded between two or three cramps and light pressure applied. Should there be any tendency for the joint to rise, either put a weight on top or cramp a strong batten across.

Both the traditional panel cramp, page 26 and the light panel cramp, page 28, are specifically designed for this work.

Luthiers' methods

Prepare a suitable board from ply, block- or chipboard and fit a strong vice strip. Glue or screw on the first clamping strip of say $1 \times \frac{1}{2}$ in (25×13 mm), Fig. 86. Now lay on the pieces to be jointed with a $1 \times \frac{1}{4}$ in (25×6 mm) strip below the joint. Press another $1 \times \frac{1}{2}$ in (25×13) strip up tightly, and pin it as in Fig. 87. Remove the $\frac{1}{4}$ in (6 mm) strip from underneath, glue the joint and press it into place with a strip of paper or thin polythene below and above the glue. Put on a weight or cramp a batten to prevent the piece from springing up, as in Fig. 88.

Another luthiers' method is illustrated in Fig. 89. Fix to the baseboard a parallel strip and a tapered one. Produce at the same time a long wedge of the same taper. Glue and assemble the joint, with paper beneath, and tap in the long wedge. Again a weight on top will probably be wanted.

Lever-cam method

The two parts of the joint can be forced against a fixed fence by several lever-cams which should not be too small. Fig. 90. The shape of the end should be a spiral. The construction of this is given on page 156. A poorly shaped cam will not retain the pressure and will spring

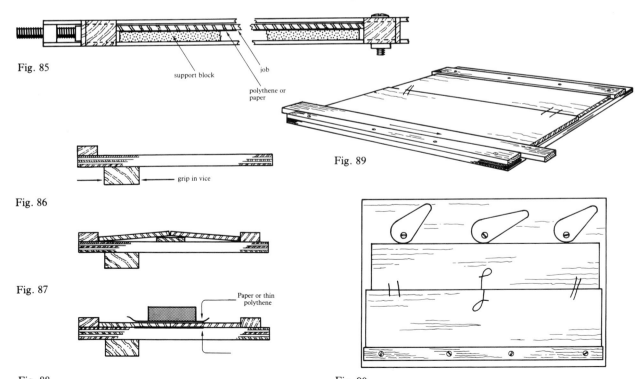

Fig. 85

support block

job

polythene or paper

Fig. 86

grip in vice

Fig. 87

Fig. 88

Paper or thin polythene

Fig. 89

Fig. 90

open again. Only part of the spiral is required. Draw the shape on card then cut out the relevant portion to use as a template. The cams and fixed fence, for strength, can be considerably thicker than the jointed components. 12 gauge screws are recommended. A weight or batten may be needed to prevent lifting.

Planing thin joints

The pieces to be jointed are laid together, suitably marked, then folded bookwise, Fig. 91. They can be cramped together between battens and hand planed or, if one of the battens is made fairly wide and woodscrews used instead of cramps, a planer may be used, Fig. 92. Working individually off the planer fence is not always so successful but if this method is used, make sure that one board is planed with the true face towards the planer fence and the other with the true face away from it. Even if the planer fence is untrue, this guarantees a joint angle of 180°.

In the same way, if the joint is hand planed using a shooting board, Fig. 130, make sure that one piece is planed true face up and the other, true face down.

In all edge jointing, and particularly when using thin wood, the accuracy of the joint is paramount. A poorly fitting joint cannot be crushed together. These tools and methods aim at lightly but firmly holding the components together while the glue hardens.

A Dovetailing Vice
Figs 93 & 94

This is a particularly useful tool and once used, readers will wonder however they managed without one for so long. Most workers who have cut dovetails on wide boards have experienced the unpleasant vibrations caused by the inadequate grip in the vice. Due to the position of the screw and slide bars, only one third of the vice jaws will grip any but the shortest of components. The dovetail vice is quite independent, merely cramping to the bench top where and when required. Out of use it stores away conveniently.

A suggested size for the jaws is 18×3×1½ in (450×75×35 mm). Naturally longer jaws can be made to accept particularly wide components, yet using the same screws. Cramp together for marking out to ensure that the pair are identical. Into one side of the fixed jaw drill two $1\frac{3}{8}$ in holes, just deep enough to accept ½ in BSW nuts. M12 nuts need a 20mm hole. Centres at 15 in (375 mm) is a convenient distance. Follow through with a ½ in wood drill. With the jaws cramped together, continue the ½ in holes through the second, or

Fig. 93 Dovetailing vice
Work set up for sawing

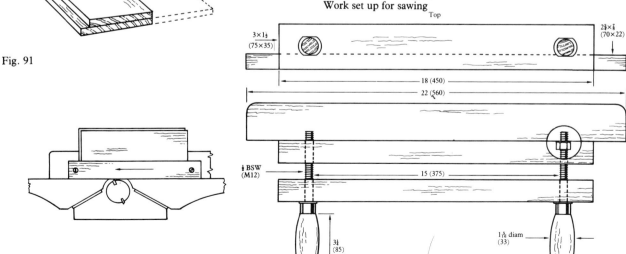

Fig. 91

Fig. 92

Fig. 94

35

moving jaw. In this way the holes are identical. The $\frac{1}{2}$ in holes are opened out to give an easy fit by running through a 13 mm drill. If this is not available, wrap glasspaper round a piece of dowelling to do the same, though somewhat slowly.

Pull in the nuts, page 155. A little epoxy resin glue may be added but generally this is not necessary. Glue the cramping piece to the fixed jaw, making sure that it projects at each end to accept G cramps or handscrews.

Prepare two pieces of screwed rod, $5\frac{1}{2}$ in (140 mm) long then turn and fix hardwood handles. These are much more effective than wing-nuts or hexagon nuts with a spanner. Turned handles can be planed flat on two faces to give a much improved grip, see page 154.

Grip the flattened handle in the bench vice and screw in the threaded rod. Two lock-nuts make this easy. Tighten until the screw reaches the bottom of the drilled hole. Assemble the dovetailing vice with good sized washers between the ferrules and the jaws. Fix to the bench with G cramps or handscrews. Alternatively the vice and the bench can both be drilled to accept $\frac{3}{8}$ in (10 mm) bolts and wing-nuts.

Angle Brackets

Figs 95 & 96

Once built, a pair of angle brackets is another workshop accessory that readers will wonder how they managed without.

Cutting a dovetail component, particularly if a dovetail vice is available, presents no difficulty. But marking pins from it, especially in the case of a wide component can. Usually the pin component is held projecting from the vice. The tail component is positioned on it. Sundry packing pieces level it up, then a couple of bricks, bits of old iron, lead piping or in fact anything heavy is used to weight the component in place for scribing. This set-up is easily jolted out of place by mere carelessness, by being in a confined space, by being in a communal workshop or by an interruption. Angle brackets prevent all this. They are the ideal method of scribing dovetails, wide, using the pair, or narrow, using just one.

The sizes given make a useful pair of brackets, but nevertheless are only suggestions. Considerable variation is possible, dependent upon the purpose and availability of materials.

For perfection, dovetail the corner. Otherwise comb or dowel joint it. Check for an exact right-angle then glue. When cleaned up, add a plywood fillet to each. Be sure to make a left- and a right-hand version.

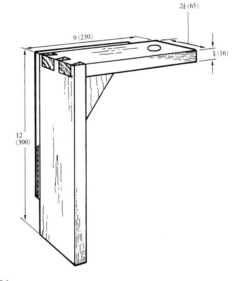

Fig. 96

Fig. 95 Large angle brackets
Large dovetailed components accurately held for scribing

To use

Having cut the dovetail, cramp one or two brackets to that component with the dovetail well overhanging the corner. Now cramp on the other component which is to be marked. This can often be held in the vice. It must firmly butt against the dovetailed member. Now uncramp the dovetailed member, slide or tap it into position, then re-cramp. Several light wooden cramps or handscrews are recommended rather than heavy metal G cramps.

Complete the marking out with an awl or scriber.

A coat of lacquer or polyurethane varnish and two hanging holes complete the job.

Ingenious readers will, without doubt, find further useful applications for these angle brackets.

An Assembly Board
Figs 97A, B & C

Items of furniture made on the lathe, country chairs, stools, small tables etc can be difficult to assemble. Although put together with a type of mortice and tenon joint, round tenons into a bored mortice, they differ from bench-made furniture in the absence of shoulders from the joints. Furthermore, chairs are wider at the back, in plan view: symmetrical trapezium. Round components are not the easiest to cramp up so all in all gluing up such items can easily result in them becoming out of square.

The use of an assembly board overcomes the problem, Fig. 97A. Saw out a truly flat piece of multi-ply or MDF. 24 in (600 mm) square is a convenient general size. With a heavy felt marker, draw in the two centre lines. Measuring from here, with a lighter pen, draw a series of 2 in (50 mm) squares covering the board, Fig. 97B.

From a previously thicknessed piece of solid wood, make four socket blocks. Prepare a strip of solid wood $2 \times \frac{7}{8}$ in (50×22 mm) and mark 2 in (50 mm) squares with space between. Find the centres of each then drill as follows, preferably in a pillar drill or drill stand: a 1 in (25 mm) or suitable hole $\frac{1}{2}$ in (13 mm) deep. Then a $\frac{1}{4}$ in (6 mm) through hole. Lastly, countersink well to accept a 12 gauge screw. Saw off the pieces. Fig. 97C.

Screw these sockets on the grid, measuring from the centre lines, to give the exact position of the legs from the drawing. When legs are splayed more than slightly, the sockets may need to be pared with a gouge to accept the legs. Thicker legs, of course, will need an appropriately bored block.

Assemble the chair in its sockets and pass a webbing cramp round board and chair to keep the whole assembly rigid. A large square can now be used to check that the legs are vertical.

Such a board will naturally be put to other uses in the workshop.

Fig. 97A   Assembly board. Gluing up a small turned table

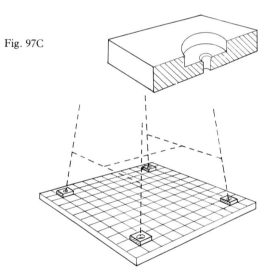

Fig. 97C

Fig. 97B

Planing Cradles
Fig. 98

A cradle for planing octagons and cylinders

This is the most common cradle and the type expected when the name cradle is mentioned. Sizes cannot be given; they depend on both available material and the size of work that the cradle is intended to hold. Probably several will eventually be constructed.

The *gutter* can of course be sawn out from the solid using a radial arm circular saw. For the hand worker accuracy is best achieved by building up.

Prepare two components to size then gauge an equal distance on the true edge (top) from the face (inside) and on the inside from the top. Mark the small housing on each piece. Saw the housing then remove the waste with chisel and router, hand or electric. Now carefully plane away the main waste, producing an accurate 45° face on each component. Check with a mitre- or combination square.

Standing on a flat surface, glue together with a plywood strip sandwiched between, as in Fig. 99. If there are not enough cramps, screw and glue together. Note the dust channel obtained in this way. Make a hardwood stop, with its grain vertical. Chamfer the trailing edge then glue in place, level with the top surface. Plane off any protrusion beneath then screw on a block to be gripped in the bench vice.

With this cradle square sections can be chamfered or reduced to octagons. Additionally, approximate cylinders can be produced by repeatedly planing off the corners then turning, to produce successively octagons,

16tagons, 32tagons and so on to an approximate cylinder. Fig. 100 shows specimen sizes

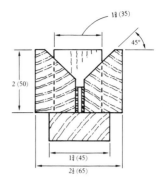

Fig. 100

A cradle for hexagons

Prepare the two components to length, width and thickness, marking the true face and true edge. Put a suitable gauge mark on the true face, the inside, and set a sliding bevel to 60°, Fig. 101A. Carefully mark the two ends then add the second gauge mark. Cut the housings for the stop then plane off the waste, checking when complete with the 60° bevel. Assemble as already described. Fig. 101B shows a less common cradle for working on the corner of a hexagon.

Fig. 98   Planing an octagon in the standard cradle

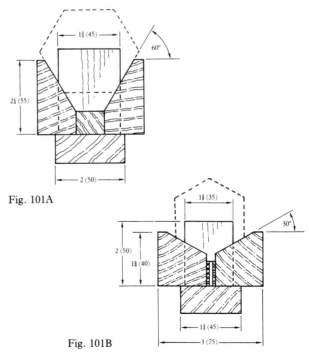

Fig. 101A

Fig. 101B

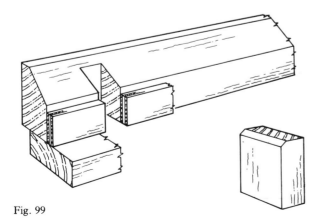

Fig. 99

A cradle for triangles

This shape is not so commonly made but is sometimes required, for example, as centring for three footed centre pedestal tables.

With a gauge and a 60° bevel mark out the waste, Fig. 102A. Mark and remove the stop housing then plane down the inner face to the gauge lines, checking from time to time with the 60° bevel.

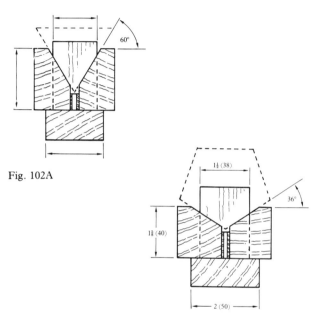

Fig. 102A

Fig. 102B

A cradle for pentagons
Fig. 102B

Though this is not often required the need does sometimes turn up when making period reproductions, for example, small twin pedestal tables.

It follows the previous pattern, the vital angle being 36°.

This permits the component held to be planed, drilled or morticed on a flat face. It is unlikely that work will be required on an angled corner.

Assemble, add the planing stop and gripping block.

In all cradle work it is important that the cradle should be of an accurate angle and that the workpiece should similarly be accurately prepared, otherwise the work will not sit firmly in the cradle.

The cradle may also be used for holding work either for morticing or for drilling.

A rough cradle can be improvised simply by gripping a suitable hardwood block in the bench-vice, as Fig. 103 shows.

Fig. 103   A quickly improvised cradle for small work

Marking

Marking Gentle Curves

Figs 104 & 105

Curves are often required of a radius far greater than it is feasible to mark with an improvised compass. For this, obtain a lath, say $1 \times \frac{5}{16}$ in (25×8 mm), of an even thickness and free from knots, in order to bend evenly.

At the ends of the workpiece tap in two thin pins on the line of the proposed curve. At the centre, lightly cramp a small pointed block. Gently tap this forward until the lath is in the required position. Cramp tightly, then draw the curve. A thin ballpoint pen is excellent if it can be certain that the marks will later be removed. Otherwise, use a pencil.

A second method is obviously more suitable for shorter curves. The requirements are a thin steel rule of 2 ft (500 mm) or 3 ft (1 m) and a length of washbasin ball chain, slightly longer than the rule. Fig. 105.

Drill out the hanging hole, if needed, so that the chain passes through freely, then file out a short narrow slot for the wire centre. At the other end saw or file a similar slot. Fig. 10.

To use, anchor the last ball at the hanging hole, bend the rule and enter the chain in the slot at the other end. The adjustment, one ball at a time, is very fine.

Sliding Bevel

Fig 107

If this tool is required only occasionally it can be made easily and economically. When used only with pencil, a thin wood blade is adequate. If much knife work is anticipated, a metal blade should be fitted.

For the all-wood model thickness some hardwood strip to $\frac{3}{16}$ in (5 mm) and cut up to size. The stock is laminated from three pieces, the inner being shorter, as shown. After gluing and cramping together clean off

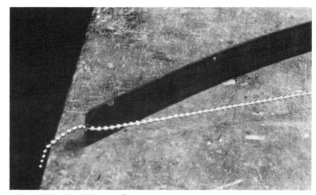

Fig. 105 Marking gentle curves

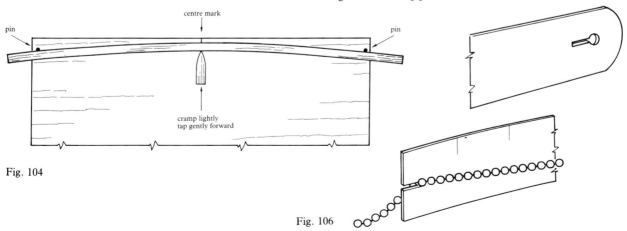

Fig. 104

pin   centre mark   pin

cramp lightly
tap gently forward

Fig. 106

any exuded glue from the slot. Then clean up to the final shape.

Cut the blade to length then plane just one shaving from its thickness to give an easy sliding fit in the slot.

Shape the ends, then rout the slot or work it by hand.

Drill through the stock at 5 mm then enlarge the hole in one outer lamination to $\frac{1}{4}$ in (6 mm). Thread the 5 mm hole at M6.

Assemble both components and secure them with a 6 mm gutter bolt, the head tightening against the threaded hole. Secure with a 6 mm washer and wing-nut. Finish with a coat of linseed or one of the proprietory teak oils.

For the metal blade model a piece of $\frac{1}{16}$ in (1·5 mm) steel strip is required. An old steel rule can be used. The slot in the stock, for the blade can be sawn but a better result can be obtained by laminating, using two thicknesses of veneer for the centre.

Secure as before.

For a photograph of the sliding bevel see Fig. 219, page 82.

Gauges

Although only three types of gauge, Marking, Cutting and Mortice, are commonly manufactured, wood-workers have devised, and continue to devise, quite an assortment of gauges to satisfy their special needs. Furthermore, with a few exceptions, the gauges marketed are of poor quality, easily bettered by quite modest craftsmen.

Before embarking on descriptions of specific gauges, it is worth considering the various methods by which the stem is clamped in the fence. According to preference and available materials or equipment, any of these clamping methods can be applied to any of the gauges which follow.

For methods of making suitable clamping screws, see page 150.

Clamping methods
Fig. 108
A Form the pressure plate, preferably from thin brass, bending up the two ends to suit the thickness of the fence block. The mortice is cut to accept the stem plus the pressure plate. A small housing is next cut to take either a square nut or a short length of steel bar suitably drilled and tapped. Finally drill to take the clamping screw.

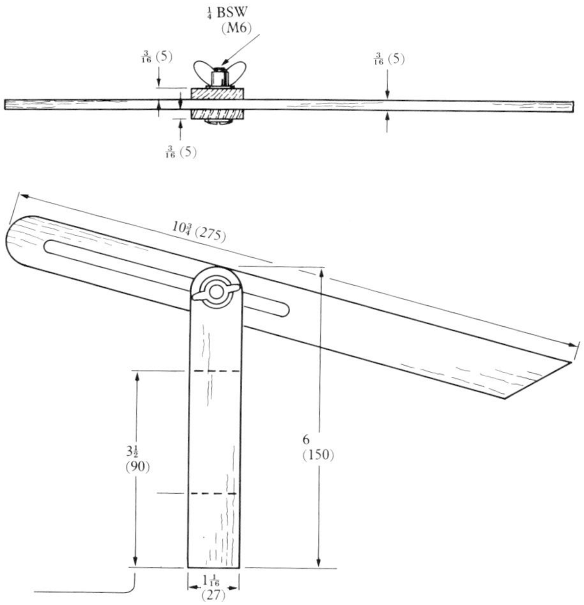

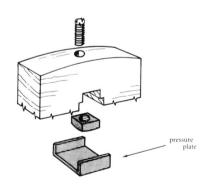

Fig. 108

Fig. 107

B A cavity is cut for a square nut and a square pressure plate which protects the stem from the screw. This is easily cut out if there is to be an applied face of very hard wood, such as ebony or rosewood. On a simpler gauge the stock can be made from two pieces glued together, in one of which the cavity has already been cut. The stock is then drilled centrally for the clamping screw. Fig. 109.

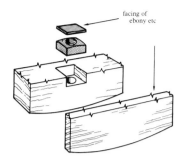

Fig. 109

C This clamping method is similar to that used in some of the commercial gauges. The thick stemmed screw necessitates either a metalworking lathe or an engineering friend. An alternative though is to solder a sleeve of brass or steel tube onto the standard thread. The cavity for a square nut and pressure plate is cut before the facing is applied. Fig. 110.

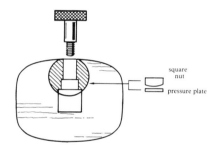

Fig. 110

D This method can be used conveniently with or without an applied facing, Fig. 111. Cut the stem mortice then, before shaping, drill the block for the screw. Drill at $\frac{1}{2}$ in when using a $\frac{1}{4}$ in screw. When other sizes are used, the drill diameter should be the same as the size across the flats of the nut, i.e. the spanner size. A $\frac{1}{2}$ in dowel is now glued into the hole. When the glue is fully dry, it is drilled centrally to accept the screw. A hexagonal nut can be pulled in, leaving space for a circular metal pellet. See Appendix 4.

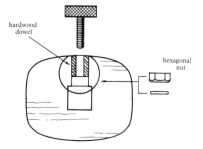

Fig. 111

E Having cut the mortice for the stem, work a shallow housing for a square pressure plate. In place of the previously used nuts, a $\frac{3}{8}$ in (10 mm) brass or steel dowel is used, tapped to suit the clamping screw. If the dowel is taken right through, as is normally done, then the gauge is worked with the clamping screw on top to offer the better bearing surface to the work. If the dowel is stopped, then the screw can again be underneath when in use, which is more comfortable, Fig. 112.

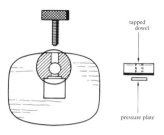

Fig. 112

F This is the wedge clamping often found on old tools which have been workshop made. Though it works satisfactorily, there is little in its favour except that it can be executed solely with woodworking tools, Fig. 112A.

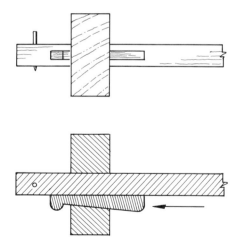

Fig. 112A

Fence shapes
Fig. 113
A This is the traditional gauge fence. Manufacturers seem slowly to be abandoning this shape. However some readers may wish still to use it, though not much can be said in its favour.

B This is the shape increasingly used by manufacturers, probably because it is an easier shape to mechanise. Originally it was used for mortice gauges but has now spread to the other forms.

C Here is the traditional form of the beautifully manufactured ebony and brass gauges of the late 19th and early 20th century. The brass facings were fixed with four brass screws, only slightly countersunk so that when filed flush the screw slots were lost.

D & E These shapes are improved in that firstly, they conveniently accept the clamping methods described and, secondly, they make the gauging process easier, particularly at the start and end of the stroke.

F Shapes A and B were often fitted with two brass strips to reduce wear. These were of $\frac{3}{8} \times \frac{1}{16}$ in. Formerly these were secured as just described, but in recent years the screws have been left boldly showing.

An Improved Marking Gauge
Figs 114, 115 & 116

As the marking gauge is in constant use, two, made to these specifications will work well, feel comfortable and provide much pleasure in use. Any of the clamping methods or styles of fence and screw described may be substituted.

The angle adjustment of the point is well worth making. A slightly trailing point is nicer to use than a truly vertical one. Readers preferring a simpler version may merely drill the stem at an angle of 5° to 10° and drive in a point. If proper points cannot be obtained, a good substitute can be ground from a thin masonry nail. Do not use soft wire nails. Left-handers will of course tilt the point in the opposite direction. It is quite wrong for the point to be projecting $\frac{1}{4}$ in (6 mm) as is often found. $\frac{1}{16}$ in (2 mm) is quite enough.

Make the gauge from good hardwood. The one illustrated is walnut with an ebony facing. When complete, soften all the corners so that the gauge feels comfortable in use. Finish with teak or linseed oil, or with several coats of polyurethane varnish.

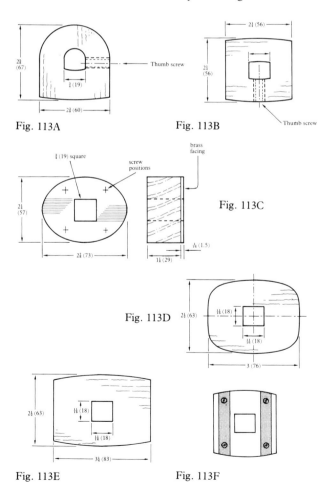

Fig. 113A

Fig. 113B

Fig. 113C

Fig. 113D

Fig. 113E

Fig. 113F

Fig. 114 Marking gauge with adjustable scriber in walnut and ebony

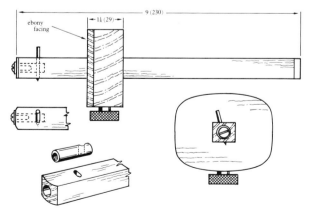

Fig. 115

Fig. 116 Marking gauge with adjustable scriber with dowel nut clamping in walnut and ebony

Fig. 117a Superior cutting gauge in ash with ebony face brass, locking screw and screw held blade

An Improved Cutting Gauge

Figs 117 & 118

This follows the lines of the marking gauge in construction. A square mortice is chopped in the stem of about $\frac{1}{4}$ or $\frac{5}{16}$ in (6 or 8 mm) to take the cutter. The face near the stock is slightly angled. The effect of this is that in use the fence is pulled close to the workpiece so that the tendency to wander is prevented. Naturally this angle is reversed for left-handers. If the clamping screw tightens directly onto the cutter it can be caused to move from the desired position. To prevent this the small brass pressure plate has been introduced, Fig. 119. Also the end of the clamping screw should be rounded, not square. A brass dowel-nut, Fig. 120, looks nice and should be finished slightly below the surface of the stem. For readers wishing a simpler solution, Fig. 128A, drill the end of the stem to take a plastic knock-down fitting, generally termed a chipboard fastener. This is glued in place then tapped to take the cutter clamping screw. A further method still, Fig. 122,

Fig. 117b Cutting gauge. Detail of clamping method

is to enlarge the mortice to accept a square nut. In all cases the brass pressure plate is essential.

The cutter itself requires a little consideration. For fine crossgrain marking, as when dovetailing, a thin

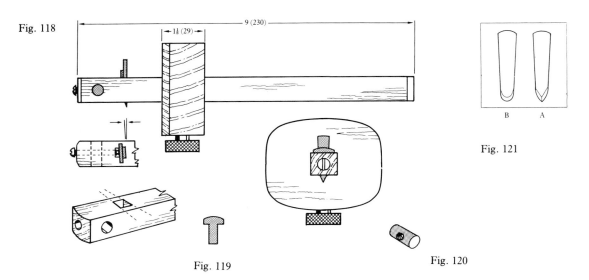

Fig. 118

Fig. 119

Fig. 120

Fig. 121

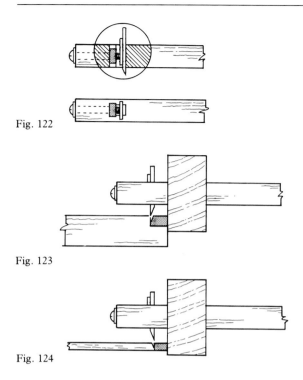

Fig. 122

Fig. 123

Fig. 124

curved work. This method permits the rolling action of the stem, regulating the depth of the cut.

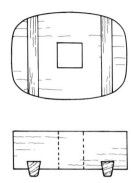

Fig. 125

pointed shape is needed, Fig. 121A. For heavier cutting a more robust, rounded shape is more suitable, Fig. 121B.

When the waste is being removed as in Fig. 123 where a rebate is being cut, the bevel faces the fence. When the wanted piece is being removed, as in Fig. 124, where an inlay stringing is being cut, the bevel is away from the fence.

Cutting gauge knives are manufactured for retail sale but are hard to track down. However, excellent knives can be made from pieces of broken or worn out power hacksaw blades. (Hand hacksaw blades are far too thin.) The high speed steel cutting edge can be broken off in a vice. The backing can generally be sawn and filed and as a rule will be hard enough for intermittent use. Should the material prove to be too hard, it can be annealed, shaped and then re-hardened, see Appendix 4, page 154.

Gauging from curves
Fig. 125
Any of the conventional benchwork gauges can be modified for use on curves. Cut two housings, ideally dovetail housings, and glue in two shaped strips of dense hardwood. If these are put on the rear side of the fence, one gauge can be used for both straight and

Into-the-corner gauge
Fig. 126
There is a restricting dead space at the end of the normal marking gauge stem. In order to gauge close to an obstruction, this gauge has a small steel cutter screwed to its end. This is easily removed for sharpening. If sharpened more keenly, it could be adopted as a cutting gauge.

Fig. 126 'Into the corner' gauge in ash with ebony face and wooden knob

A pencil gauge
Figs 127 & 127A
The pencil gauge, Fig. 127, will be found to be extremely useful for the earlier approximate marking out, both on boards and on sheet material. It is well worth making the tool specifically rather than just boring a hole in the back end of a marking gauge. The stock is made considerably longer than that of the marking gauge. A rebate is worked on the lower edge. This makes the working very comfortable but means that very small measurements cannot be gauged. This is no great disadvantage. The stem can be locked by any of the methods already described.

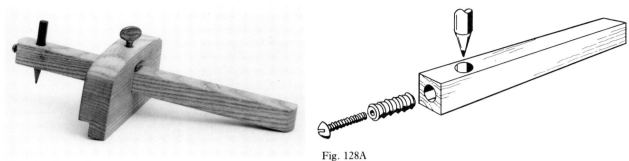

Fig. 127   A pencil gauge

Fig. 128A

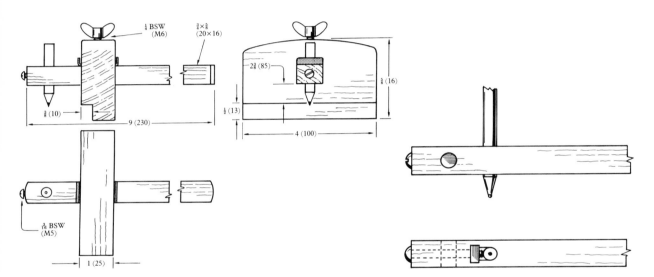

Fig. 127A

Fig. 128B

The pencil can be held by either of two methods. Fig. 128A. The stem is drilled to accept a plastic chipboard fastener which is glued in, then tapped. Fig. 128B. The pencil hole is enlarged to take a square nut. Make the hole large enough for the standard cheap ball-point which shows more clearly than pencil when marking along the grain.

In Figs 129 & 129A the rebate has been replaced by two short dowels. This is a convenient method of marking from a curved or circular edge.

Note that this same method can be applied to a cutting gauge. In this case though the cutter must be held in a small applied block similar to that in Fig. 130.

A convenient stem length is 12 in (300 mm). An extra, longer stem might be considered useful.

Fig. 129   A pencil gauge for curves

Fig. 129A

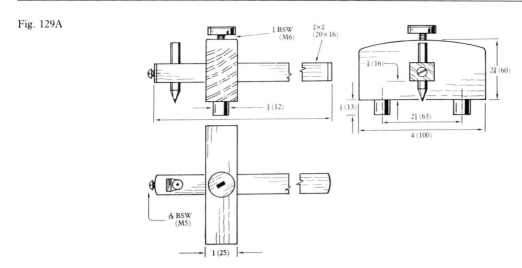

Fig. 130 Panel gauge in mahogany

A panel gauge
Figs 130 & 131

Formerly there was a limited production of panel gauges. The Tyzack catalogue of 1938 shows one priced at 5 shillings and 6 pence (27½p). However, by the time production had resumed after the war, the panel gauge had been eliminated. In fact though, the majority of these gauges had always been workshop made, so there is no difficulty in repeating the project.

Generally the stem was locked by means of a captive wedge, Fig. 112A. This method was common to all hand made gauges. For more convenience any of the screw fastenings can be used. A very wide rebated stock is essential. A wide variety of shapes is possible but the comfortable form drawn is hard to improve on, being

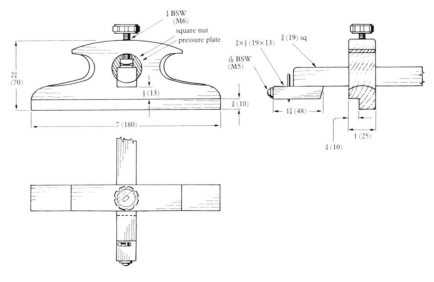

Fig. 131

equally suitable for left- and right-handers. Nicely round-off the area of the thumb socket.

The stem has an added block of a thickness equal to the distance between the rebate and the mortice. With such a long stem, it is vital that the point should trail, hence the method of Fig. 115 has been used. A general stem length is 21 in (530 mm) but this will depend on the work anticipated.

Readers may find it convenient to adapt the other end of the stem for the pencil, Fig. 128, which will be found useful for approximate marking on plywood sheets.

The long mortice gauge
Figs 132 & 133

In carcase work it is often required to mark mortices and tenons well in from the edge of, for example, ends and partitions. Obviously the standard mortice gauge will not reach, so various improvised methods are resorted to. This long stemmed mortice gauge makes such marking easy and standard.

In view of the increased distance to the points, a somewhat larger stock is required. Any suitable clamping method may be used.

Brass strip is marked out as illustrated and drilled before being cut into two smaller pieces. Exact sizes are not important. If, however, the points are set in too far from the ends, the gauge cannot be adjusted to the smaller chisels. The points are most conveniently turned, or filed in a woodturning lathe, or less conveniently, rather slowly filed to shape. The holes for them in the brass are slightly countersunk so that the spigot of

132A   A long mortice gauge

132B   A long mortice gauge. Details of the metal parts

the points can be riveted over to secure them. During this process the points are held on an end grain block of dense hardwood. File this underside smooth and fit in place. The fixed block is simply screwed to the stem. The moving block is held by a machine screw operating in a short slot through the stem, Fig. 134.

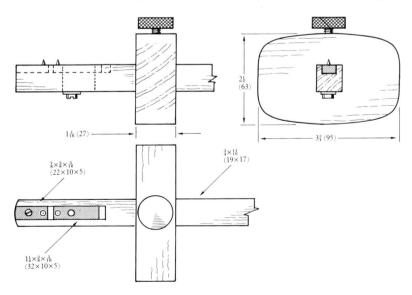

Fig. 133

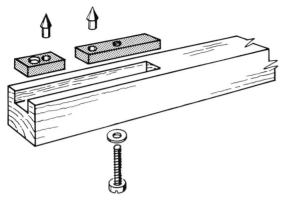

Fig. 134

Fig. 135   A 'grasshopper' gauge

The stem is prepared, 21 in (540 mm) is a convenient length, and a small housing is routed or carved out at one end to the size of the brass strip available. A short slot is routed or chopped for the locking screw.

The gauge is used exactly as is the standard mortice gauge, being rolled slightly to regulate the depth of the marking. A two-handed technique is recommended, one hand for the stock and one controlling the points.

Grasshopper gauge
Fig. 135

The term *grasshopper* is applied to a gauge which is able to jump over an obstacle, generally in the form of a lip or overhang. It is very doubtful if such gauges were ever manufactured. Nevertheless, craftsmen have often found a use for them and over the years have constructed for themselves a variety of different shapes and styles.

There are two distinct basic forms. Fig. 135A shows a gauge able to mark across an upstanding lip. Fig. 136 shows the other application where the gauge is marking across an overhang. An example of this would be

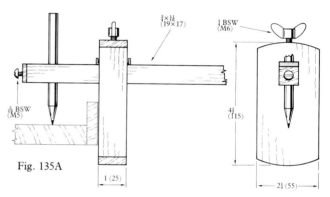

Fig. 135A

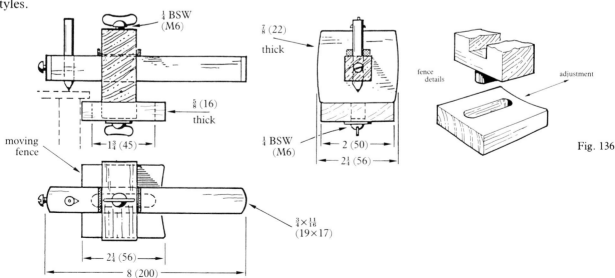

fence details

adjustment

Fig. 136

marking for a line of pins where a plywood lid, slightly over-size, has been lightly pinned at two corners, and will later be planed flush. In this second case, a small subsidiary fence, A, has been added. In order to operate similarly from a curved edge, its other face has been suitably curved, as B.

Laminate cutter
Figs 137 & 138
It is often required to cut parallel strips of plastic laminate, such as Formica, generally for edge lippings on table tops, shelves etc. A saw will both splinter the work and quickly become blunt. A scriber and straight-edge is tedious and not all that accurate.

This tool follows any of the gauge patterns described, with the difference that a tungsten carbide cutter is fitted. Laminate cutters of the style illustrated, Fig. 139, are freely and cheaply available. All that is required is to saw off the short straight end and to arrange a clamping method.

Fig. 137   Plastic laminate cutter

Naturally the fence will quickly become scored from the laminate, so it will need protection. Face the fence with either a piece of the laminate, or of brass, or even steel. $\frac{1}{16}$ in, 16 gauge or 1·5 mm will be suitable.

Start by checking or planing one straight edge, then with the tool set, deeply scribe on both sides of the material until it separates or may be snapped off. Plane up the remaining edge once more then repeat.

It is a help if a screwdriver slot can be made in the bar holding the tungsten carbide tip. It can then easily be turned to the most effective cutting position.

Fig. 139

A double cutting gauge
Figs 140 & 141
This gauge generally has two purposes. One is the cutting of the channelling to accept an inlay banding, often in a veneered surface. The other is the cutting of the veneer banding itself, often cross-grained. An alternative for this latter purpose is given on page 133.

The tool follows closely the cutting gauge on page 44. The slot for the knives, either routed or chopped out, is $1\frac{1}{8}$ in (28 mm) long. This makes possible the cutting of bandings up to 1 in (25 mm) wide. The end is again slightly angled at about 5°.

For bandings, the knives are set with the bevels outward. For cutting channelling, the reverse, the

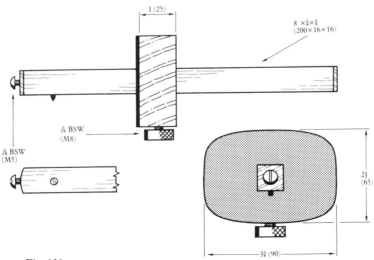

Fig. 138

Fig. 140   Double cutting gauge

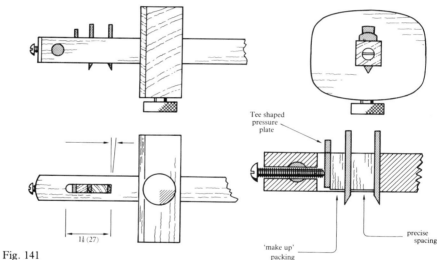

Tee shaped
pressure
plate

precise
spacing

'make up'
packing

1¼ (27)

Fig. 141

bevels are inward. On no account must a bevel be allowed to develop on both sides of the knives.

Between the blades is the precise packing, which decides the width of the cut. This can be one piece or built up from blocks and slips of veneer. This block should be slightly angled to match the end of the slot, so that the cutters pull the gauge into the work.

A similar pressure plate is used, Fig. 119, which prevents the rotating screw from disturbing the set of the knife. When making the narrower cuts some approximate packing is needed to part fill the gap. Otherwise an excessively long screw would be needed. The knives are held firmly in place by any of the clamping methods described earlier.

Fig. 142 shows an alternative and very basic form of the tool. No metalwork is required. The stem is somewhat longer and in this case was built up from strips, giving an immediate slot. A wedge holds the knives and a captive wedge secures the stem. A dowel through the stem end is intended to stop splitting if the wedge is driven in too enthusiastically.

The fence is larger and rebated which gives an advantage when working well in from the edge. However, the convenience of controlling the cut by rolling the stem is lost.

Circular cutting gauges for one or two knives
Figs 142 & 143

These gauges, at the cutting edge, follow the pattern of the previously described cutting gauges. Instead of a fence, there is a pivot.

A good firm pivot is essential for circular work so the cutting end is designed with this in mind. $\frac{5}{16}$ in (8 mm) or $\frac{3}{8}$ in (10 mm) is about the right thickness. $1\frac{1}{2}$ in (40 mm) square is the minimun size. Drill the block centrally, countersink well and screw in a machine screw of about $\frac{3}{16}$ in (5 mm). Formerly the pivot block was glued in place with a paper joint for easy removal. Now double sided tape saves all the drying time.

The arm is produced to size and a block added at the cutting end of the same thickness as the pivot block. Holes are drilled to suit the pivot screw at $\frac{3}{4}$ in (20 mm) intervals. The cutting end is reduced in thickness and the cutting unit, for one or for two knives, is arranged as described on pages 50 to 51. There is no need to angle the knives. The slot, however, must be made long enough to set radii between the drilled holes.

When only one knife is fitted, cut towards the end grain, in the manner shown in Fig. 144. When two cutters are fitted, one of them is always cutting the

Fig. 142   Simple double cutting gauge with wedge locking

wrong way so the cut is made in the directions which give the sweetest cut.

A refinement. A wing-nut and washer prevent the arm from inadvertently slipping off the pivot.

A Dovetail Marker

The average dovetail marker, Fig. 145A, though simple to make and use, is at a distinct disadvantage when used near the edge of the workpiece, where it has an inadequate bearing surface, Fig. 145B.

The greatly improved version, Figs 146 & 147, looks best made from sheet brass, though aluminium, steel, acrylic or polythene sheet can equally be used. The

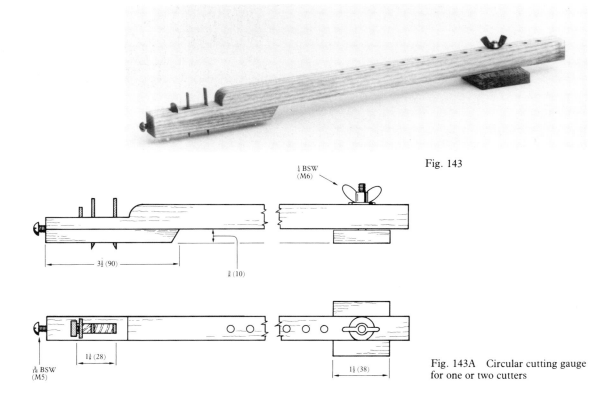

Fig. 143

$\frac{1}{4}$ BSW (M6)

$3\frac{1}{2}$ (90) $\frac{3}{8}$ (10)

$\frac{3}{16}$ BSW (M5) $1\frac{1}{8}$ (28) $1\frac{1}{2}$ (38)

Fig. 143A   Circular cutting gauge for one or two cutters

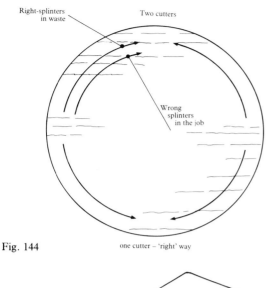

Fig. 144

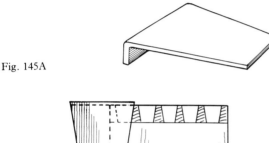

Fig. 145A

Fig. 145B

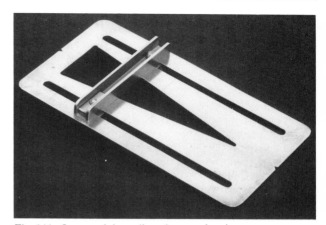

Fig. 146   Improved dovetail marker. under view

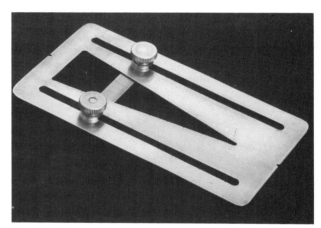

Fig. 146   Improved dovetail marker. Top view

customary dovetail slopes are 1:8 for hardwoods and 1:6 for softwoods. The drawing shows 9° which is an acceptable compromise, easily set out with an adjustable set square or combination square.

The adjustable fence, of metal chanelling, Fig. 148, is set both to the chisel size and square to the edges. By means of the sliding nut, Fig. 147A, the tool can be set up for angled dovetails. It also serves as a small square.

Brass electrical terminal screws were used on the tool illustrated but any suitable small knobs, wing-nuts or even slotted screws will serve.

A dovetail marking system

First make a *divider* from plywood, cardboard or acrylic sheet. It is probably best to make a smaller one for say drawer construction and a larger one for carcase work. Fig. 149. With this mark out the centres of the dovetail *pins*, Fig. 150. Note that the end half-pins are generally

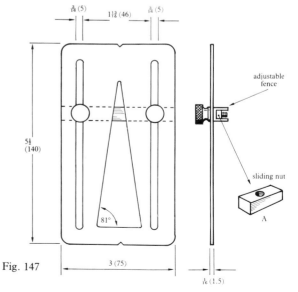

Fig. 147

Fig. 148

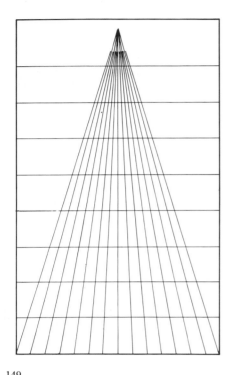

Fig. 149

made slightly larger than half, hence a centre line is drawn close to each edge. Set up the marker by adjusting the fence so that it is square to the edges and accepts the chosen chisel, with a fraction to spare, at the marked shoulder line.

Mark the centre lines onto the face and from them, using the centre nick, mark the pins, Fig. 151. A fine ballpoint or felt pen is ideal so long as it is certain that the marking can later be planed off. Angled dovetails are marked out in exactly the same way, the fence being set to the angle of the workpiece.

Fig. 151   Dovetail marking system. Method of use

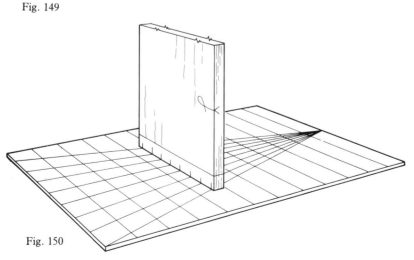

Fig. 150

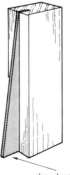

slope about
1 in 6
end square   Fig. 152

A dovetail halving marker

Though some sliding bevels can be set to the very acute angle needed, this marker, Fig. 152, is permanently set and is much more convenient.

Work a groove in a hardwood stock to accept the blade. This can be from thin metal, acrylic or polythene. Glue or pin in place, or both.

This joint is generally marked as in Fig. 153A. A better method is to slightly set in the dovetail line, Fig. 153B. This allows the saw to start conveniently and continue the cut, a more acceptable method than whittling with a chisel as Fig. 153A necessitates. If the end of the blade is finished accurately, it can be used as a small square.

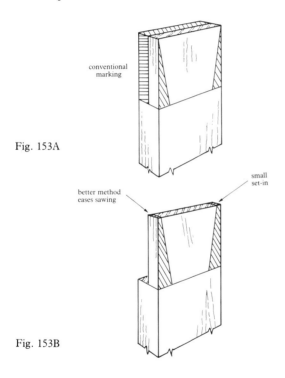

Fig. 153A

Fig. 153B

conventional marking

better method eases sawing

small set-in

Fig. 154A   Depth gauge for bench work

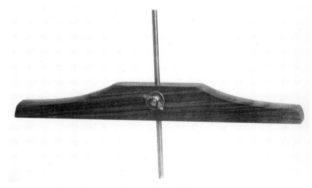

Fig. 154B   Depth gauge for bowl turning

Depth Gauges for the Lathe and Bench

Figs 154 & 155

Metalworkers use depth gauges constantly. For the woodworker something better can be arranged than poking a pencil down a hole with the thumb nail held in place.

The main feature of this type of gauge is a draw bolt. Any round bar, brass, steel or aluminium, can be used to make this to suit the size of gauge planned. Turn or file a spigot on the end of the piece of bar, (Appendix 2).

This is threaded to suit an available wing-nut or knob. A garage will generally do this if the reader lacks the necessary die.

The length of the wooden stock will vary with its purpose. Quite a small one will do for bench work. For bowl turning a much longer span is required. The height of the bar must be such that the wing-nut well clears the work.

The stock should be shaped sufficiently so that it is obvious from which face the depth is being measured. Drill a horizontal hole for the draw bolt and a vertical to accept the depth rod.

Drill the drawbolt to take the rod with an easy sliding fit.

If a bar of larger section is used, it can be drilled to accept a ballpoint pen. When cutting housings by chisel and hand router, this can be constantly tried in the housing. If it marks, the housing is still not to depth.

Use in bowl turning

Having turned the outside of a bowl, Fig. 155A, remove it from the faceplate, invert it on the bench or a flat board and place a stick across the base, Fig. 155B. Measure the height from the bench and deduct the depth of the turned base. Next deduct the required thickness of the bowl and set the gauge to this measurement.

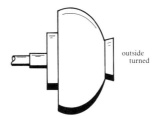

Fig. 155A

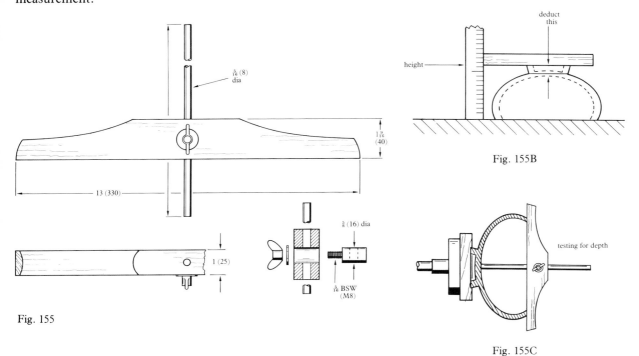

Fig. 155

Fig. 155B

Fig. 155C

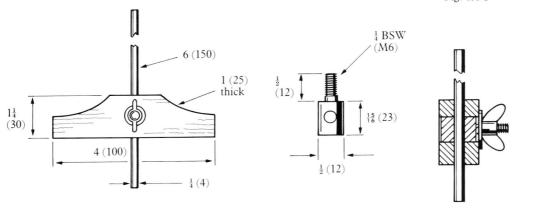

Replace in the lathe reversed, i.e. held by the base ring. While turning out the inside, test frequently, Fig. 155C. This method guarantees never cutting through the bottom and obviates massively thick bottoms, the result of over caution. The rim must not be cut until final depth has been checked.

Large compass
Figs 156 A & B

Big radii can of course be marked with the circular cutting gauge, but in many cases a pencil or ballpoint is all that is required. This simple tool will cope with most workshop requirements.

Produce a pair of stems of different lengths. Drawing modest circles with a very long arm is inconvenient. Secure the pencil in one of the several ways already described.

The pivot is simply built up using offcuts of stem material for the two centre blocks. A cavity for the nut and pellet can easily be cut before gluing up. Clean up and add the spike. A hanging hole should be drilled in the side of the stem.

Plotting an ellipse
Fig. 157

Geometry books show several methods of plotting an ellipse, most of which are quite unsuitable for the workshop situation. The well known string and pins method is accurate enough for a garden flower bed but certainly not for a table top.

The two basic dimensions required are the major diameter, D, and the minor diameter, d. A rectangle of timber is prepared, just larger than D × d. The centre lines are clearly and accurately drawn, A.

Prepare a trammel from suitable thin material, B. From point P, the plotting position, mark off half of the major diameter, D/2 and also half of the minor diameter, d/2. Line up the trammel with d/2 on the minor diameter and D/2 on the major diameter, C. Make the plot at P. Continue in each of the four quarters, clustering the plots where the curve changes most rapidly. Join up the plots, completing the required shape.

Fig. 157A

Fig. 156a   A long marking-out compass

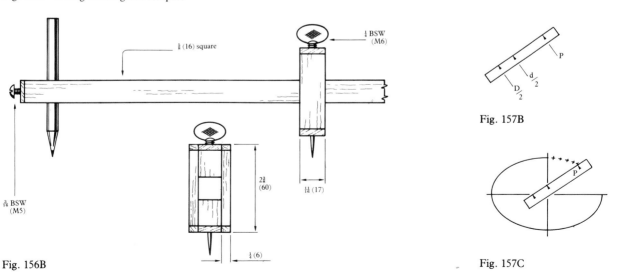

Fig. 156B

Fig. 157B

Fig. 157C

A smooth curve through three points
Figs 158 & 159
Let the points be A, B and C. Join A and B then square from AB to give CD. D is assumed to be midway between A and B, Fig. 158.

Make a template from plywood or hardboard. The length is just greater than AB. The width is CD plus a small allowance. Join AC then cut and plane there. Drive in three thin pins at A, B and C. Make a small notch in the template at C to just accept a pencil point.

The template is moved round anti-clockwise, being always held against pins A and C, with a pencil or ballpoint held in the notch. When pin A is reached, turn over the template and proceed clockwise to B, Fig. 159.

If the use of pins is not acceptable, cramp in their places sharp pointed strips.

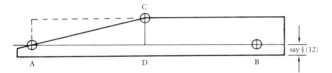

Fig. 158

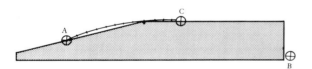

Fig. 159

An arc through three points
Fig. 160
Let the points be A, B and C. Join AB and BC. Right bisect each line. Normally the construction of X would be used but frequently in the workshop situation, as for example cutting the curved end of a table top, one pair of arcs would be off the timber.

More conveniently, strike large arcs from A and B, joining up this intersection with the mid point, (by measurement), of AB. Repeat for BC.

There will be a further intersection at P, which is the centre of the circle which passes through A, B and C.

This is a handy method for arranging such an arc to be cut by a portable jigsaw or power router, pivoting on a long arm.

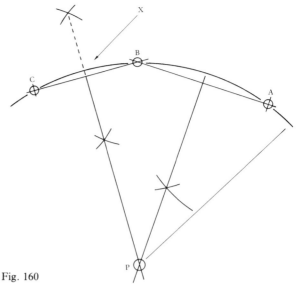

Fig. 160

Angles from simple trigonometry
Fig. 161
This is not as frightening as may at first appear to readers with but the haziest schoolday memories of the subject. The simplified table, page 59, gives enough accuracy for woodworking purposes. Of course, the bigger the project, the greater the accuracy will be. The small protractor is quite inaccurate for large scale work. However, very great accuracy can be obtained using the tan table (or a suitable calculator). The principle is this:

The tan of an angle equals $\dfrac{\text{opposite side}}{\text{adjacent side}}$

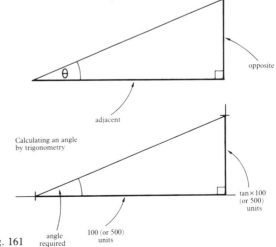

Calculating an angle by trigonometry

Fig. 161

Suppose the angle required is 9°. The tan of 9° is .1584, therefore

$$\frac{\text{opposite}}{\text{adjacent}} = .1584 \text{ or } \frac{.1584}{1}$$

so opposite = .1584 and adjacent = 1

For workshop purposes two decimal places are enough, so the tan may be taken as .16.

The method for use on the bench then is

1 Look up the tan of the angle, e.g. 9° = .1584
2 Correct this to two places of decimals, i.e. .16
3 Multiply this by 100 (or 500) = 16 (or 80)
4 Draw a line 100 (or 500) units long
5 At right angles at one end, draw a line 16 (or 80) units high.
6 Join the ends to get the angle required. Fig. 161 shows the idea. In practice, multiply by the largest number which will fit on the workpiece.

Angles from a folding rule
Fig. 162

Accurate large scale angles cannot be set out from the average protractor. Twelve inch and larger protractors are rare and expensive. Fortunately there is the perfect tool already in the workshop; the folding metre rule. There is not much use for the computer in the small workshop, but here for once it has come in very handy in saving an immense amount of boring calculation to provide the following table.

Simply open the rule at its centre joint and measure off the required distance at the inner tips. Half degrees may be obtained by interpolation.

For readers still loyal to imperial measurements the fractional calculations are much more involved. However, a simplified table is given for use with the folding two foot rule. (NB. – not three foot), calibrated in sixteenths.

Natural tangents	0′	30′		0′	30′		0′	30′
0° 0.0000	0087		32 0.6249	6371		64 2.0503	0965
1 0.0175	0262		33 0.6494	6619		65 2.1445	1943
2 0.0349	0437		34 0.6745	6873		66 2.2460	2998
3 0.0524	0612		35 0.7002	7133		67 2.3559	4142
4 0.0699	0787		36 0.7265	7400		68 2.4751	5386
5 0.0875	0963		37 0.7536	7673		69 2.6051	6746
6 0.1051	1139		38 0.7813	7954		70 2.7475	8239
7 0.1228	1317		39 0.8098	8243		71 2.9042	9887
8 0.1405	1495		40 0.8391	8541		72 3.0777	1716
9 0.1584	1673		41 0.8693	8847		73 3.2709	3759
10 0.1763	1853		42 0.9004	9163		74 3.4874	6059
11 0.1944	2035		43 0.9325	9490		75 3.7321	8667
12 0.2126	2217		44 0.9657	9827		76 4.0108	1653
13 0.2309	2401		45 1.000	0176		77 4.3315	5107
14 0.2493	2586		46 1.0355	0538		78 4.7046	9152
15 0.2679	2773		47 1.0724	0913		79 5.1446	3955
16 0.2867	2962		48° 1.1106	1303		80 5.671	5.976
17 0.3057	3153		49 1.1504	1708		81 6.314	6.691
18 0.3249	3346		50 1.1918	2131		82 7.115	7.596
19 0.3443	3541		51 1.2349	2572		83 8.144	8.777
20 0.3640	3739		52 1.2799	3032		84 9.51	10.39
21 0.3839	3939		53 1.3270	3514		85 11.43	12.71
22 0.4040	4142		54 1.3764	4019		86 14.30	16.35
23 0.4245	4348		55 1.4281	4550		87 19.08	22.90
24 0.4452	4557		56 1.4826	5108		88 28.64	38.19
25 0.4663	4770		57 1.5399	5697		89 57.29	114.6
26 0.4877	4986		58 1.6003	6319			
27 0.5095	5206		59 1.6643	6977			
28 0.5317	5430		60 1.7321	7675			
29 0.5543	5658		61 1.8040	8418			
30 0.5774	5890		62 1.8807	9210			
31 0.6009	6128		63 1.9626	0057			

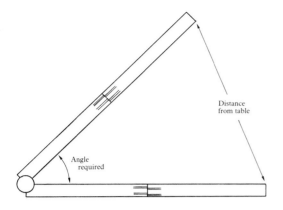

Fig. 162

Angles and distances made by a 2 ft folding rule
(*distances correct to $\frac{1}{16}$ in*)

Angle	Distance	Angle	Distance
10	$2\frac{1}{8}$	40	$8\frac{3}{16}$
15	$3\frac{3}{16}$	45	$9\frac{1}{8}$
20	$4\frac{3}{16}$	50	$10\frac{1}{8}$
$22\frac{1}{2}$	$4\frac{11}{16}$	60	12
25	$5\frac{1}{16}$	$67\frac{1}{2}$	$13\frac{5}{16}$
30	$6\frac{1}{4}$	90	17

Angles and distances made by a 1 metre folding in rule
(*distances correct to 0.1 mm*)

Angle	Distance	Angle	Distance	Angle	Distance
1	8.7	31	267.2	61	507.5
2	17.5	32	275.6	62	515.0
3	26.2	33	284.0	63	522.5
4	34.9	34	292.4	64	529.9
5	43.6	35	300.7	65	537.3
6	52.3	36	309.0	66	544.6
7	61.0	37	317.3	67	551.9
8	69.8	38	325.6	67.5	555.6
9	78.5	39	333.8	68	559.2
10	87.2	40	342.0	69	566.4
11	95.8	41	350.2	70	573.6
12	104.5	42	358.4	71	580.7
13	113.2	43	366.5	72	587.8
14	121.9	44	374.6	73	594.8
15	130.5	45	382.7	74	601.8
16	139.2	46	390.7	75	608.8
17	147.8	47	398.7	76	615.7
18	156.4	48	406.7	77	622.5
19	165.0	49	414.7	78	629.3
20	173.6	50	422.6	79	636.1
21	182.2	51	430.5	80	642.8
22	190.8	52	438.4	81	649.4
23	199.4	53	446.2	82	656.1
24	207.9	54	454.0	83	662.6
25	216.4	55	461.7	84	669.1
26	225.0	56	469.5	85	675.6
27	233.4	57	477.2	86	682.0
28	241.9	58	484.8	87	688.4
29	250.4	59	492.4	88	694.7
30	258.8	60	500.0	89	700.9
				90	707.1

Routing Methods

Routing on edges
Figs 163 to 167

This useful device developed from the need to rout a finger groove round the edge of a rectangular bread board. There are obviously many other applications.

Though apparently very simple, a few words of explanation are required. Very stable solid wood may be used but blockboard or multi-ply is more reliable.

Pin or cramp together the two cheeks, A, and drill the bolt holes so that they are identical. The precise method is this. Having marked the centres, drill first with the tapping drill for the screwed rod which has been chosen, for example if it is $\frac{1}{2}$ in screwed rod, drill through both at 10·5 mm. Separate the pieces, tapping one and redrilling the other at 13 mm, giving an easy fit. The table, B, is now glued to each cheek. If preferred, this can be additionally screwed or dowelled. Check very carefully that the two components are truly square and plane the joint level. Bolt the two parts together and skim over the combined table if it is not completely flat. With the circular saw or by gauge and hand planing, bring both tables to the same width.

Screw in the rod to the threaded holes and lock by means of a washer and nut.

To operate, assemble the two jaws with the work-

Fig. 163 Routing on edges. The method of operating

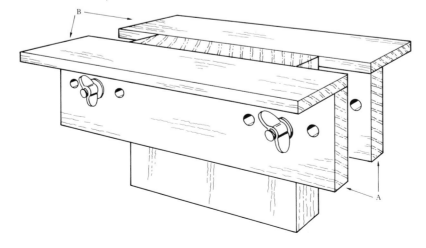

Fig. 164

piece between and tighten finger tight. Upend this assembly on a machine table or piece of truly flat blockboard, press down firmly then tighten fully. Hold this in the vice and operate the router with its fence running along the outer edge of the table. On occasions it will be found necessary to operate from each edge, Fig. 165.

Angles of 45°, Fig. 166, can be worked on in this way if the fixed jaw has a thin 45° block screwed to it, as in Fig. 167.

Routing small components

The holding of small components for routing does present a problem. This permanent solution is both convenient and time saving.

All that is involved is a slight modification to one of the wooden vice jaws. Fig. 168 clarifies this. Part A, the inner or fixed jaw, remains unaltered but when fitting new jaws some extra length is an advantage. B is the moving jaw and onto this is glued a strong lipping, C. which is, say, $\frac{1}{4}$ in (6 mm) greater than the metal jaw thickness. The lower the metal jaw is from the bench top, the stouter this lipping will be.

Having glued C to B and screwed on the wood jaws, plane the tops of both jaws accurately level with the bench surface. Now set the router fence to slightly less than the combined thickness of B and C. Run the fence of the router along the *inner* face of jaw B, thus trimming the outer face of the lipping C exactly parallel with the inner face of the moving jaw.

In use, the workpiece is held lightly in the jaws and with two short straight edges is pushed down level with the bench and vice jaw tops. Check this before starting work. The router's cutter depth is set and the fence is

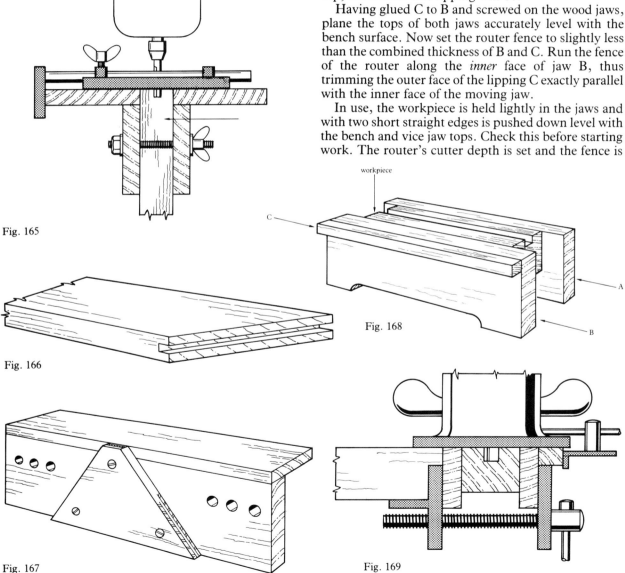

Fig. 165

Fig. 166

Fig. 167

workpiece

Fig. 168

Fig. 169

adjusted from the outer edge of the lipping, C. The section, Fig. 169 shows the set-up clearly. Both grooving and morticing are easily undertaken in this manner. Rebating is carried out by adding a parallel piece of waste, then proceeding as for grooving. Fig. 170 shows this with the vice omitted for simplicity.

As the lipping is intended to be a permanent feature, the reader will soon find further applications of this method of working.

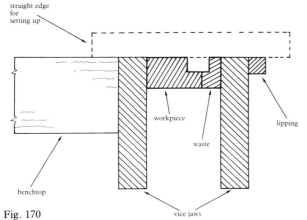

Fig. 170

A hinging aid for the router

This device will successfully cut the hinge sockets for doors when half the hinge is let into the door and half into the frame or carcase. It does not cope with the sloping sockets needed in the best cabinet making where the whole thickness of the hinge is let into the door. It is particularly useful in joinery, where numbers of similar large doors are to be hung.

Glue up the top frame, A, Fig. 171, leaving enough gap to accept the thickest doors to be considered. Attach to this a wide fence, B, which must project beyond the top frame at each end. The door is cramped to this fence. One end of the top frame acts as a stop; the other end is fitted with the sliding stop, C.

All sizes are but suggestions. Those given permit a

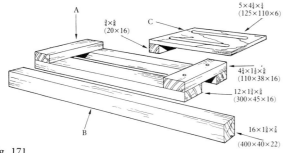

Fig. 171

Bosch router with a ½ in (12 mm) cutter to deal with hinges up to 3 in (75 mm). With other makes, draw the top view out full size with the router in place at each end and with the chosen cutter fitted – allow, say ¼ in (6 mm). This will be the maximum distance from the fixed to the moving stop, as shown in Fig. 172.

In use, set up and cramp to the previously marked door, Fig. 173. Remove the waste, preferably with a rough cut followed by a fine finishing cut. Before removing for a trial with a hinge, knife in a reference mark across both the top frame and the door. This enables the device to be accurately repositioned if necessary for a further cut. The mark on the top frame can be re-used for any other cut using the same router, cutter and hinge size.

The top frame is inevitably cut into but this is no disadvantage since it helps to set up for the next cut.

The normal router fence controls the width of the hinge socket. The rounded corners will need to be trimmed square.

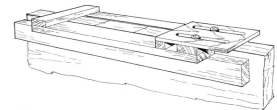

Fig. 172

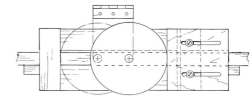

Fig. 173

Big circles with a small router
Figs 174 & 175

Some routers come with a circle cutting device, but its range is generally small and it relies on driving a point into the work, which is not always acceptable. This inexpensive device is an improvement.

Carefully measure the diameter of the sliding arms on the router's fence: generally about $\frac{5}{16}$ in (8 mm). Buy a pair of these in BDMS (bright drawn mild steel), not black steel, which is too rough. They should be a little longer than the diameter of the circle required. Prefer-

Fig. 174 Big circles with a small router. Moulding a table-top edge

Big circles with a small router
The router arms and pivot

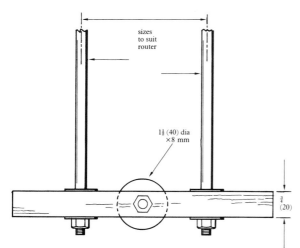

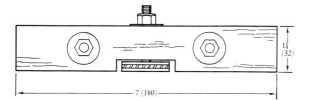

Fig. 175

ably they can be neatened by turning down one end of each to $\frac{1}{4}$ in (6 mm). An engineering friend or school-child metalworker is useful here. Thread these ends to $\frac{1}{4}$ in BSW (Whitworth) or the metric M6 and find for each a suitable nut and two large diameter washers. If it is not possible to turn the ends, thread at full size and use a second nut to provide the shoulder. While set up for this work, it is not a bad idea to make several pairs of differing lengths, which will cope with the most common sized jobs.

The general dimensions of the wood block are not critical, so the sizes given are only suggestions. What is important is the centre distance between the router arms, (measured from the router itself), and the height of these centres above a flat surface on which the router stands. Mark these sizes accurately on the wood block and, to allow for any slight error, drill the block a drill size larger than the thread chosen. Cut out the centre notch, then drill the pivot hole centrally with the tapping size for the pivot screw. For a $\frac{1}{4}$ in thread drill $\frac{7}{32}$ in or 5 mm; for a 6 mm thread, drill 5 mm. If the pivot is made from screwed rod or a large screw, turn $\frac{1}{4}$ in (6 mm) of it down to $\frac{3}{16}$ in (5 mm). If plain rod is to be threaded, leave this end unthreaded. Make a screwdriver slot at the threaded end and assemble. Lastly, turn a $1\frac{1}{2}$ in (40 mm) disc from good quality plywood and drill it centrally to suit the end of the pivot pin. Assemble with the whole appliance standing on a flat surface, then tighten the nuts fully.

To use, stick double-sided tape to one side of the disc and cut the middle clear. Peel off the backing, sight through the hole and position the disc over the marked centre of the job, tapping it firmly in place. Adjust the pivot pin to just clear the work, then adjust the diameter by means of the clamping screws on the router.

Remember that at two positions on the circle the router is cutting very much against the grain, so proceed with a number of fine cuts, finishing with a particularly fine, fast cut.

Big circles with the small router – further thoughts
Fig. 176

Readers lacking suitable metal or metalworking facilities may find this variation convenient. It applies to the Bosch router but can no doubt be modified for others.

Withdraw the fence then re-insert it the other way up. With the router standing on a flat surface the lowest part of the fence should remain clear. Obviously this will or will not be so, depending on the router being considered. If it can be so arranged, screw a wood block to the fence, just clear of the surface.

Into this block, tenon or lap dovetail the pivot bar. Arrange matters so that the pivot bar will be a full $\frac{1}{2}$ in

above the work surface. Drill a row of $\frac{1}{8}$ in holes along the centre line. Make a pivot block from $\frac{1}{2}$ in ply.

To use, fix the pivot block in place on the job, using double-sided tape. Attach the router by a $\frac{1}{8}$ in dia. pin in the most convenient hole in the pivot bar. Make the final adjustment by movement of the router along the fence bars.

Multiple grooves with the router
Fig. 177

Provided the grooves are not required too close together – nor too far apart – the simple device of Fig. 178 does an excellent job of cutting parallel housings. It is, essentially, no more than a fence, but by using the previous groove as a guide this method saves much setting up time.

First obtain two steel rods, of the same diameter as those on the router fence. Turn down one end of each to $\frac{1}{4}$ in (6 mm) and thread about half of this length. Prepare the wood block to size, depending on the router

Fig. 177 Multiple grooving with the small router. The basic adjustable model.
The fence

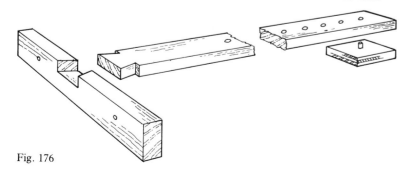

Fig. 176

Fig. 178A   Multiple grooving with the small router. The basic adjustable model. Not suitable for closely spaced grooves

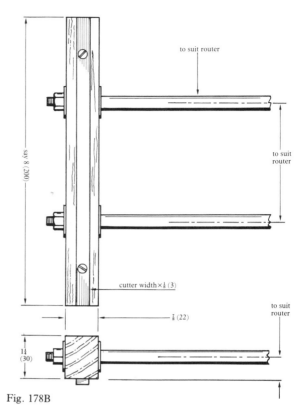

and the work. Measure carefully and mark out the centres of the holes to take the rods, and drill these one size above the nominal diameter of the thread, giving a slight adjustment if necessary. Stand the router and the block on a flat surface and assemble. If the bottom of the block and the base of the router do not align perfectly, slightly elongate the holes with a round file until they do. Secure each rod with two large diameter washers and a hexagon nut.

The guide bar is now screwed to the bottom face of the block. Ideally this is a $\frac{1}{8}$ in (3 mm) mild steel strip, the same width as the cutter. If this is unobtainable, make a wooden guide. Naturally various widths of

Fig. 178B

Fig. 179A   Multiple grooving with the small router
The fully adjustable model.
The set-up

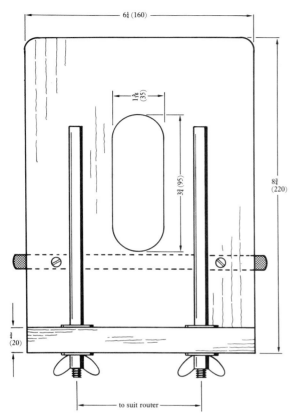

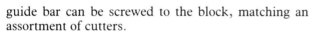

Fig. 179B

Fig. 180A   Multiple grooving with the small router
The simple 'one-off' system

guide bar can be screwed to the block, matching an assortment of cutters.

Make the first cut with the guide bar acting as a fence, running along the end of the work. For subsequent cuts, adjust the bar length where necessary, insert the guide bar into the first groove cut, and make the second, repeating the process as required.

More closely spaced grooves require a more elaborate method, Figs 179A & 179B. Make another block, as in Fig. 178 and secure to the ends of the round steel bars. Check for level with the router base and assemble. If satisfactory, dismantle and glue on the false base. This should be no thinner than $\frac{5}{16}$ in (8 mm) as suggested in the drawing. The holes in the block may need slight elongation to obtain a smooth sliding fit between the false base and the router base.

Screw the guide bar to the underside of the false base either with woodscrews from below, or more preferably, with machine screws from above, entering tapped holes in the bar. Either $\frac{1}{8}$ or $\frac{3}{16}$ in (3 or 4 mm) are

suitable diameters for the screws. Eventually an assortment of guide bars will be built up to match the cutter sizes.

For a 'one-off' job a simple non-adjustable model, Figs 180A & 180B, can quickly and easily be produced. Make a baseplate from good quality $\frac{5}{16}$ in (8 mm) plywood. Bore a central hole to accept the cutter and discharge the waste, and two countersunk holes to suit holes in the router base. If no suitable holes exist, the router base must be drilled and tapped, or at least clear drilled to accept screws and nuts.

A metal or wood strip to match the router cutter is screwed to the baseplate as already described. This is located to give the spacing required.

As stopped grooves or housings cannot be cut in this manner, a strip is first sawn from the edge of the component, the grooves worked then the strip glued back in place. For less important work, a separate strip can be made and applied to the job.

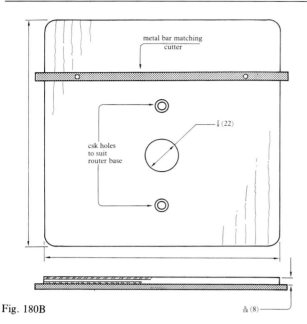

Fig. 180B

Bevelling and fielding with the small router

Rectangular work
Fig. 181

This method is particularly useful in the fielding of panels. These should be gauged first. A marking gauge marks the final edge thickness. To avoid an unsightly scar, the width of the fielding is marked with a pencil gauge, Fig. 182.

Produce a full size sectional drawing of the relevant part of the job, Fig. 183, and from it note the amount of slope for a given distance, i.e. the gradient. For example $\frac{3}{8}$ in : $1\frac{1}{2}$ in (10 : 40mm). Multiply this figure by, say, five, giving $1\frac{7}{8}$ in : $7\frac{1}{2}$ in (45 : 190 mm). This will be used in planning the device, so is drawn out full size, with $\frac{1}{4}$ in (6 mm) added as illustrated, Fig. 184. A tapered block is prepared to this size and with a width adequate to take the router base. True this up carefully

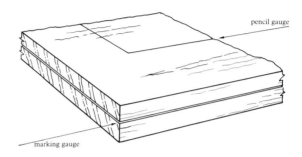

Fig. 182

Fig. 183

Fig. 181 Panel fielding or bevelling with the small router
The device

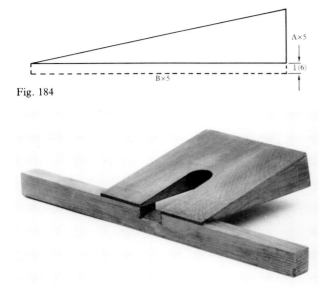

Fig. 184

Fig. 185   Aid for straight bevelling

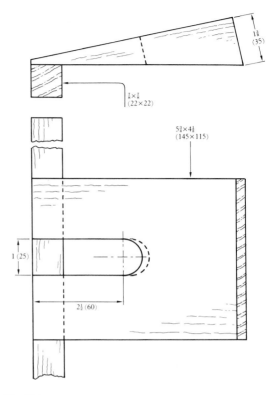

then trim the thick end square to the upper, sloping surface, not to the base. Take out a slot, say $\frac{1}{2}$ in wider than the cutter size.

A wood strip fence is glued and screwed under the block at the thin end. Make this longer than the block width. This helps to keep the router on line at the end of the cut, Figs 185 & 186.

Fig. 186

Fig. 187

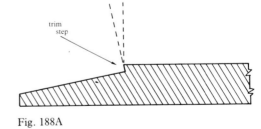

Fig. 188A

The router with its cutter and fence is assembled on the sloping face. Most fences have holes for the attachment of a larger wooden fence. Use these to screw the fence to the thick end of the block.

Adjust the depth of cut, then begin work at the outside edge, gradually bringing the router up the block until the cut runs out. Increase the cut, repeating the process until the gauge mark is reached. A gentle clean up will be required, using a sharp, finely set

smoothing plane followed by glasspapering down the grades.

When cutting a step fielding in this manner it is inevitable that the step will not be at right angles to the face of the panel. This can be overcome either by first routing a narrow plain groove in the normal way or by later trimming square with a shoulder plane. Another alternative is first to rout a groove using a half round hollow cutter, Fig. 188B.

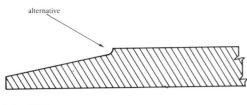

Fig. 188B

Circular work
Fig. 190

One useful purpose for this is the undercutting of the edges of circular tables to give an impression of lightness.

For this a similar block is prepared, Fig. 189. A housing is routed in this to take the radial arm. This is glued in and the base skimmed flat again. Note which way up the block goes, i.e. the thick end is at right angles to the sloping top, not to the base. Naturally this component may be built up if that is more convenient. When quite dry and true, a slot is routed out, a little wider than the cutter to be used. It is suggested that a $\frac{5}{8}$ in or $\frac{3}{4}$ in (16 or 20 mm) cutter be used, being about the biggest available with a $\frac{1}{4}$ in shank.

Position the assembly so that the router will have the required movement while still running completely on the sloping face. Mark and drill the pivot hole in the radial arm. If the work is being down on the underside of a table top, it is acceptable to put in a pivot screw. Where this cannot be done, fit a $\frac{1}{4}$ in (6 mm) plywood pivot block by means of double-sided tape and notch the radial arm to fit over it.

Small tops are conveniently held on a baseboard of ply or chipboard by means of two strips of double-sided tape. A bar screwed to the underside of the baseboard can be gripped in the vice.

Make a number of modest cuts, starting at the

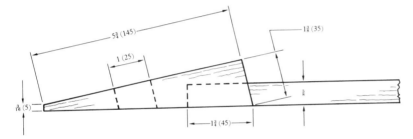

Fig. 189

Fig. 190   Circular bevelling with the small router undercutting a small table-top

periphery and bringing the router up the slope for subsequent cuts. Finish with a fine fast cut. This method removes the waste quickly and accurately but on difficult or stringy woods it may be necessary to finish with a finely set flat-faced spokeshave and then down through the grades of glasspaper.

Bevelling and fielding curved work

When such work is required, as for example on a curved or elliptical table top, the device shown in Fig. 186 is modified to that of Fig. 191. The straight fence has been replaced by the curved shape shown.

Where there are distinctly sharp corners where one of the two contact points will leave the work, the routing must be stopped just short and the shape finished by hand.

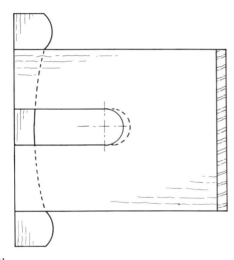

Fig. 191

Routing for tambours

Nowadays fewer workers will want to plough or scratch out grooves for tambours. The power router is so quick, neat and accurate that when one is available it is obviously the tool to be used. And many workers will use it, though not completely. The majority will be happy to work the straight grooves this way but lack the confidence to work the corner quarter circles. Working these freehand is somewhat risky, particularly on expensive material or when much work has already been done. So generally these curves are chiselled out, a time consuming though thoroughly safe method. Some routers are provided with a pivot pin for circular work but generally the radius required for tambours is too small to be arranged.

However, help is at hand in the form of the very

simple jig or template which follows. To make it, first collect the data as shown in Fig. 192. This will come from the working drawing and is width of groove; depth of groove (not immediately required); distance in from the edge; the radius proposed and the diameter of the router's guide ring.

Make the template from a piece of plywood very slightly greater in thickness than the height of the guide ring. Prepare an accurate square. The size will vary to suit the particular router. It must be big enough to permit the router movement required and also provide room for the two cramps holding it in place.

Fig. 193 shows the construction. Mark out with a fine ballpoint pen as this gives a consistent thin line. Mark the two centre lines to give the point C. On centre C, draw a circle which is the centre line of the groove. Stab in two centres P^1 and P^2. From them, with any convenient radius, strike two arcs, B. Join to C, bisecting the right angle then extend beyond C. On this 45° line, stab another centre, D, about $\frac{1}{4}$ in (6 mm) from C. This distance is related to the width of the slats. A later test run on some scrap material will confirm this distance. Now drill two holes on centres P^1 and P^2 of the

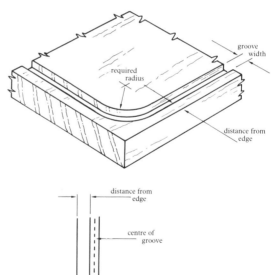

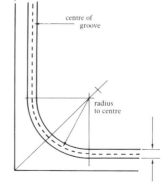

Fig. 192

same diameter as the guide ring. From centres C and D draw arcs between the two drilled holes. Shade in the waste then saw out carefully with a coping saw and file accurately to the lines. Drill C suitably to take a panel pin.

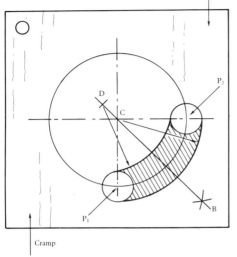

Fig. 193

On the actual job, gauge the distance to C from the two edges, and lightly stab their intersection. Locate the template on this point by a pin through C. Do not hammer in the pin. Square up the template with one edge of the job and secure there with handscrews or cramps, which must be positioned clear of the router.

Now simply fix the required cutter, generally $\frac{1}{4}$ in or 6 mm, adjust the depth and proceed to cut the groove. Two finer cuts are to be preferred to one heavy one.

That extra removed from the inside of the curve makes it easier for the slats to negotiate the corners. Test out the resultant groove and should there not be an easy fit, re-draw the inside curve with a slightly increased radius.

Now, having confidence in the template, it is preferable to cut the corner curves first and then join up with the straight grooves.

Finish by drilling a hanging hole as the template may well be used again. Write on it the width of slat used.

A router shooting board
Fig. 194

End grain often has to be planed. Simple jack planing in the vice can be hazardous for the less experienced. Concentration and effort are required. The need for so much concentration and skill can be eliminated by the use of a shooting board with the jack plane. The same system has been developed to make use of the router, giving great accuracy with even less effort.

Even the smallest router can be used, and any straight cutter, but the very smallest is suitable. The device is particularly useful to workers having no other machinery. As is generally the case, readers will find further uses for this device, Fig. 195.

Prepare the baseboard, A, from $\frac{3}{4}$ in (19 mm) multiply or MDF (medium density fibreboard). With the router cut a slot to accept a G cramp. Attach a rebated

Fig. 194   Router shooting board

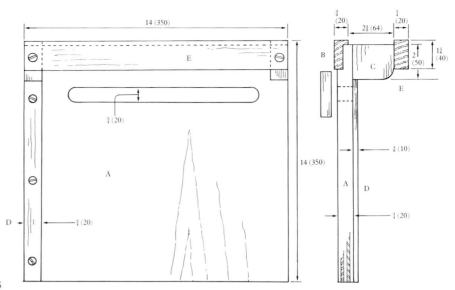

Fig. 195

strip, B. (This is not essential but is recommended.) Two spacing blocks, C, are glued and screwed in place accurately square to the top edge. The thinner strip, D, is screwed on in continuation of the spacing block. This must be checked for squareness to the top edge with a very accurate large tee-square or a large draughtsman's set square. The guide rail, E, is screwed in place with No. 10 screws, checking that the top, working surface is square to the baseboard. If necessary a planer may be used. Note that sizes given are only suggestions and will depend mainly on the router to be used and on the material available.

To use, lay the workpiece on the baseboard, A, pressed firmly against the strip, D, and level with it but not above the top of B and E. Slip a cramp through the slot, and with a small block behind it, cramp the workpiece firmly in place. The whole assembly may now be gripped in the bench-vice.

Fit up the router with the fence and a largish cutter. Tungsten carbide cutters are preferred since much end grain work will quickly dull a high speed steel cutter. It is now simply a matter of running the router and its fence along the guides. Either or both sides may be used. The depth of cut is slowly increased until the workpiece is squared down to the marked line. Finish with a slow moving fine cut to obtain the best surface.

In a similar way grooves or rebates in the end grain can be worked.

A router shooting board for 45°
Fig. 196

This 45° shooting board produces accurate mitres on board and flat material for either plain mitres or the reinforced mitre joints described later.

It is suggested that one be made with an internal capacity of 13 in (325 mm), capable of handling $\frac{7}{8}$ in (22 mm) material. Later a larger model may be required for work on carcases. Figs 197, 198 & 199.

Prepare a base from multi-ply or blockboard with a hardwood lipping. Plane the two long sides exactly parallel. This is very important. Machines may help here. Mark out with a knife and try-square, then cut the

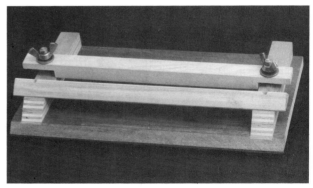

Fig. 196A Router shooting board for 45 degrees

73

Fig. 196B Router shooting board for 45 degrees. Router in place to cut the mitre

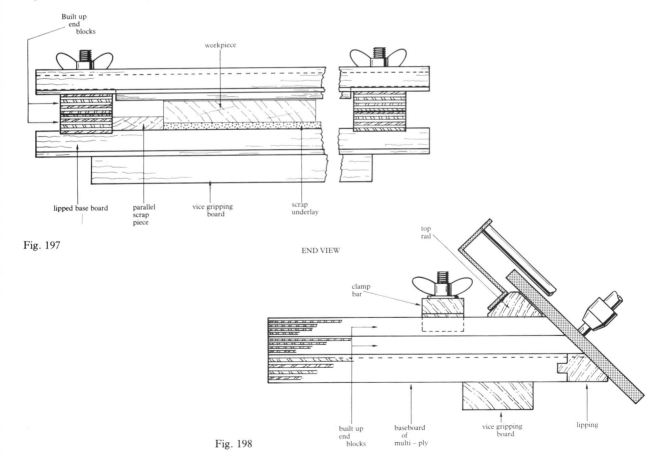

Built up
end
blocks

workpiece

lipped base board   parallel
scrap
piece

vice gripping
board

scrap
underlay

Fig. 197

END VIEW

top
rail

clamp
bar

built up
end
blocks

baseboard
of
multi – ply

vice gripping
board

lipping

Fig. 198

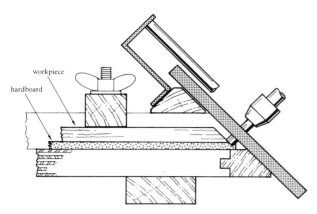

Fig. 199   End view with end block removed

two $\frac{1}{16}$ in (2 mm) housings for the end blocks. Angle the lipping to exactly 45° either by hand, machine or both. Leave a small amount of the original edge.

The two end blocks are built up from two layers of 13 mm ply (or more of thinner material). Solid wood may shrink, increasing the 45° angle. The blocks are brought to width then glued and screwed into the housings, checking that they are truly square (using the parallel back edge) before final fixing.

The top rail is prepared to triangular section, avoiding sharp corners, and with the screw holes bored and counterbored. Cramp in place and check the 45° by setting a bevel accurately to a draughtsman's set square. Then screw in place. Do not glue at this stage in case later correction is required.

Drill for the clamping screws and tap, using the taper tap only, until the bottom face is reached. Using two lock-nuts, screw in the two lengths of $\frac{1}{2}$ or $\frac{3}{8}$ in (12 or 10 mm) screwed rod. Two washers and nuts, or preferably wing-nuts complete this stage.

The clamp bar is notched and drilled at each end to a sloppy fit. Fig. 200. The under, or gripping, face should be planed to a slight curve giving a good grip in the centre. If preferred, a glasspaper or rubber facing can be applied.

A gripping bar for the vice is screwed underneath.

To use

Assemble in the jig with a scrap piece of hardboard or plywood underneath to protect the base. A second scrap piece, a spacer, cut truly parallel, is placed between the work and the end block. Its purpose is similarly to prevent damage to the shooting board. A scrap of multi-ply is held against the 45° face. The workpiece is pressed hard against this and also against the spacer. While the work is so held, the clamp bar is tightened. The mitre can now be cut with the router as illustrated in Fig. 196B, ending up slightly below the 45° plane. A better finish is obtained by taking several lighter cuts. It helps in the setting up if the end of the workpiece has been sawn dead square before inserting into the shooting board.

Use the largest cutter which the router will accept.

Routing gauges

To take the thinking out of routing

From time to time grooves and housings are required where the distance from the true edge to the groove is greater than the router's fence will cope with. The usual remedy is well known. A wooden straight-edge is cramped or pinned to the work and the router, with its fence removed, runs along this wooden fence, whose exact position is found by a niggling process of trial and error. This will be repeated for each operation.

The distance of this fence from the marked out groove is well known: radius of base minus radius of cutter, i.e. half of the base diameter minus half of the cutter size. With this worked out there are still the possibilities of miscalculation or mismeasurement. But things can be worse. For example, the base size might be 125 mm and the cutter $\frac{7}{16}$ in. Furthermore, some routers, like the Bosch, have a flattened side which runs very conveniently along the wood fence.

There is an accurate and permanent solution to this problem in the form of the following simple wooden gauges.

Put together, from scrap, a temporary construction table. No sizes are important. The fence needs to be

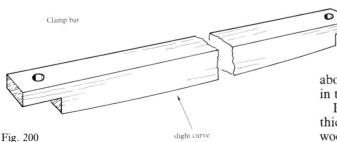

Clamp bar

Fig. 200

slight curve

about $\frac{1}{2}$ or $\frac{5}{8}$ in (12 to 15 mm) tall. A block below to grip in the vice obviates the use of cramps, Fig. 201.

Prepare an offcut of plywood $\frac{3}{16}$ or $\frac{1}{4}$ in (4 or 6 mm) thick with one edge planed accurately. Do not use solid wood which may shrink and so become inaccurate. The ply is pinned down with this true edge firmly in contact with the fence and the heads punched below the surface, Fig. 202.

With the selected cutter installed, run the router along the fence, cutting off the excess ply. Fig. 203. Rather than take a heavy cut, work in the following stages. Interpose a thin steel rule between the router and the fence then cut through the plywood. Remove the steel rule and make a fine finishing cut. Make a second pass in case the router has strayed from the fence on the first cut. Prize off the plywood gauge, label it with the size of cutter used and drill the customary hanging hole, Fig. 204.

To set up the work, lay the fence on the job with the gauge at each end in turn, Fig. 205. For real accuracy, hold a marking knife on the line and push the fence and the gauge up to it. Repeat at the other end. When both ends are satisfactory, cramp the fence and proceed to cut the groove or housing.

Sometimes odd sizes are required for which a cutter is not available, or larger grooves are required from a router taking only $\frac{1}{4}$ in shanks. In such a case it is useful to collect offcuts of bright drawn mild steel, say $\frac{3}{8}$ or $\frac{1}{2}$ in (10 or 12 mm) wide and in thicknesses of $\frac{1}{16}$, $\frac{1}{8}$, $\frac{3}{16}$ & $\frac{1}{4}$ in or metric equivalents. To cut for example a $\frac{5}{8}$ in groove when only a $\frac{1}{2}$ in cutter is to hand, proceed as already detailed then interpose a $\frac{1}{8}$ in strip between the router base and the fence and make a second cut, thus widening the $\frac{1}{2}$ in groove to an accurate $\frac{5}{8}$ in.

As in all routing, it is essential to concentrate well and not let the router wander from the fence.

Having made the construction table, it is worth spending a little time to make a gauge for each size of one's stock of straight cutters.

Routing housings of odd sizes
Fig. 206
The power router is probably the ideal tool for cutting a housing or dado. It is both quick and accurate. The method is simple and well known. A batten is pinned or cramped at right angles across the workpiece and the router is run along this.

Unfortunately, wood is not as co-operative as it could be. Frequently, by the time the wood has been cleaned up or reduced to its required size, it does not match the sizes in which router cutters are made. Also, expense limits the number of router cutters kept. This means that two or more cuts will need to be made to cover the required width. This in turn means that the guide batten must be moved to a second position and, what is more, it must be moved absolutely parallel and for the same distance for each housing.

This easily constructed device overcomes these dif-

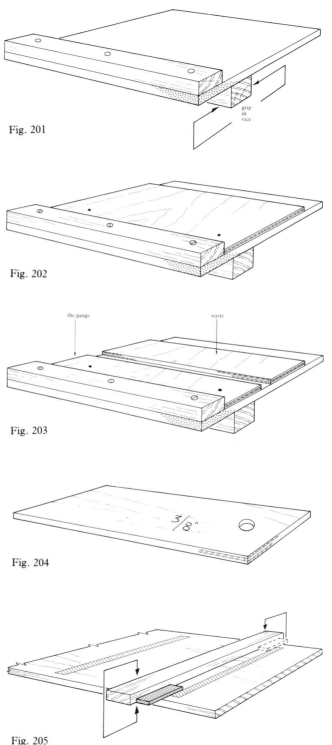

Fig. 201

Fig. 202

Fig. 203

Fig. 204

Fig. 205

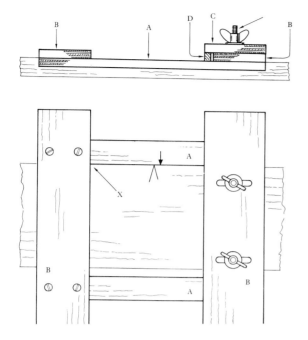

Fig. 206

ficulties. Sizes will vary according to the model of router employed and the size of work undertaken. The longitudinal pieces, A, can be about $1\frac{1}{2}\times\frac{1}{2}$ in (40×12 mm) and of a length to suit the router, say 13 ins (330 mm). The cross members, B, can be $3\frac{1}{4}\times\frac{1}{2}$ in (80×12 mm). Choose a length which will be convenient for the majority of the work expected. On the model shown they are $15\frac{3}{4}$ in (400 mm). In due course, several devices will probably be constructed in different sizes.

Glue and screw together components A and B, taking great care that the joints are accurate right angles, particularly the joint marked X.

The sliding component, C is made $3\frac{1}{2}\times\frac{1}{2}$ in (90×12 mm) and is slotted to give an easy fit to $\frac{5}{16}$ in (8 mm) screws. A lipping piece, D, fills the gap between C and A. Drill the cross member, B, with two holes to match the slots. Use a $\frac{1}{4}$ in ($6\cdot5$ mm) drill then tap to take $\frac{5}{16}$ in BSW or M8 screws. Countersink underneath and screw in two captive countersunk machine screws. Now secure C using wing-nuts and large diameter washers.

The gap is set using this simple formula:

$$\text{width} = \text{size of router base}$$
$$+ \text{size of housing}$$
$$- \text{size of cutter}$$
$$or\ W = b + h - c$$

It is worth inscribing this somewhere on the device.

Try this out on a scrap piece. Cramp on the job with the longitudinal piece, A, against the true edge. Make a trial cut, adjusting C as necessary. C and the opposite B must be truly parallel. Aim for a very tight fit so that the shelf, for example, needs the finest shaving off to enter. When satisfied with the adjustment, take cuts right through A and use this cut to subsequently line up on the workpiece. When the job is completed, fill in with a glued block and trim level, ready for the next project.

A parallel or a dovetail cutter can be used. On a wide component a dovetail takes a lot of pushing in, so C can be set slightly out of square to produce a tapered dovetail housing. An alternative method of cutting dovetail housings is given on page 90.

Using this device, any width of housing may be cut, using for example, only a $\frac{1}{4}$ in (6 mm) cutter.

To avoid the use of G cramps, a batten can be arranged underneath. Coach bolts through pieces A with washers and wing-nuts can secure the device to the workpiece. This is not shown in the diagram. A strip of fine glasspaper glued to the underside of pieces B reduces any tendency to move during fitting. It must be kept well back from the edges.

Other uses will no doubt be found for this device.

Odd angles with the small router
Figs 207 & 208

From time to time angles other than 90° are required. Admittedly 45° cutters are available though not commonly owned. Other angles are not provided by the cutter makers. Fortunately a simple device can be constructed which will enable the worker to cut any angle using the Bosch router or any similar machine which can be fitted to a drill stand, Figs 209 & 210.

A baseplate of multi-ply, blockboard or MDF is

Fig. 207   Odd angles with a small router. The jig

Fig. 208 Odd angles with a small router The method

suitably drilled to secure it to the drill stand. An adjustable worktable is hinged to this. Two slotted metal or plywood stays lock this table at the desired angle. It will be found convenient to drill two holes in the table to give screwdriver access to the screws securing the baseplate. These holes are opened out slightly on the underside to give adequate clearance.

The fence is secured with a woodscrew pivot at one end and at the other with a wing-nut operating in a slot, thus giving fine adjustment. A central notch is cut out to accept the router cutter. The method of use is clearly shown in the photograph.

For circular work, the fence is removed and replaced by two dowels inserted into the worktable.

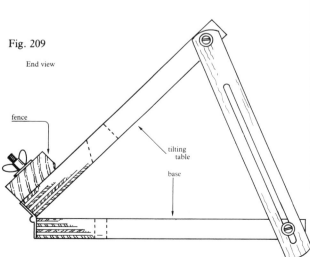

Fig. 209

End view

fence

tilting table

base

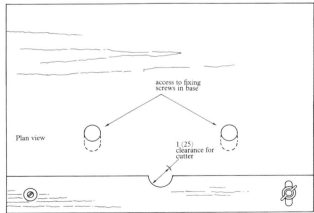

access to fixing screws in base

Plan view

1 (25) clearance for cutter

Fig. 210

SECTION 4 **Machine Made Joints**

Splined Mitre Joints with the Router
Figs 211 & 212

There are times when making a box, casket or small carcase, that a corner joint is required between a concealed dovetail and a rebated and nailed job. This

Fig. 211 Splined mitre joint with the router. Specimen joint

may be for lack of time, lack of skill, lack of funds or a special need might call for a considerable number of identical boxes.

All these requirements are catered for by a splined mitre joint which has the additional virtue of not demanding heavy machinery. A router, even the simplest and smallest, is the only essential power tool.

The jig, Fig. 213, is basically the 45° router shooting board described on page 73. This should be read before any construction is begun.

Time and effort is saved if the mitre is sawn approximately first. It can then either be planed using a sharp jack plane on a mitre shooting board, page 132, or else cut in the jig with the router, using the biggest cutter available. Thicker components or smaller cutters require several cuts.

To set up for grooving the waste piece underneath is not necessary. Hold a piece of multi-ply against the 45° face and press the workpiece hard against this. If the groove is to run right through, a parallel spacer is needed to prevent the corner from breaking out so the work must also bear hard against this. With the work so held, tighten up the clamp bar. Grooving can now

Fig. 212 Splined mitre joint with the router.
Routing the groove

commence. Note that the grooves are not cut centrally on the mitre. By moving it closer to the inside, a deeper groove is possible. Repeat the process on the other components. When a number of components are required with concealed splines, two adjustable stops can be screwed to the end blocks to limit the router movement.

The ideal splines are cut from plywood to match the router cutter. The best plywood for this purpose is 'stoutheart' which gives an almost cross-grained spline. If made from the solid, cut out across the grain. This spline is quite fragile until glued in place, but produces a stronger joint than a long grain spline which can split.

Solid wood splines are easily made using the small router overhead, in a drill stand, as a miniature thicknesser. To make accurate splines by hand, plane them to thickness in the simple jig, Fig. 214. This can be made quickly and easily and will always come in handy again.

The joints can be glued up using wire cramps, page 30, for smaller jobs. But for larger boxes and carcases cramp with triangular blocks, Fig. 215. These are made

Fig. 215   Splined mitred joint. Gluing up method

by sawing square stock diagonally and gluing onto the corners. This is generally a 'five o'clock job', to be ready for work next morning. Light wood hand-cramps, (pages 17 onwards) keep down the weight and expense. Allow 24 hours for the joint to harden before splitting off the blocks and planing clean, to produce a simple, strong joint.

More splined mitre joints: an adjustable device
Fig. 216

A device has been described for cutting and grooving a mitred joint at 45°. Other angles are required from time to time, for example, when making boxes and tubs in hexagonal, octagonal and irregular forms. A similar though adjustable device enables any angle to be mitred then strengthened with a spline. Figs 217 & 218.

First prepare a baseboard. This can be multi-ply, blockboard or MDF. For modest work an overall length of 18 in (450 mm) is suggested. Otherwise make to suit the expected jobs. The front edge is thickened by the addition of a hardwood lipping. This is planed truly straight then formed to a semi-circle section with the router. A shallow housing is next formed at each end of the baseboard. Make the end blocks, either by routing a slot or by building up as in the photographs. The height shown will accept $\frac{7}{8}$ in (23 mm) material. Increase this height if thicker material is expected. Drill a $\frac{1}{4}$ in (6 mm) hole centrally in each housing and tap for a $\frac{5}{16}$ in BSW thread or similar. Do not tap fully but stop when the taper tap just protrudes. Insert screwed rod, or long

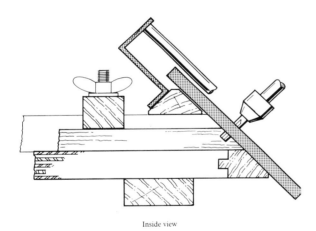

Inside view

Fig. 213

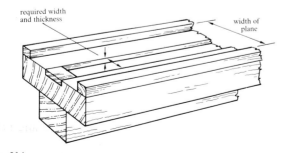

required width and thickness

width of plane

Fig. 214

Fig. 216 Adjustable router shooting board for splined mitres etc

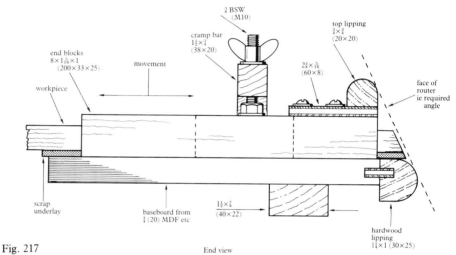

Fig. 217

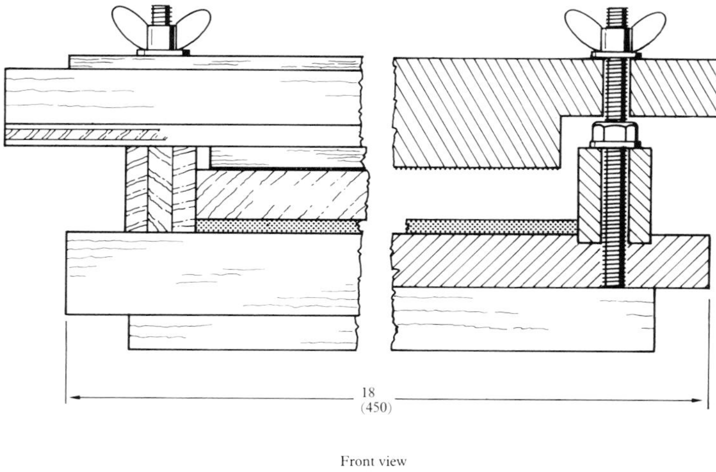

Fig. 218

roofing bolts. Clamp the end blocks, using large washers and hexagon nuts.

Prepare the top rail, rounding with the router as illustrated. Glue this to a strip of good quality $\frac{1}{4}$ in (6 mm) plywood and this in turn to the end blocks.

Underneath the base screw a thick strip to be gripped in the vice.

Produce the cramp bar to size, then drill and notch the ends. Drill over-size to give a sloppy fit. Plane the underside very slightly curved then face it with glass-

Fig. 219 More splined mitre joints. A bevel to set the angle

build up the stock. A shaving off the blade gives an easy fit. Drill the stock at $\frac{3}{16}$ in (5 mm) then tap at $\frac{1}{4}$ in (6 mm). Enlarge the hole on one side of $\frac{1}{4}$ in (6 mm). Secure the blade by using a large headed *gutter* bolt, washer and wing-nut. One hole only is needed in the blade.

Making ready Set the bevel precisely to the mitre angle, preferably from a large scale template. Remove the cramp bar, slacken the hexagon nuts, then line up the top rail as illustrated, Fig. 219A, by sliding the end blocks. Check at both ends, check yet again then tighten the hexagon nuts.

The workpiece must be planed truly square at the ends to be mitred. This is most important. Do not rely on the small end blocks to give accuracy. Clamp the workpiece in the centre of the baseboard with a scrap of hardboard underneath.

Hold a flat setting board against the upper and lower rails, pull the workpiece and the hardboard firmly against this, then tighten the clamp bar. With a steel rule check that the work is correctly held.

Work can now begin either in the vertical or the horizontal mode, according to preference and the size of the workpiece.

In the case of small routers fit the largest available cutter, probably $\frac{3}{4}$ in (20 mm) or $\frac{5}{8}$ in (16 mm). With a series of cuts, adjusting both fence and depth, cut the mitre, finishing with a fine cut. Repeat the process on all the other components. When the last mitre has been cut, notice that the mitred face is behind the line joining the upper and lower rails. So, slacken the clamp bar and bring forward the mitre to the setting board as before.

Change to a $\frac{1}{4}$ in (6 mm) or $\frac{3}{16}$ in (5 mm) cutter, adjusting both depth and fence. The groove is arranged slightly inwards of the centre to give a greater depth and hence a bigger spline. Cut in one pass. Do not take the router back through the groove as this is likely to make it over-wide.

paper. Position the cramp bar in its place and add two large-diameter washers and wing-nuts.

To set up, a large sliding bevel is required. Such a tool can easily be made, Fig. 219. See page 40. Thickness a piece of hardwood to $\frac{1}{4}$ in (6 mm) then

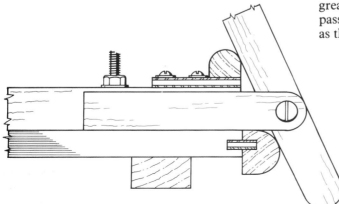

Fig. 219A Setting the angle

Splines can be cut from plywood, (stoutheart is best having a strong long-grain core), or from short-grained hardwood strips, page 000.

Clean and polish the inside surfaces to prevent a build-up of glue in the corners. For best results, glue on some angle blocks then nip up the dry joint with a spline in place. If all is well, complete the glue-up. When using thinner materials it is an advantage sometimes to make the glue-up on a temporary former.

Where necessary, stop and start the groove short of the ends, giving an invisible joint.

The Keyed Mitre Joint

An alternative box joint
Fig. 220
Neat boxes are frequently required with joints other than through dovetails. A plain mitre is particularly weak. It is occasionally strengthened with keys of veneer. This is not much stronger and the difficulty is always met of finding a saw to match the veneer thickness. The Keyed Mitre joint nicely fits the bill and, once again, no great skill is required.

Prepare the components accurately to width and thickness, ensuring a good finish, particularly on the inside. The mitred ends can be sawn by hand, by radial arm saw or by a circular saw having a tilting arbor. However they are sawn they will not be good enough for jointing. They should be cut very slightly long and brought to size using either an accurate mitre shooting board, (page 132 or router equivalent, page 73).

Grooves or rebates for the bottom or the top, if applicable, can now be ploughed, routed or sawn, taking great care of the mitres.

When the top and bottom have been prepared, the whole structure can be assembled dry, using two wire cramps, (pages 30 & 31) or by the use of triangular glue blocks and cramps as in Fig. 215. If all is well, the top and bottom are polished and the whole job glued together. Later any glue must be removed from both the inside and the outside.

At this stage the joint is very fragile, requiring the addition of strengthening keys. Veneer keys, used extensively by the Victorians provide but little strength and one or two thicknesses seldom match the saw kerf. Something stronger is required, from, say, $\frac{1}{16}$ to $\frac{1}{8}$ in (1.5 to 3 mm) in thickness. These keys form quite a decorative feature either of the same or of a contrasting

Fig. 220   Keyed mitre joint

wood. End grain in any case will darken with polishing. The slots for the keys can be cut in one of three ways. Choose the most convenient.

An overhead router or a hand router set in a drill stand is very effective. A slotting cutter on an arbor is used. This gives a limited depth of cut, but for small decorative boxes is generally enough. The work is fed into a vee-shaped guide positioned precisely below the cutter, Figs 221 & 222.

A small radial arm saw set horizontally, using wobble washers, works in much the same way with a similar vee guide, Figs 221 & 222. Here, there is no limit to the depth of cut.

The table saw with wobble washers is equally successful but necessitates the construction of the simple jig shown in Fig 224A & B. It is essentially a vee-shaped cradle mounted on two runners, one of which is fitted with a metal bar to match the groove in the sawbench. Inside the cradle is fitted a movable

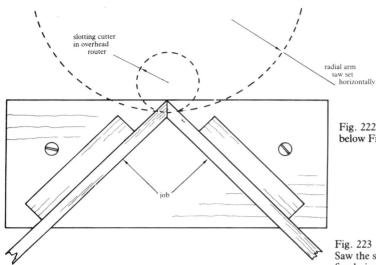

Fig. 221

Fig. 222 Push block for feeding in work. View of underside see below Fig. 223

Fig. 223 Keyed mitre joint
Saw the slots by moving the saw. The push block holds the work firmly in the jig. See Fig. 222

fence. Having completed its construction, the jig is passed over the saw set to the required height. The fence is removed and a locating key glued in place. When cleaned up the fence is repositioned having been moved across to give the required spacing.

The first cut is made with the box against the projecting key. This cut is then located on the key to make the next cut and the process repeated. Cuts can be evenly spaced or grouped in pairs and so on.

The key material is prepared in strips either by hand planing or using the overhead router as a miniature thicknesser, (pages 80–85). If the strips are too tight a

Fig. 224A The keyed mitre joint. Cutting the key slots in the table saw

Fig. 224B

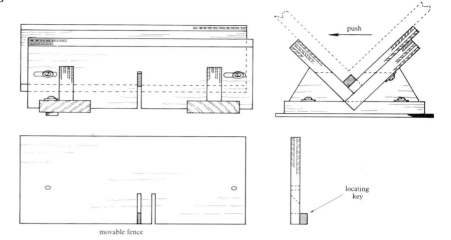

movable fence

locating
key

fit, they will swell slightly with the glue and become difficult to insert. Cut the strips into rectangles rather than triangles as tapping in with the hammer will break off the apex of triangular keys. Fig. 225.

When dry saw off the keys and plane flush, then finish as for any other type of small box.

Where there is to be a sawn off lid, remember to give extra space between two keys so that after the sawing and planing has been done, the spacing appears even.

To avoid having to do precise marking out, cut at the first setting, invert the box and repeat. Continue in this way for subsequent settings. This gives two clusters of keys, Fig. 226. This technique also permits deeper boxes to be made with the router since, after a few cuts, the work fouls on the router body and no deeper adjustments can be made.

Small carcases can be jointed in this way if the jig, Fig. 224, is scaled up in size to give adequate support and if the saw table is big enough.

Attempts to use this jig on a router table will not be successful since the cutter will not protrude high enough above the table.

Splines and keys from the router

The slender material for splines and keys, to be effective, must be most accurately prepared to thickness. Although this can be made using the circular saw or by hand planing, the router is the most precise and finely adjustable tool.

A modern variation is needed of the traditional sticking board, to hold the material. Fig. 227 shows this in section. Length is a matter of preference. It can be built up, as drawn, or routed out.

Fig. 225   Keyed mitre joint. Rectangular keys glued in place

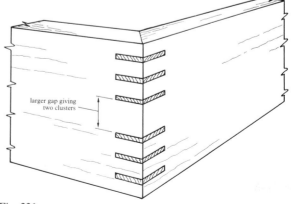

larger gap giving
two clusters

Fig. 226

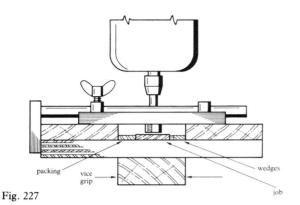

Fig. 227

The board is held in the vice by the usual vice batten and the material itself gripped between a thin packing piece and wedges.

The router is guided along the work by its fence. The largest available cutter should be chosen, its depth being very slowly regulated as the material is tried for thickness in a specimen groove or sawcut.

The Comb Joint
Fig. 228

The comb or finger joint is made commercially with quite sophisticated and expensive machinery. Nevertheless, satisfactory joints can be produced using very simple equipment, i.e. the small circular saw with wobble washers. Using modern adhesives the joint is comparable in strength with the through dovetail. It is hardly worth making by hand since the time and skill required is the same as for the more decorative dovetail.

The simple tool to make this joint, Fig. 229, is best constructed from one of the man-made materials rather than from solid wood, to avoid warping and to preserve the flat working surfaces. Sizes are only suggestions and will depend mainly on the sizes of the sawbench and the expected work, Fig. 230.

Rout or chop the slots in the working face and drill the base plate for the screws securing the metal guide strip which is positioned so that the saw should line up

Fig. 229a Simple comb jointer

Fig. 228   The comb joint

Fig. 229b Simple comb jointer

Fig. 230

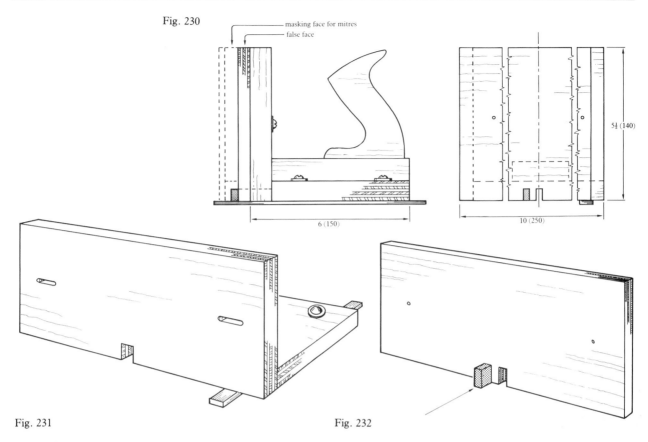

masking face for mitres
false face

5½ (140)

6 (150)

10 (250)

Fig. 231

Fig. 232

approximately central. Drill over-size so that the strip can later be adjusted truly square to the working face. Glue together the working face and the base, ensuring an accurate right angle, Fig. 231. A glued-in fillet may be added if it is thought necessary. A strong block is glued centrally on the base and the handle fitted to it. This can be a spare for a Record type plane, hand-made or simply a turned knob.

A false face is now made from thinner material and screwed onto the working face. The wobble saw is now adjusted to give the size of kerf required. The height is next set by trial. It should be lower than the thickness of the material to be used. A trial cut on an offcut should not quite sever the piece. There should be a paper thin connection. The saw is locked at this height.

Obtain a piece of bright drawn mild steel strip to suit the groove in the sawbench. Formerly and frequently this was $\frac{1}{2} \times \frac{1}{8}$ in. Modern benches are likely to have metric grooves. Preferably tap the bar and screw from above. Adjust for squareness with the working face. Alternatively, screw with countersunk woodscrews, but here later adjustment will be difficult, Fig. 231.

Now position the tool and pass it over the circular saw making a groove right through. Safety will be discussed later and a guard described.

The false face is now removed. A hardwood locating pin, the exact thickness of the saw kerf is glued in place. When dry the back face is planed level and the false face repositioned, moved along by the thickness of the saw kerf, Fig. 232.

Make tests cut on offcuts from the job, adjusting the false face until the joint meshes perfectly along the width required. A test of two or three cuts is not enough. Obviously a sloppy joint is undesirable but a joint which is very tight will swell when dampened with glue. When a successful test has been made, start on the job itself.

Method. Start with a long side. Place the true edge firmly up against the locating pin and make a cut, Fig. 233A. Place this cut over the pin and repeat successively, Fig. 233B. The piece must end with a pin, not a slot. This means that often it is quicker to slightly modify the job width to match the set-up rather than tediously to adjust for the planned width. Repeat the process until

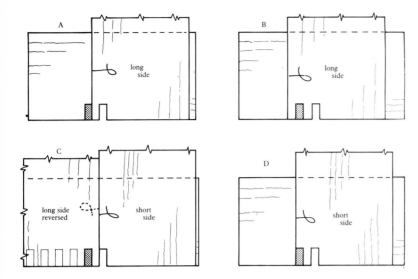

Fig. 233

the four ends are jointed. Note that the first cut must always be made at the true edge.

Now place the first cut of a long side on the register pin, hold a short side firmly against it and make a cut, Fig. 233C. Hold this cut against the pin and make another cut, Fig. 233D. Continue as normal across the width. Repeat on the other ends. Again, the true edge must lead.

Polish the insides, protecting the pins with plastic tape. Glue and cramp together with waxed wood blocks providing pressure along the joints. Lightly plane the sides flush.

When a mitred corner is required, a further loose masking face, Fig. 234, is cramped in place. This must

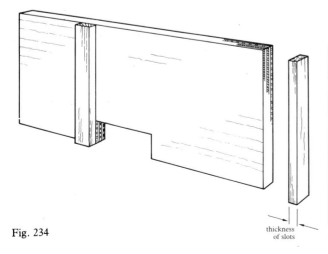

Fig. 234

thickness
of slots

Fig. 235 Improved comb jointer with fine adjustment

be just thicker than the locating pin. Also prepare a strip, exactly the thickness of the slots. Once the first cut has been made, the masking face is removed and the joint is cut as normal on all the long sides. Add the thin strip, Fig. 234, and make the first cut on all the short pieces. Now remove the masking face and continue as normal, stopping short of the if a second mitre is required.

When the mitre is required on one edge only, as for example on the top edge of a box, or the front edge of a carcase, use the normal method and stop cutting short by the size of mitre required. To cut the mitres, see page 134.

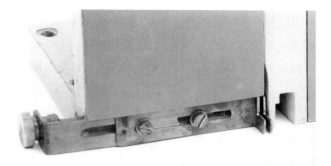

Fig. 236 Improved comb jointer. Details of the mechanism

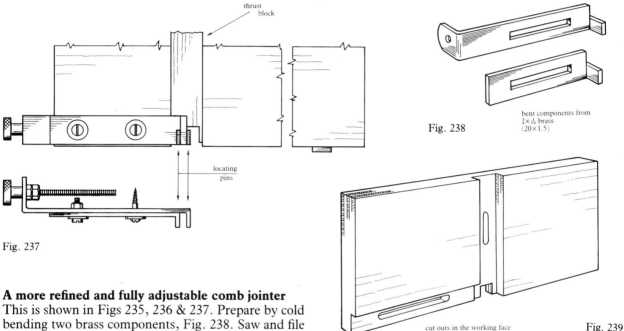

Fig. 237

Fig. 238

bent components from ⅜ × 1/16 brass (20 × 1.5)

Fig. 239

cut outs in the working face

A more refined and fully adjustable comb jointer

This is shown in Figs 235, 236 & 237. Prepare by cold bending two brass components, Fig. 238. Saw and file the two locating pins and work the slots. Remove a rebate for them on the working face. Cut the housing, with its slot, for the thrust block in the working face and prepare a block to fit it. This prevents spelching when cutting the sockets. A woodscrew with washer secures it, Fig. 239. Solder a brass nut behind the larger, moving strip. The smaller fixed strip is fastened to the larger, preferably with a cheese headed screw. Both components are secured to the working face with a round headed woodscrew. Both screws require washers. The adjusting knob can be either of metal or a radio knob. Two lock-nuts secure it to the moving strip. A hole tapped in the wooden working face will be adequate for the small amount of movement which will take place.

To use. Make a cut in scrap wood, unfasten both screws and adjust the two locating pins to be a good fit in the slot. Tighten the cheese headed screw. With the knob, adjust the pair of locating pins in the manner already described until a good joint is obtained. Tighten the round headed screw, make a final test of the joint, then go into production.

Do not forget constantly to re-adjust the thrust block, otherwise the sockets will all have a splintered back corner.

The same method may be used with a router inverted in a router table, providing of course, that the table has a machined groove to accept the metal guide bar.

Dovetail Housings with a Small Router

Fig. 240

With these two simply made aids this joint can be made repeatedly, accurately and without special skills. Minor details will vary according to the router used and the scale of work attempted, so any sizes given are but suggestions.

Cutting the housings

This device consists of two guide pieces of multi-ply secured to two hardwood battens. One guide is fixed by gluing; the other is adjustable, locked with screws and wing-nuts. One of the battens is assembled below two plywood spacing pieces, to prevent the router cutting into the batten, though this is a refinement rather than an essential. When gluing the two battens to the guide piece, be sure to get exact right-angles.

Tap the hole in the moving guide so that the countersunk screw, when fully inserted, cannot turn. A slot can be routed in each batten to accept the screw: use a large diameter washer to prevent the wing-nut chewing up the wood, Figs 241 & 242.

To set up the aid, close up the guide pieces tightly on the router's template guide or bush, but still permitting easy movement. This will cut a housing of precisely the diameter of the dovetail cutter. If a wider housing is required, close up the guide pieces onto the template guide, having inserted a small strip of wood or metal which, when added to the diameter of the cutter, will give the required housing width.

Fig. 240   Dovetail housings with the small router
Detail of a stopped joint

Fig. 242   Dovetail housings with the small router
The housing aid – view of the under side

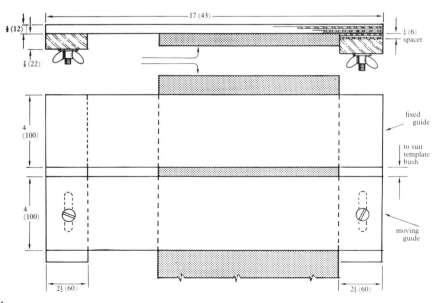

Fig. 241

Fig. 243A Dovetails housings with the small router
left – the first parallel cut
right – assembling a stopped joint

Fig. 243B Dovetail housings with the small router.
Cutting the housing

Take the first cut with the largest suitable straight cutter, following with the dovetail cutter, Fig. 243. The cut may either go right through, or be stopped short of the far edge. A handy rule is that the depth should not be more than a third of the component thickness.

When marking out components it is easier not to mark out the housing itself, but rather the width of the template guide as set up. The device can then easily be positioned and cramped. When all the housings have been cut, make a specimen cut on some scrap material, with which to test the dovetail component as it is cut.

Cutting the dovetail component

This aid is quite straightforward: see the device in Fig. 164. Assemble as described, level the top faces and trim them truly parallel with the router. Thread each bolt into one jaw and lock it, then pass it through an over-size hole in the other jaw.

The inner jaws also have comfortably over-size holes. They are lightly screwed to the main jaws and must be thicker than the diameter of the dovetail cutter to be used, Figs 244 & 245.

Fig. 245 Dovetail housings with a small router. The dovetail aid

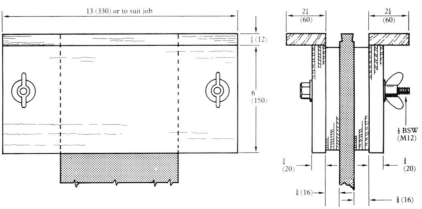

Fig. 244

Fig. 246   Dovetail housings with the small router.
Cutting the dovetail

Fig. 247   Dovetails housings with the small router.
Assembling a stopped dovetail housing

Next, remove the router's template guide and stand the switched off router over one of the completed housings. Plunge the cutter to the bottom of the housing and lock it there. It is probably wise to extend the router fence by attaching a wood strip.

The router fence runs along the outer edge of the working surface, the cut being made on the nearer side of the workpiece, as shown in Fig. 246. This ensures that, should the fence drift away from the edge giving an incomplete cut, no harm is done and another cut corrects. Work in this way on both sides of the aid, not necessarily expecting to complete in one cut. Use the specimen housing to test for fit as work proceeds.

Notch this component when making invisible stopped dovetail housings, Fig. 247. Should the dovetail component be slightly warped, cramp to a strong batten when tapping the joint together. Do not knock up the joint more times than is necessary as it will loosen slightly each time.

A simpler, non-adjustable aid for cutting housings, Fig. 248, can be made by gluing a piece of plywood, thicker than the template guide height, to a substantial batten. Rout a slot in this, using a cutter of precisely the same diameter as the template guide. For the Bosch router illustrated, this is 12 mm. The purchase of this cutter will be justified by the ease with which special templates can be made.

Tapered dovetail housings

These joints can be cut with slight modification of the existing devices. To cut the dovetail component, one of the packing pieces is planed to the required taper, Fig. 249. This is more easily done if it is made from solid wood as distinct from the plywood previously shown. The work is cramped in as before and the taper is automatically obtained.

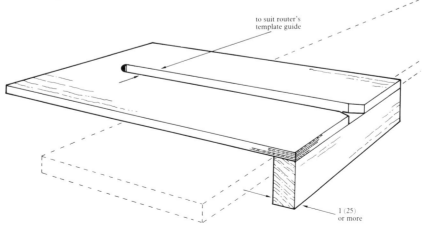

to suit router's
template guide

1 (25)
or more

Fig. 248

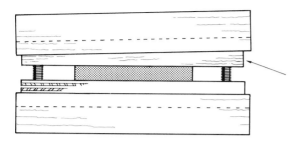

Fig. 249

Fig. 250B   Morticing with the small router. The wooden jig

To cut the dovetail housing the existing jig is used, the moving face being set out of parallel by the same amount as the tapered packing piece. It may be possible in some cases to use this piece as a spacer to obtain the precise angle. The work must be done in this order since there is no adjustment of the tapered packing, while the housing device adjusts, within limits, quite easily.

Morticing with the Small Router

Figs 250A & B

For the small workshop, unable to justify an expensive morticer, there is another way of cutting mortices without having to resort to hand work. The small router can do the work quite well, though it may need some modification.

Morticing on a wide component presents no problems. However on a narrow edge, for example when making a flat frame construction of say ¾ in (20 mm)

thickness, there is a problem; that of settling the router base on such a narrow edge. The fence will of course locate the cutter, but does little to help keep the tool steady. On a narrow face it is always possible for the fence to make insecure contact with the work, resulting in the mortices being off centre or out of place, so simple adaptation is needed.

Two rods are required, Fig. 251, of bright drawn mild steel of about 10–12 in (250–300 mm) long, and of the same diameter as the fence rods supplied with the router. A number of routers have rods of 8 mm diameter, which is very convenient, since this size is virtually indistinguishable from $\frac{5}{16}$ in. Four clamp screws are also required, Fig. 252. These are made from ½ in dia. mild steel bar, or the nearest metric size available. A metal-turning lathe or an engineering

Fig. 250A   Morticing with the
small router

friend would be useful, but not essential. The spigot can be filed in the manner described in Appendix 2. The thread is cut either $\frac{1}{4}$ in BSW or M6. Four wing-nuts with large diameter washers will also be required.

The two wood fences are built up, the sizes depending mainly on the particular router. Piece A is straightforward, simply a piece of good quality $\frac{1}{2}$ in (12 mm) plywood. Block B, which contains the two clamping screws, will need to be very carefully marked out, Fig. 253. Measure the distance between the fence rods of the router so that the centres of the holes in B are exactly the same distance apart. Mark this distance with a knife on two adjacent sides, then mark the centres on these lines. Drill the holes for the rods first, then fill them in temporarily with dry dowels while drilling the holes for the clamping screws so preventing splintering. Ease the clamping screws into their holes, which have been slightly enlarged, (see Appendix 3).

When assembled, the clamping screws and the bars in them should be an easy sliding fit. Glue A to B then glue on the actual fence, C, and clean up all the joints. Arrange matters so that the plywood pieces, A, slide snugly along the base of the router. Assemble both fences on the router, push them together so that the faces of both pieces, C, touch. If these do not close perfectly, adjust by careful planing until they do. If the end grain surfaces of the plywood are unacceptable, a thin face, D, can be glued to each fence, Fig. 254.

The standard router cutters must have end cutting capacity, but often are not long enough to achieve the required mortice depth. To obtain a good depth, use a long series engineer's end milling cutter instead. Unfortunately though, these are made parallel, so owners of small routers are restricted to $\frac{1}{4}$ in or 6 mm cutters. (The larger routers will accept $\frac{3}{8}$ and $\frac{1}{2}$ in shanks.) It is, however, possible for an engineer to grind down the larger sizes to give a $\frac{1}{4}$ in shank.

To set up for morticing, carefully drill a small hole with the router central in the marking, Fig. 255, switch off and lock the plunging mechanism with the cutter in the hole. Then close up the two fences for a fairly tight fit on the job. If a thin piece of paper is placed between one fence and the job, a comfortable sliding fit will be obtained when it is removed.

Cut the mortice by making a number of overlapping borings, and then traverse the length of the mortice to give clean sides. Do not plunge and make a sideways cut. This will break the cutter and is the main reason why manufacturers are reluctant to produce long large cutters with the $\frac{1}{4}$ in shank. Remember that only one mortice needs to be fully marked out with the mortice gauge – the others require only the length marks.

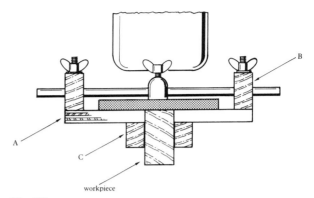

workpiece

Fig. 251.

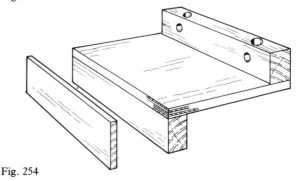

an alternative clamping using bolt & wingnut

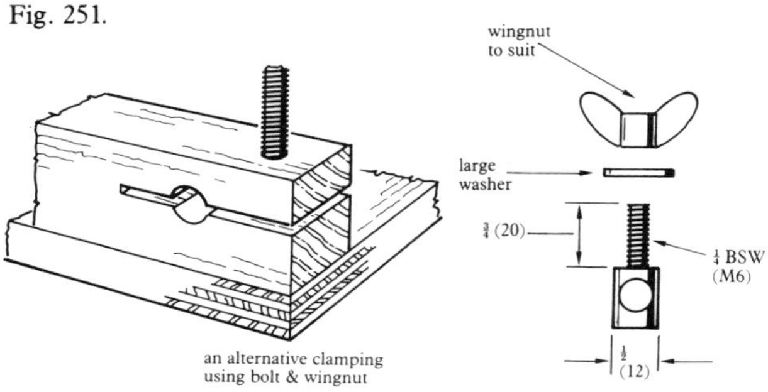

wingnut to suit

large washer

$\frac{3}{4}$ (20)

$\frac{1}{4}$ BSW (M6)

$\frac{1}{2}$ (12)

Fig. 252

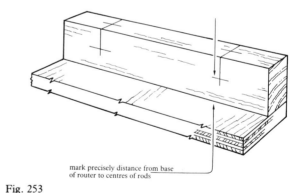

mark precisely distance from base of router to centres of rods

Fig. 253

Fig. 254

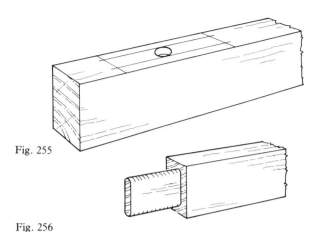

Fig. 255

Fig. 256

Fig. 257   Morticing with a small router in a drill stand

The rest is fairly obvious. The workpiece may be held in the vice or cramped either to the benchtop or to a piece held in the vice. The fences keep the router firm, steady and square to the job. Naturally the mortice ends are rounded, giving the option of either chopping the mortices square or rounding the tenons, Fig. 256, which is quickly done with a rasp and file.

For some makes of router with a fence which slides along the bars, it is possible to buy a second fence. If both fences are lined with hardwood faces, the technique is considerably simplified.

Morticing with the small router in a drill stand

Fig. 257

The router in this case is the Bosch POF 52 fitted in a drill stand. An old type Wolf drill stand has been used. This method may be adopted for any other router which can be held in a drill stand as distinct from being mounted in a router table. The original depth stop has been removed from this drill stand and replaced by a short piece of $\frac{1}{2}$ in BSF screwed rod. This is held permanently in the stand and is fitted with two nuts, preferably anti-vibration nuts, which control the depth of cut and also position the cutter just to clear the workpiece. The convenient advantage of this particular thread is that one turn advances the nut one sixteenth of an inch.

Standard router cutters will only cut shallow mortices. Extra long cutters are available, however, with a 1in (25 mm) cutting edge. Beyond them use must be made of engineers' long series end milling cutters. As these are made parallel, larger sizes will require the assistance of an engineer to grind down their shanks to

$\frac{1}{4}$ in (6 mm). Most work is commonly accomplished with the long router cutters.

For normal overhead routing the inconvenient handle of my drill stand has been shortened to about 6 in (150 mm). For morticing, a length of $\frac{3}{4}$ in electrical conduit is slipped over the stump.

The morticing table is built on an adjustable board of $\frac{3}{4}$ in (20 mm) MDF. The main fence, L-shaped in section, is pivoted at one end and held at the other by a screw and wing-nut operating in a slot. Rough adjustment is obtained by moving the whole table. Fine adjustments are achieved by movement of the pivoting fence. Fig. 258.

The clamping table is slotted with the router and then has a similar fence glued to it. The base board is drilled and tapped to take two countersunk machine screws, fully tightened to prevent rotation. Wing-nuts and large washers secure the clamping table.

Adjust the base-board and the fence to locate the workpiece below the cutter, then move up the clamping fence to hold it in place. Clamp as tightly as possible while still allowing free movement.

Cut the mortice by drilling a series of connecting holes then clearing out the residue by sideways movement. *Do not* drill one hole to depth then move the workpiece along to complete the mortice. This is liable to snap off the cutter.

Naturally this set-up can equally well be used for grooving, particularly when settling the router base on a narrow edge is impossible.

NB. The cutout on the pivoting fence, as illustrated, serves no purpose in this operation.

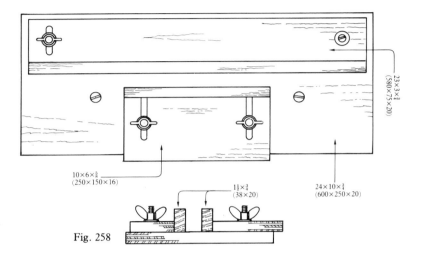

23×3×¾
(580×75×20)

10×6×⅝
(250×150×16)

1½×¾
(38×20)

24×10×¾
(600×250×20)

Fig. 258

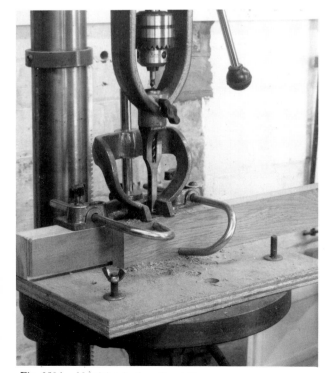

Fig. 259A   Morticing in the pillar drill
Method as recommended by the makers

Fig. 259B   Morticing in the pillar drill
Improved method, using a second and sliding fence

Morticing in the drilling machine

More and more woodworkers are equipping their workshop with simple imported pedestal drilling machines. The accuracy of these tools is quite adequate for woodworking. Many of the makers supply a hollow chisel morticing attachment, which certainly has an appeal to the small workshop and the amateur.

On the machine illustrated, while the drilling operation was quite satisfactory, the holding method, Fig. 259A, was far from so. Though the holding down device was acceptable, the fence was low, inadequate and difficult to bolt accurately to the drilling table. The work was held against the fence by the customary two hooks of round steel bar. The ends had been roughly chopped off. They damaged the work and even when corrected by filing, failed to hold the work well. It was thought best to scrap all this and rebuild a more effective system, Fig. 259B.

A stout fence is glued to a blockboard or plywood base, which can be bolted to suitable slots in the drilling table, giving complete adjustment to position the workpiece where it is needed, under the chisel. Two blocks are glued to this fence to accommodate the hold down casting, Fig. 260.

A sliding section, again with a stout fence, adjusts across the baseplate to grip the workpiece, Fig. 261. Two wing-nuts secure its position. If the work is

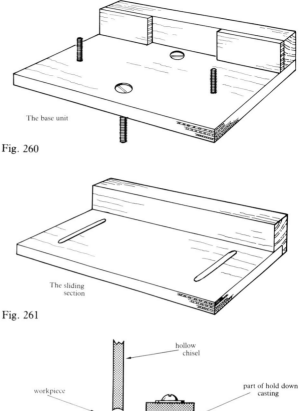

The base unit

Fig. 260

The sliding section

Fig. 261

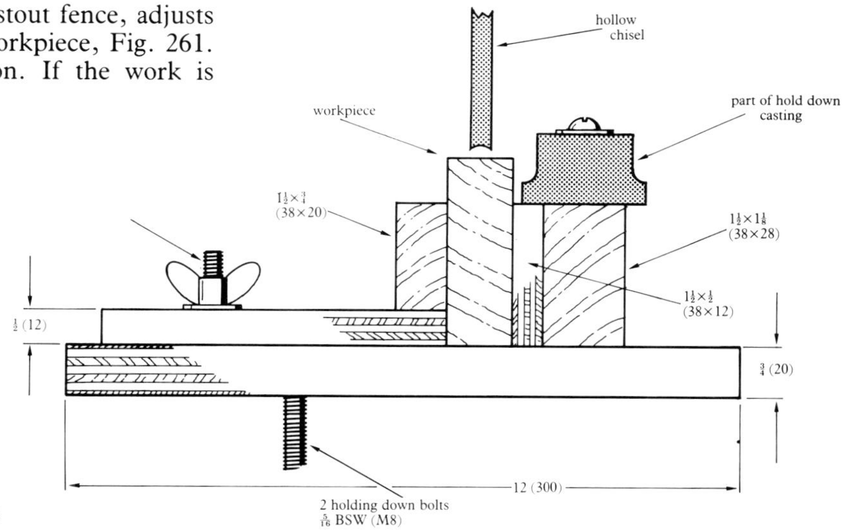

Fig. 262

hollow chisel

workpiece

part of hold down casting

$1\frac{1}{2} \times \frac{3}{4}$ (38×20)

$1\frac{1}{2} \times 1\frac{1}{4}$ (38×28)

$1\frac{1}{2} \times \frac{1}{2}$ (38×12)

$\frac{1}{2}$ (12)

$\frac{3}{4}$ (20)

12 (300)

2 holding down bolts $\frac{5}{16}$ BSW (M8)

gripped tightly with a slip of paper between it and one fence, when the paper is removed, a nice sliding fit is obtained. The makers' hold down system is quite satisfactory, so is screwed to the fixed fence, Fig. 262.

This arrangement works as a normal morticing machine except that the workpiece is moved laterally either by hand or with a light tap with a scrap of wood. The machine's depth stop controls the mortice depth.

Tenons with a Small Router

This device will accurately cut one tenon or a number of identical tenons. Very fine adjustments can be made to trim over-thick tenons to fit.

The vital requirement is to hold the router truly level during the process. This is achieved by building and fitting a levelling foot, Fig. 263.

First obtain a pair of bright mild steel rods of the

Fig. 263   Tenons with a small router.
Close-up. The set-up, showing the levelling foot

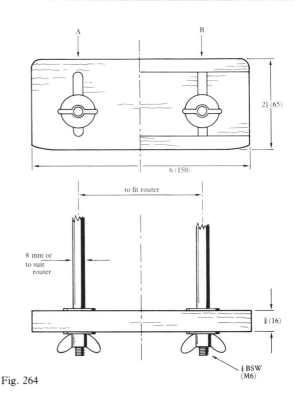

Fig. 264

same diameter as those of the router's fence, commonly 8 mm. Turn these down at one end to give a shoulder, then part thread either ¼ in BSW or M6. If turning is not possible, thread to the full diameter and use a hexagon nut to form the shoulder. Also needed are four large diameter washers to fit and two wing-nuts. Be sure to have these first and thread to suit them.

Now make the levelling foot, Fig. 264. Either rout the slots, A, or build up the foot, B, giving ready made slots. Whichever method is used, start by most carefully measuring the distance between centres, with the rods held firmly in the router.

Assemble standing on a flat surface. Stand the router on the workpiece with the bars overhanging. Fit the levelling foot, standing it on the flat surface, then tighten the wing-nuts.

To use, fit the largest cutter available, with small routers having only a ¼ in (6 mm) chuck, this will probably be ⅝ or ¾ in (16 or 20 mm).

Cramp the workpiece firmly to the bench and carefully saw the shoulder by hand. Now use the router to remove the waste. The rod length should be so adjusted that the router can work the whole length of the tenon. Set the depth stop to the final depth then remove the waste in stages, ending with a fine cut. Having cut the first tenon, try it diagonally in a pre-cut mortice, adjusting the depth stop where necessary. Take particular care to avoid confusion when the tenon is not set centrally on the component, in which case, two final settings will be required. Other uses will no doubt be found for the device, such as working rebates on narrow components.

Edge Jointing by Router
Fig. 265

The edge jointing of boards is a time consuming operation. Not every small workshop has a planer, nor has every reader the requisite skill in hand jointing, initially. However, the versatile router can be brought to the aid. A very elementary, quickly and easily made piece of apparatus is all that is required, Fig. 266.

MDF or any of the man-made boards is the most suitable material for the work surfaces. Length and width will depend on the work planned and the material to hand. Screw the two boards onto two battens. A gap of 1 in (25 mm) allows the bulk of the waste to fall through. The width of the battens is not important. Their thickness, or height, is. It should exceed the thickness of the handscrew or cramp jaws which widl hodd the work in place. This way the job sits conveniently flat on the bench. Screw on a lengthwise batten which can be gripped by the bench vice. Finally make a fence as long as the work surface. This must have a good, true and smooth edge so hardwood is probably to be preferred. In all cases the fence should be substantially longer at each end than the wood to be jointed, to eliminate wobble at each end of the stroke.

Fig. 265   Edge jointing by router

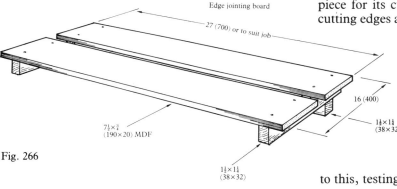

Fig. 266

Edge jointing board

27 (700) or to suit job

16 (400)

7½×¾
(190×20) MDF

1½×1¼
(38×32)

1½×1¼
(38×32)

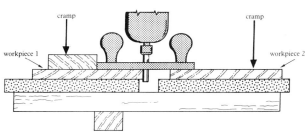

cramp   cramp

workpiece 1   workpiece 2

Fig. 267   The first cut

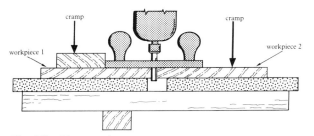

cramp   cramp

workpiece 1   workpiece 2

Fig. 268   The second cut

Grip the apparatus in the bench vice. Put together the pieces to be jointed, marking the jointing edge and the true face. Cramp on the first piece, face down, with the fence above it. The jointing edge must overhang the gap. The fence is positioned so that the router will take a very fine cut. A cutter of say ⅜ in (10 mm) or above is preferable to the smaller sizes. The greater part of the cramps should be below for convenience.

The second board is cramped on, true face down, clear of the first, merely to keep the router level. First make a mark with a carpenter's pencil right along the edge. Switch on and run the flat edge of the router (if it has one) along the fence from right to left. Make sure that all the pencil mark has been removed. A second pass can be made if it is shown that all of the pencil has not gone, that is, that the router has left the fence at some point. Fig. 267.

Now slacken its cramps and move up the second piece for its cut. Turn the router cutter so that both cutting edges are clear of the work. Move the board up to this, testing several times at each end. This method ensures a very fine cut. Cramp firmly. Here, cramps standing above the work are no obstacle. Pencil on the jointing edge as before.

Check that the cramping is firm, then take a cut from left to right, Fig. 268. It is very easy for the router to drift away from the fence so place the feet in such a position that an uninterrupted clean cut can be made. Exert firm pressure against the fence throughout. Any momentary drifting away from the fence will spoil the joint so that the component will have to be re-positioned and cut again.

The two components should now fit. The technique is particularly useful for thin components which always present a problem for hand planing.

A variation
For panels and similar components an interesting decorative effect can be achieved by using a gently curved fence and joining, say, two boards with close grain with a centre board of more open grain. Colour variations can be used in the same way, Fig. 269.

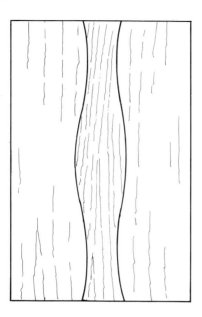

Fig. 269

Morticing round components with the router

A basic cradle is required similar to that in Fig. 99. This is mounted on a base of man-made material with a gripping board for the vice underneath. Two strips fixed to the base form a track for the carriage. Figs 270A & 270B.

These should be adjusted so that the carriage can slide sweetly. The carriage sides are glued to a top of plywood which must be as thin as reasonably possible to permit the maximum depth of cut. Alternatively, this may be made from clear acrylic sheet, in order to observe the operation. In this case, the top will be screwed rather than glued, then suitably drilled for the attachment of the particular router. The standard stirrup clamp, Fig. 283, completes the assembly.

The work is cramped as for drilling, then the carriage is slid into position and the mortice is cut. Use long *series* router cutters or, failing that, engineers' long vertical milling cutters.

Form the mortice by making a series of linked vertical cuts. Then gently traverse to clean out the mortice. Attempts at a heavy sideways cut will possibly break the cutter.

If the clamp needs to be moved during the operation, hold the work firm by locking the stationary router cutter in a mortice.

Dovetail housings for pedestal tables

This is virtually the same as the device for morticing round components, Figs 270A & B. It will probably need to be scaled up in size. The carriage should just clear the cramped cylinder being worked on. It is advisable to cut the housings while the pedestal is still in the cylindrical form. Alternatively, either leave at the top end, a short cylinder of the same diameter, or, if the tenon has been turned, prepare and slip on a massive wooden washer of the same diameter.

To mark the centres of four housings, cut a strip of paper to make exactly one lap of the base cylinder. Fold this in half, then half again. Replace on the job and mark from the four creases. For the more common three housings, divide the strip into three then transfer to the work.

With the work firmly clamped, make initial cuts to remove most of the waste, using a straight cutter.

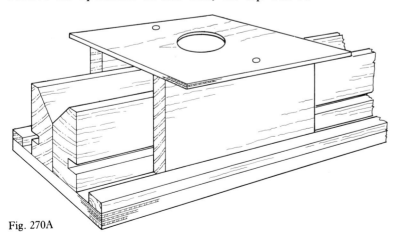

Fig. 270A

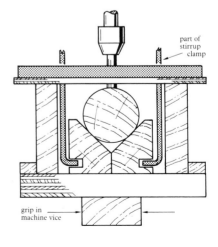

part of stirrup clamp

grip in machine vice

Fig. 270B

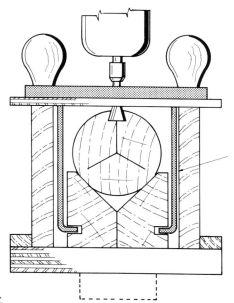

Fig. 270C

Replace with the dovetail cutter and complete the housings, Fig. 270C. The dovetails on the feet can be cut as described on page 91.

Morticing round components in the morticer

This is virtually the same process as drilling cylinders, page 106. A similar cradle is made to accept the same stirrup clamp.

However, in order to grip the device in the machine's vice, without trapping the clamp, the cradle is mounted on a substantial base, whose sides must be truly parallel with the cradle sides. The width of this base should be the minimum which allows a clear run for the clamp, Fig. 271.

The cradle can be slid along in the vice to allow a succession of mortices to be cut. When the clamp is found to be in an inconvenient place, it can be safely moved by holding the work firm by means of the chisel in an already cut mortice.

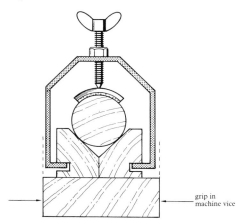

grip in machine vice

Fig. 271

SECTION 5 The Sawbench

Mouldings from the Sawbench

Many readers will be familiar with the principle that if wood is passed diagonally across a circular saw, a hollow cut will be made. Not many though will have had personal experience of the technique. The need to produce large hollow mouldings when constructing a grandfather clock case led to the development of this device, Fig. 272.

Planning. It should be said at the outset that the circular saw is not capable of producing either a true ellipse or any hollow shape drawn. It is likely, however, to be able to produce something quite close to it. As successive cuts must of necessity be very fine, this is rather a slow process. In order to see in advance what is feasible and to save time spent experimenting, it is well worth making the following drawing.

Bear in mind that there are three variables. These are:

    The height of the saw above the table
    The angle of approach to the saw
    The diameter of the saw

The first two are infinitely variable; the latter is much more restricting. The smaller is the diameter, the more concave is the shape produced.

Some readers will remember a typical school technical drawing exercise: to find the true shape of an object viewed from other than the front or side. Here the reverse is the case. The shape is known, and the angle of view is required.

Begin by drawing a full size sectional view of the moulding required. Fig. 273. This will give the height and the width of the portion to be removed.

Draw a vertical. Mark on it point P and with this centre, draw an arc of the saw diameter, cutting the vertical at A. Remember that the saw becomes smaller with sharpening, so measure rather than accept the nominal diameter. From A, mark down the height, giving point B. Draw a horizontal here, which is the table surface, cutting the arc at C.

Set a pair of compasses to width and strike arcs from B and C. Draw tangents from B and C and continue these as shown.

At right angles to these draw DE. Above this draw another right angle at a distance equal to the height.

Divide BC and DE into the same number of equal parts, in the example this is ten. Draw perpendiculars here and number them. On a strip of paper or with dividers, measure the height of each from BC and plot these heights from DE. Join up the plots to find the

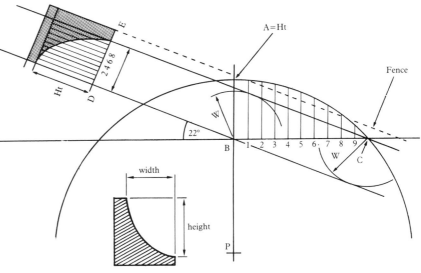

Fig. 272 Mouldings on the sawbench
A commonly required moulding particularly
for restoration and reproduction work

Fig. 273 The required shape

shape produced. The required angle may be measured at B. The fence will be fixed at this angle but displaced as shown, to produce the moulding required.

Operation. This method will generally work with the saw guard in place. Otherwise an improvised guard must be arranged.

Cramp on a stout fence at the angle required, displaced from the saw, point C, to suit the moulding planned. Wind the saw right down. Lay in place the material to be moulded and cramp on a second, short fence. This should be as tight as possible, yet permitting free movement. If needed a piece of ply can be screwed to the main fence, above the saw, to give protection.

Fig. 274   Mouldings from the sawbench
The sawbench arrangements. The guard has been removed for clarity

Fig. 275   Sawbench taper jig

Saws are not built to saw diagonally so slow careful progress must be made with quite a fine cut. Tungsten carbide tipped saws, being more robust, are the most successful.

Slowly raise the saw for the first cut. The successful depth of cut will depend on both the angle of approach and the hardness of the particular timber. Feed through slowly, steadily and without a halt, using appropriate push-sticks. Take a cut on each component, raise the saw and repeat. Continue until the desired shape is obtained. The last cut must be very fine and under no circumstances should the movement of the piece be allowed to stop as this will produce a blemish. Fig. 274 shows the operation.

Clean off the saw marks with a scraper ground or filed very slightly more convex than the moulding shape, as one will not be strong enough to push a shaving of the full shape. Make a sanding block to fit the moulding and finish down the grades of abrasive paper.

After the mouldings have been applied, any slight irregularities at the mitre can be corrected by further use of this sanding block.

Carvetto, Hollow and Fascia mouldings can all be produced in this way. The Scotia shape is planned by making a similar drawing but with point A moved, in this case, slightly to the left.

A Sawbench Taper Jig
Fig. 275
The taper job which most readily springs to mind is a stool or a table leg. There are others but they can all be handled in the same way. Basically it is a matter of removing rather a lot of wood, either by planing or by sawing. In either case, working by hand is slow, tedious and hard work. A surface planer is much quicker, but has shortcomings, and in any case, the finish planing must be done by hand. Sawing may also be done by hand but again it is hard work, requiring a sharp ripsaw.

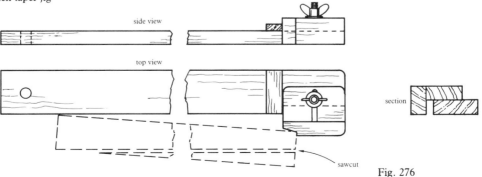

side view

top view

section

sawcut

Fig. 276

The circular saw makes light work of this. It is obviously preferable and more economical to remove the waste material as a piece of wood rather than as a bucket of shavings. The finish is good, needing only light hand planing to clean up an already true surface.

Figs 276 and 277 show the jig required. No sizes are critical; use what material is to hand. The jig should be long enough to handle a dining table leg, which is the longest job the amateur workshop generally encounters.

Except in certain reproduction work, legs are tapered on the inside only, from below the joint. Tapering the outsides too gives to a table a somewhat pigeon-toed appearance.

Saw the waste from the foot and mark the finished size on the end, Fig. 278. Invert the jig, holding the leg in place. Two small wood blocks may be needed to level the two. With a gauge, rule or caliper, measure the jig plus leg at A, Fig. 278. Adjust the stop so that jig plus leg at the finish mark, B, is the same. Re-check before starting to saw.

Adjust the fence of the sawbench, Fig. 279. Saw as close as possible to the finish line, leaving just enough to hand plane to a finish. Do not remove the guard. Use two push sticks when approaching the end of the cut.

Plan carefully which cut to make first so that the true face or true edge is always on the table, otherwise the leg will rock on the first cut when making the second.

A convenient method of holding the leg for hand planing is a screwed down sash cramp. Fig. 280. Two packing pieces are needed for the cramp jaw to just clear the bench. Three screw holes into the bench will cover all sizes of work.

A guard for sawbench jigs

Some of the machine made joints described can be worked with the sawbench guard in place. This will depend of course on the particular machine. When, however, this is not practicable, an alternative guard must be devised, since on no account can working without a guard be justified.

This general purpose guard, Fig. 280, will operate on several of the jigs described. Perhaps a little modification will be required. Fig. 280A shows a baseboard of multi-ply cut to suit the sawbench to be used. A notch is cut out to accommodate a wobble saw and two grooved slide blocks, Fig. 280B, are glued in place. The guard itself, Fig. 280C, is simply a plywood strip to which two cheeks have been glued. Fig. 280D shows this in section.

Drill two holes for the fixing screws, then drill and tap the table to take $\frac{1}{4}$ in (6 mm) round head fixing screws, with washers. Two headed pins are driven into the slide blocks and one into the tail end of the guard.

A strong elastic band positions the guard, at rest, covering the saw, Fig. 281. It can move back with the work, returning to the rest position.

Most dimensions are at the discretion of the reader, being dependent on what material is available and the restraints of the particular machine. Weak coil springs will be more durable than the rubber bands.

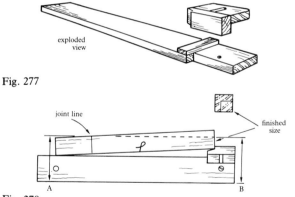

exploded view

Fig. 277

joint line

finished size

A B

Fig. 278

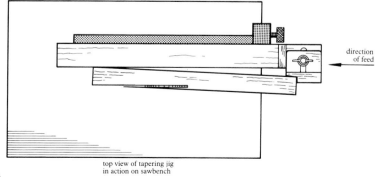

direction of feed

top view of tapering jig in action on sawbench

Fig. 279

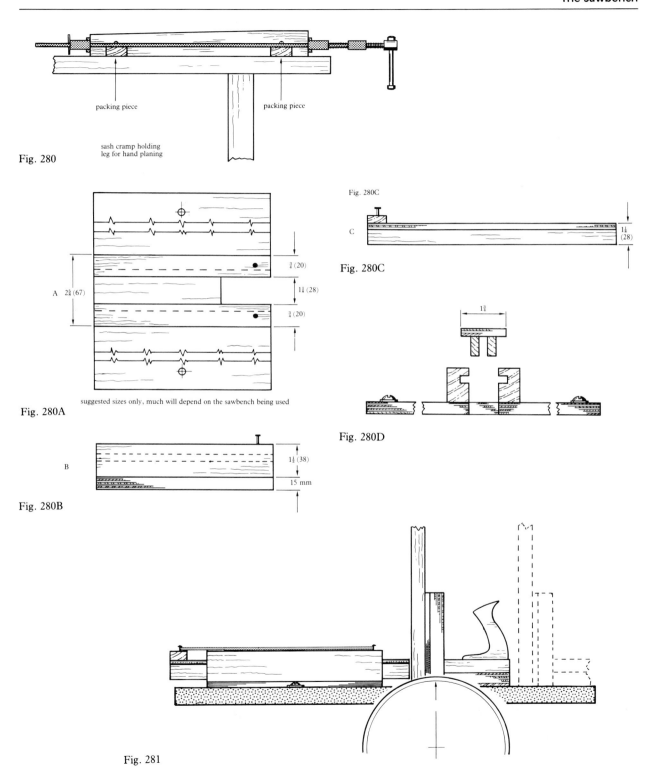

Fig. 280

packing piece

packing piece

sash cramp holding
leg for hand planing

Fig. 280C

C

1⅛ (28)

Fig. 280C

A   2⅝ (67)

¾ (20)

1⅛ (28)

¾ (20)

suggested sizes only, much will depend on the sawbench being used

Fig. 280A

1¾

Fig. 280D

B

1½ (38)

15 mm

Fig. 280B

Fig. 281

The Drilling Machine

Drilling Cylinders at 90°

This is a process needed when making turned stools, tables with round legs and certain parts of traditional rush seated chairs. It is assumed that a drilling machine or an electric drill in a drill stand is available.

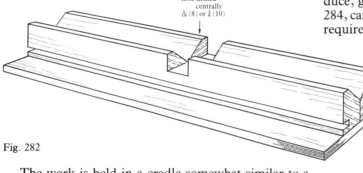

hole drilled
centrally
$\frac{5}{16}$ (8) or $\frac{3}{8}$ (10)

Fig. 282

The work is held in a cradle somewhat similar to a planing cradle. A wide plywood base makes it easy to cramp the cradle firmly in place, Fig. 282. Additionally, two $\frac{1}{4}$ in (6 mm) grooves are worked to take a stirrup cramp. A notch is removed from the centre, the

purpose of which will be described later. A hole of say $\frac{5}{16}$ in (8 mm) or $\frac{3}{8}$ in (10 mm) is centrally drilled with great accuracy, its purpose being to locate the cradle exactly under the drill chuck.

The stirrup cramp in the photograph, Fig. 283, is an aluminium casting which any small foundry will produce, given a wooden pattern. A simpler version, Fig. 284, can be bent from mild steel strip. Some heat will be required for the sharp bends. A nut is brazed or silver

Fig. 283   Stirrup clamp

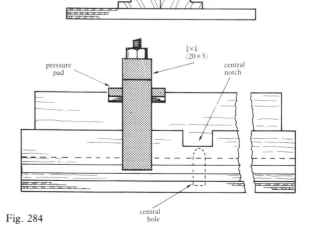

brazed
on nut

pressure
pad

$\frac{3}{4} \times \frac{1}{8}$
(20×3)

central
notch

central
hole

Fig. 284

soldered in place and the thread continued through the strip.

Pressure pads will be required to prevent damage to the work by the cramp screw. These can be made in several sizes by sawing short pieces of scrap iron pipe into three. Drill a dimple to accept the rounded end of the cramp screw and line the inside with rubber. A piece of old car inner tube is suitable material. Make a locating pin from a short length of bright drawn mild steel of the same diameter as the hole drilled in the cradle.

To set up. Fit the locating pin in the chuck and bring it down into the hole in the cradle. With the chuck held firmly down, cramp the cradle in place. Replace the locating pin with the chosen drill and with the workpiece located and held firmly by the stirrup cramp with its pressure pad, drill the hole.

To drill several holes in line. Locate the cradle as described but do not cramp. Instead cramp a batten against it. The cradle can now be slid back and forth along the batten. To drill successive holes when insufficient movement can be obtained, hold the drill firmly in a hole, slacken the stirrup cramp and move the cradle to a new, more convenient position. Reposition the stirrup cramp. Thus at all times the workpiece is held and prevented from turning *either* by the stirrup cramp or by the drill in a hole. Both must not be released at the same time.

Drilling cylinders at other angles
Fig. 285

For this purpose a tilting cradle is required. Fig. 286 shows the construction. The pivots can conveniently be large brass mirror (or glass) plates. The twin stays can be of plywood or mild steel strip. The end of the cradle must be cut back to permit movement. Using the locating pin, the cradle is set up in the closed position. The most convenient method of setting up the angle is to make a plywood or hardboard template of the angle

Fig. 285   Adjustable cradle.
Drilling around component at an angle

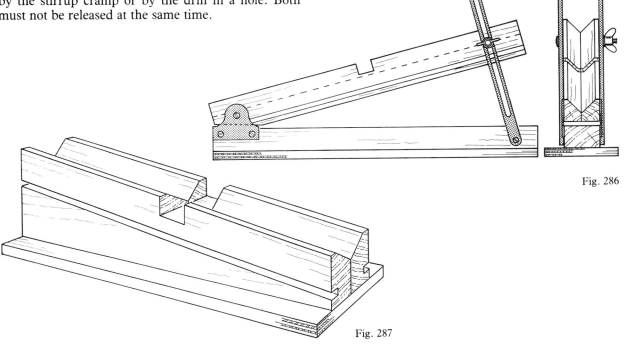

Fig. 286

Fig. 287

required and to insert this between the cradle and the base. In this way, the angle may be exactly repeated if needed later.

When a job is being repeated often, as, for instance, when making a set of chairs, it may well be worth making a permanent cradle for a particular angle, as in Fig. 287.

Drilling a second angle at 90°
The basic cradle is set up and the first hole drilled. Uncramp the workpiece and insert a short length of tightly fitting dowel in the hole. Suitably locate the workpiece and turn the dowel into the notch. Using a

small spirit level, (preferably with a vee channel base), set the dowel horizontal. Cramp here and drill the second hole, Fig. 288.

Drilling a second hole at other than 90°
This routine is the same as that just described except that an angle template is held between the dowel and the spirit level. When drilling the legs of traditional turned chairs, by reversing the template, holes for both the front and back may be drilled, i.e. an acute and an obtuse angle, Fig. 289.

Templates. When making such templates do not attempt to obtain the angle by protractor measurement. Much greater accuracy is obtained by measuring from the drawing a displacement left or right in a given length, Fig. 290.

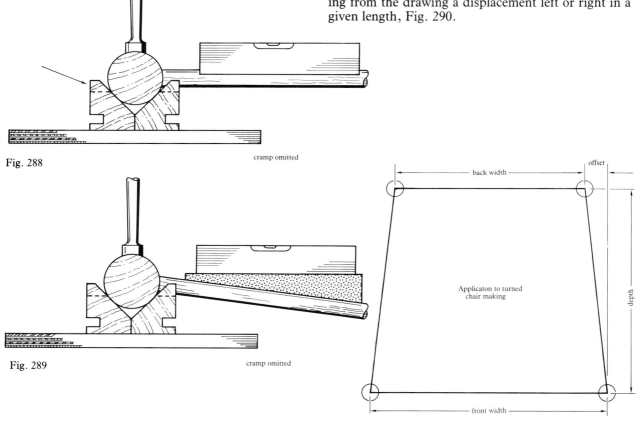

Fig. 288   cramp omitted

Fig. 289   cramp omitted

back width
offset
Applicaton to turned
chair making
depth
front width

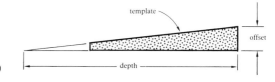

template
offset
Fig. 290   depth

The Lathe

Driving Cups for the Lathe

Fig. 291 and 293

This device for turning derives from a traditional method used in the past by ball turners. The cups hold the work by friction. The grip is far stronger than one would ever expect.

Driving cups solve many of the common problems with normal driving centres. Such centres are impossible for small work; work once removed and later replaced never runs true (particularly important in an educational setting, where work is done in a number of small sessions).

With driving cups, round or square work may be held securely without slipping under normal conditions. Work can be removed and replaced as often as desired, yet it always runs true. This means that turned tenons can be repeatedly tried in their mortices or ferrules until a perfect fit is obtained. Previously turned work can be set up for boring or further turning.

The cups can be made from aluminium alloy, steel or cast iron. Aluminium or mild steel bar can be used but this is not cheap and a great deal of metal needs to be removed. Alternatively and probably most conveniently, they can be cast from aluminium. The patterns for the castings are quite simple; they follow the drawings of the finished cups with an allowance on each surface of a good $\frac{1}{16}$ in (or 2 mm) to allow for machining. If cast iron is contemplated, this allowance should be more

Fig. 291   A set of driving cups
The number 1 morse taper is shown fitted. The number 2 is loose

generous in view of the thick skin to be removed. A small local foundry will cast the cups quite economically.

The diagrams, Fig. 292, are self explanatory, and the job is well within the capacity of anyone with access to a modest engineering lathe: otherwise a model engineer friend is useful. It is just possible to turn in aluminium using hand tools. The normal routine is as follows.

Grip by the larger diameter and turn a flat base. Into this drill an 8·5 mm tapping hole and put through a $\frac{3}{8}$ in × 24 UNF (not NF) tap. The taper tap alone is sufficient if buying is necessary.

Most of the smaller lathes take a No. 1 morse taper in the headstock; larger lathes will take a No. 2 or No. 3. Threaded arbors of No. 1 and No. 2 morse tapers are made with $\frac{3}{8}$ in × 24 UNF threads: No. 2 and No. 3 tapers are made with $\frac{1}{2}$ in × 20 UNF threads. Where head- and tailstock bores differ, conversion sleeves are available, converting 1 to 2 MT and 2 to 3 MT.

The threaded cup is screwed on to the arbor and inserted into the headstock. It is now possible to turn the inside and the remainder of the outside. Keep to the dimensions given so that the walls do not get too thick. The sizes have been chosen to accept the common sizes of timber available, i.e. 2×2, 1$\frac{1}{2}$×1$\frac{1}{2}$, 1×1 and $\frac{3}{4}$×$\frac{3}{4}$ in. Metric sizes copy the imperial. These, when full, are gripped about $\frac{1}{8}$ in (3 mm) from the lip. There is a slight overlap of the sizes, i.e. the 2 in cup will accept 2×2 and 1$\frac{1}{2}$×1$\frac{1}{2}$ in material.

Using the driving cup

A good centre is required, preferably a revolving one, at the tailstock end. Saw the ends of the spindle material square. A very badly sawn end will not grip well. If well sawn, the grip will be adequate for a square section to be roughed into a cylinder without slipping. Previously bored pieces can be turned or re-turned.

Though it is generally unnecessary to plane down to octagons, as books so often recommend, when a large number of similar spindles is to be turned, and a sawbench or bandsaw is available, much time (and sharpening) can be saved by sawing off the corners. See

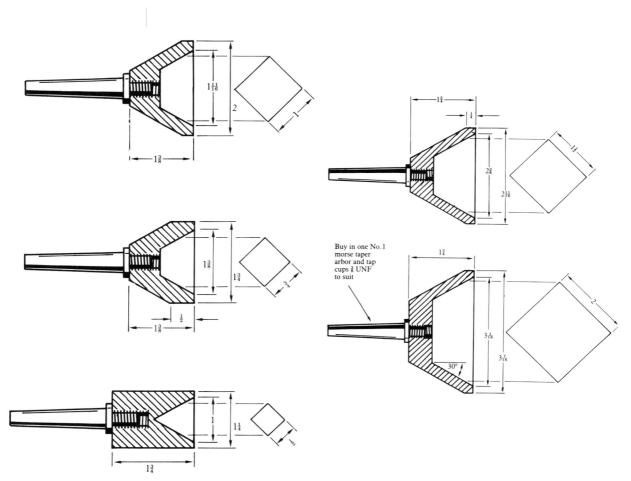

Fig. 292

page 139. Octagons are satisfactorily gripped by the driving cups.

It may sometimes be preferable to mark a centre at each end, turn the tailstock end and then reverse the spindle to turn the other half. With a tool handle, the rounded end can be turned and parted off; the finished end can then be gripped in the driving cup while the ferrule end is turned, tested and then drilled.

Boring of spindles and squares can be considerably eased by using a driving cup in the tailstock with the drill chuck in the headstock.

For larger diameter timber, saw a 2×2 in square on one end, say about $\frac{1}{2}$ in (13 mm) long. The reader will quickly get used to the driving cups and hardly use the standard driving centres. Other applications will no doubt soon occur.

For all but the smallest cup, castings should be available from any small foundry, provided a simple pattern is first made in wood. There is no casting for the

Fig. 293 Component reversed and held in the driving cup by the tenon

smallest cup as this is most easily made from bar material.

The Lathe Hammer

Fig. 294

Removing lathe centres and drill chucks is always rather a messy business. That piece of metal has to be hunted for which is not too thick to go through the head- or tailstock, not too thin as to bend and long enough to do the job. A hammer must be borrowed and then returned. All this perhaps for a moment's work. In a communal workshop it is even harder to find and retain the metal bar. All this can be avoided by making this lathe hammer which will conveniently hang with the other lathe tools.

The sizes given, Fig. 295, are for the Myford ML8 lathe but they can easily be modified for any other lathe. A good hefty block of mild steel is the first requirement. With luck, a cast iron or brass doorknob may be found.

Fig. 294   Lathe hammer

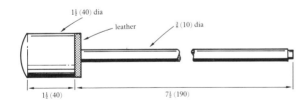

Fig. 295

Otherwise this weight is made from round mild steel bar. It is drilled and tapped to take the steel rod. Alternatively the rod may be brazed or welded in place. With a centre in place, the weight should be about ½ in (15 mm) clear or the head- or tailstock spindle, whichever is greater. The striking end of the rod should be turned down to a step. Since the rod diameter should be as large as will enter the bores, this small step obviates, for a long time, swelling of the end to a size which will cause the rod to jam in the bore.

The threads on the headstock ends are protected from damage by a thick washer of leather or rubber, fixed with an epoxy resin glue.

The reader who makes this tool will wonder how he struggled for so long without it.

Marking Barleysugar Twists

Fig. 296

Readers involved in reproduction work or repairs will, from time to time, want to produce twist turnings. The standard method for marking out single, double or triple twists is dealt with in numerous textbooks and involves quite an elaborate ritual to produce the required helices. The alternative of winding strips of paper round the work hardly produces accuracy. The following well tried method is worthy of recommendation.

The method was described by Paul Hasluck, a well known woodwork and metalwork writer of his day, in his *Woodturner's Handybook* of 1887. The tool he used is illustrated in Fig. 297. His original instructions were as follows:

The diagrams illustrate an instrument for marking out a spiral at any angle that may be required. It can be made as follows. Cut a piece of mahogany three inches in diameter and five-eights-of-an-inch thick. Cut off a segment and cut a groove [*sic* rebate]. The blade can be made from an old chisel or flat file. A hole must be bored large enough to admit the ferrule part of the handle. The thumb screw is to fix

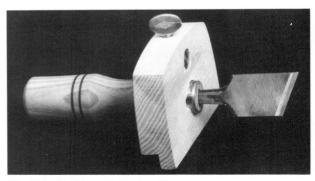

Fig. 296   Marking spiral twists. The marking tool

the cutter at the desired angle. An ordinary tool handle, to hold the cutter, completes the instrument. In order to use it, put on the T rest and rest the groove [*sic*] upon it even with the wood to be marked.

Having determined the angle you wish to twist, loosen the thumb screw, turn the cutter round until the desired angle is obtained and tighten the screw. The edge of the cutter should now be touching the wood to be marked. Hold the handle in the hollow of the right hand and press gently to the work; turn the pulley with the left hand, at the same time sliding the cutter along the T rest. Do not hold the instrument stiffly, but let it work freely at the same time as it marks.

Fig. 297

While Hasluck's original drawing may be followed, a simpler bench-made version is shown in Figs 298 to 300. This construction is quite straightforward. Naturally any species of wood may be used for the fence. The thread for the thumbscrew may be merely cut in the wood, or, as shown, a cylindrical nut may be let in. Slots cut from the ferrule hole permit the tool to be easily withdrawn for sharpening. As the pulley and belt are not generally accessible on modern lathes a convenient method for rotating the work is to fit on an outside faceplate to which a long bolt has been fixed, to serve as a turning handle.

¼ BSW (M6) screwed rod and wing-nut

$\frac{3}{4} \times \frac{1}{2}$
$\frac{1}{20} \times 12$ dia tapped to suit

to suit ferrule

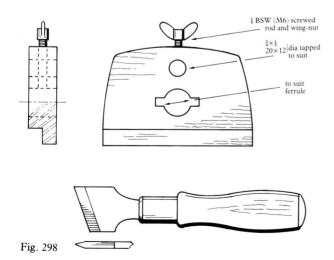

Fig. 298

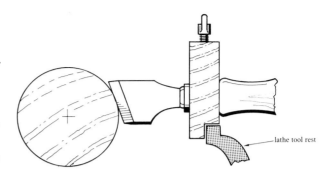

lathe tool rest

Fig. 300 Marking spiral twists
Method of use, hand removed for clarity

An Inexpensive Stand for a Lathe

Most woodturning lathes seem now to be sold without a stand. Stands supplied by the makers are often over-priced and in the case of one manufacturer his stands were obviously designed for dwarfs. There is no need to go to this expense when a very satisfactory stand can be tailor-made at no great cost, Fig. 301.

The raw material is bed irons. These can be found in most scrapyards though there is a growing tendency for scrap dealers to overvalue them, probably because of the steady demand. The steel in them is of good quality. They are thin enough to give easy hacksawing, drilling and filing while remaining amply strong. Common dimensions are $1\frac{1}{2} \times 1\frac{1}{2} \times \frac{1}{8}$ inches.

The centre height is a matter of personal preference. Fred Pain in his book *The Practical Woodturner* advises elbow height when the forearm is horizontal. Bowl turning tends to benefit from a highish centre while spindle turning from a lowish centre.

Having made this decision, saw out the two end frames, Fig. A. Drill the corners and bolt together

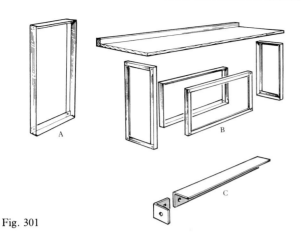

Fig. 301

using $\frac{1}{4}$ in or 6 mm bolts. The front and back frames are similarly made to nicely fit into the end frames. Where it is applicable, the bottom rails of the end frames can be drilled to screw or bolt to the floor.

The bolted frames can now be welded, with no chance of the welder getting it wrong. Many garages will undertake this in the absence of a welding service. Have the welder check the diagonals and for twist. The bolts can now be removed as they serve no useful purpose.

After a clean up the frames should be carefully drilled then bolted together, Fig. B. Now unbolt, paint the frames and re-assemble.

A good top board can be made up by glueing together two pieces of $\frac{3}{4}$ in (19 mm) blockboard. The width will be decided by the exact location. It is a good idea to fix a small back strip to stop small articles rolling down behind the lathe. The top can now be bolted to the end frames and the lathe itself bolted in place.

When the exact location of the machine has been settled it can be fixed to the floor. Use rawlbolts for a big lathe. Smaller, lighter lathes can be quite well secured by using coachbolts or large woodscrews in rawlplugs. Two chipboard shelves can now be fitted.

Where possible the end frames should be secured to the wall. Bed iron can make the necessary two bars with a small offcut bolted to the wall end, Fig. C. In some cases these may be used to support the top board.

Lathes are generally fitted against the wall. This is satisfactory for lathes with a rotating headstock. When there are outboard turning facilities the lathe must be far enough from the wall to allow a right-handed turner to work unhampered.

Stability is further helped by storing turning blocks and other heavy material on the shelves.

A demountable structure of this kind is easy to get in and out of small restricted workshops.

A High Speed Steel Parting Tool

The obvious advantages of this tool are its almost negligible cost and its long duration of sharpness.

Make the body of the tool, Fig. 302, from bright drawn mild steel, (available in imperial and metric sizes), by hacksawing and filing. Make a central slot to take the high speed steel insert. The handle, to personal preference, will be a straightforward turning job.

The most common source of HSS is power hacksaw blades, discarded by small engineering firms, schools and colleges when blunt or broken. These must not be confused with the much smaller and thinner blades for the hand hacksaw. They are of two types. One has a HSS strip of about $\frac{1}{4}$ in (6 mm) wide containing the teeth. The remainder is of softer material, useful for making scratch tool and gauge cutters. The HSS strip can be broken off in the vice. A suitable length can be ground part way through on the corner of a grinding wheel and then snapped off. When this technique is used, for safety, the steel must be wrapped in cloth.

The cutting insert, a little over-size, is fitted into the slot. Gentle filing with a needle file may be needed. It can then be fixed permanently, preferably by silver soldering, or else by brazing.

After cleaning off the scale, the tool is neatened up by grinding. Good clearance when working is achieved if the insert projects very slightly at the sides. Finally grind the cutting edge. High speed steel is not harmed by heat when grinding, so there is no need for frequent dipping out in water.

Blades made entirely from HSS can be used to produce the inserts by edge grinding and snapping. The process, though, is a little more time consuming.

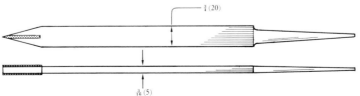

Fig. 302

High Speed Steel Scrapers

The basic shape, Fig. 303A, is formed from mild steel. The HSS cutting face can be made from a variety of sources. Apart from the 'all HSS' hacksaw blades, broken or worn out blades from planing machines or engineers' milling machines are possibilities. Suitable portions can be extracted by the grind and snap technique.

Having obtained the insert, a suitable rebate is formed in the tool. Milling is the easiest method though the slower handfiling will produce the same result. To avoid this work, a poorer looking tool can have the HSS insert merely fixed onto the top surface. Solder or braze the HSS in place then grind to shape. There is of course a wide variety of shapes. That shown is useful for gentle hollowing. For turning the insides of boxes use Fig. 303B. After cleaning up, the cutting edge is ground. Here, tastes differ but an angle of about 70° seems average.

A superior tool can be produced if arrangements can be made for the top surface to be machined on a surface grinder.

is convenient. Wires of several thicknesses are useful too.

Mark the position of the burn with a tiny chisel groove, or if a number of burns are to be made, use a pair of dividers on the tool rest. The points must definitely be below centre height. Clear the lathe of shavings and remove the tool rest.

Switch on with the wire across the lathe bed. Lift up into the mark, then slowly wrap about half way round the spindle and apply pressure. Do not be upset by the smoke and smell. Make sure that all the burns are of equal strength.

Before polishing, lightly sand off any roughness and clean while still revolving with a rag and a piece of string.

Different patterns burnt on lathe tool handles are an aid to finding the right tool quickly from amongst the shavings.

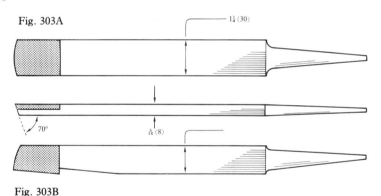

Fig. 303A

Fig. 303B

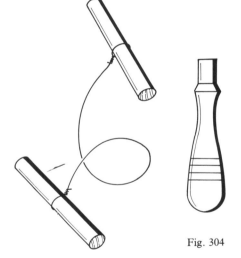

Fig. 304

Burning Wires

Figs 304 & 305

In the past burning was a more commonly used turning decoration, not only on tool handles, but also for small domestic articles. It gives the impression of a fine black inlay, more decisive than just a touch with the point of a chisel, which gives a line that eventually looks grimy.

The wire must be without spring and of single strand. Excellent material comes from old night storage heaters. Metalworkers' soft iron binding wire and florists' wire are two other possibilities. The dangerous practice of forming a finger loop at each end cannot be condemned too strongly. Go to the trouble of making a pair of toggle handles. A span of about 20 in (500 mm)

Grinding Devices

Most woodworkers, probably on grounds of economy, appear to grind their edge tools on high speed grinders, not the perfect appliance for the job. Probably the bulk of woodturners, who need to grind much more often, will use and prefer the high speed grinding wheel. However, with frequent dipping out into water to avoid drawing the temper, a satisfactory result can be obtained. Wheels below a diameter of 6 in (150 mm) are not to be recommended as the bevel produced is too hollow ground.

The very small tables supplied with these tables, though convenient for engineers, are virtually useless for woodworking tools. The simple devices described, not only give a precise and uniform angle, difficult to achieve hand held, but ensure that the same angle is produced at every grinding. Not only is there a considerable saving of time, but the amount of metal removed is greatly reduced.

To begin with some form of rest is required. Fig. 306 shows a simple wood angle piece which can be adjusted to and from the wheel and removed entirely if inconvenient.

The device of Fig. 307, made from wood or metal, is suitable for bench chisels, lathe chisels and lathe scrapers. Fig. 308 shows a variation for grinding plane cutters. If Fig. 307 were made to accept the widest plane cutter, it would become inconveniently large, particularly so when grinding narrow chisels.

Sizes and methods of construction will greatly depend upon the materials available.

Gouges, and in particular turning gouges, require considerable rotation when grinding, hence the modification in Fig. 309. Use a good dense hardwood and remember that considerable over-tightening will break the turned block. This device will permit all the rotation required while retaining the required angle.

When starting out, gauges of thin sheet metal will be useful to establish the angles, Fig. 310. Repetition of the chosen angle is assured by making in wood, a simple positioning gauge for each type of tool. Fig. 311 shows a gauge combining two sizes and the method of use.

These devices are equally successful when used on any horizontal wheel having a tool rest.

Fig. 305 A turning tool handle with burnt decoration

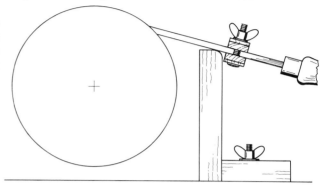

Fig. 306

Fig. 307

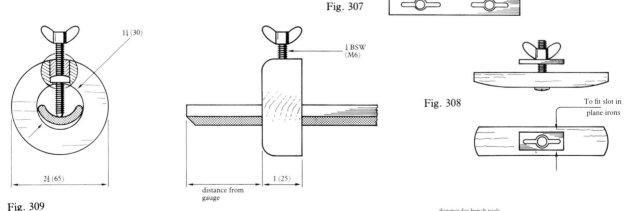

Fig. 308

Fig. 309

Fig. 310

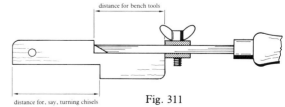

Fig. 311

Tools

Planes

Adjustable wooden planes
Fig. 313 & 314

It is always a pleasure to make something which actually performs – even more so if it performs well. That is why planes are such satisfying projects. The sweetness in action and the very feel are the attractions of wooden planes, but when it comes to easy and convenient adjustment, the metal plane is generally the winner.

Before World War II there was an attempt to bridge the gap by fitting Norris mechanisms to otherwise standard wooden planes, but the idea did not survive the war. Continental makers are producing adjustable

parallel in thickness, but in practice the more common tapered blade seems to work, since the amount of taper in the length of movement required is negligible. The smoothing plane shown here takes a 2 in cutter and the jackplane a $2\frac{1}{4}$ in, not the $2\frac{3}{8}$ in of the iron planes. Beech and maple have been the common woods. Fruitwoods and oak are also particularly successful but do not discard a nice block of imported timber, either.

Ideally the body should come from a quarter-sawn board, as in Fig. 315, but in the past, wooden planemakers frequently ignored this. If the material is old and dry, it will hardly distort anyway. Quarter sawn, of course will not distort, but as these planes are not intended to be used on their sides, a slight distortion should not affect the performance.

Fig. 313   Fully adjustable jack plane in mahogany with ebony sole length 17" thick cutter $2\frac{1}{4}$

wooden planes but their mechanisms do not lend themselves to one-off making with tools which the woodworker is likely to have. The mechanisms to be described here, plus the laminated construction of the planes themselves, put these fully adjustable tools well within average capacity so long as care is taken. See page 157 (Appendix 8) for scale drawings.

The basic requirement, before any woodwork starts, is an old, thick plane blade. In theory this should be

Fig. 314   Fully adjustable wooden smoothing plane

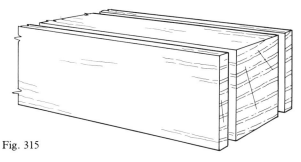

Fig. 315

The Body

The entire plane can be cut from one block, or if timber of this size is not available, the two sides can be cut from 1 in (25 mm) material. A single piece of thick material is cut into two for the front and rear blocks while a further piece of about 1 in (25 mm) is required for the handle. Be sure to arrange the grain of the blocks so that when the sole is planed to finish it, it is worked from front to rear.

Face and edge the main block, then carefully thickness it to $\frac{1}{8}$ in (3 mm) more than the cutter width. Saw it in two, at the angles shown and plane the bed face to 45°. If desired, the smoother may be given the cabinet-makers' 'York pitch', of 50°. The front block is planed to its 60° then reduced in height, Fig. 316.

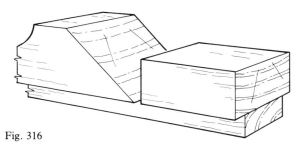

Fig. 316

Now shape the handle, from 1 in (25 mm) material; hands differ as widely as preferences, so the handle is such an individual matter that only approximate guidance can be given. Do not skimp on the time and work on the handle, for a really comfortable handle goes a long way towards making a plane a firm favourite.

The rear block nears completion when it is cut away to take the low-set handle. Clean up the curve, then mortice it and glue in the handle. Skim over the 45° bed again finishing the handle in line.

The Mechanism
Figs 317 to 320

It is wise now to put aside the woodwork and make the mechanism, about which there is nothing particularly difficult. All the work can be done with hand-tools,

though access to a lathe is a help. Two versions are shown in Fig. 318A & B; the double screw gives the finer adjustment, but there is more slack in the mechanism. Be sure that the central block, Fig. 318C, is a match in size for the bit which is to drill the hole in the angled face of the handle/bed.

Preferably draw a full size view, Fig. 317, of the blade, cap-iron and mechanism, which enables the hole in the bed to be bored with accuracy. Cut a groove from this hole to take the mechanism – a router is best.

Assembly

The front and rear blocks can now be cramped in position together on a building board, Fig. 316. Lay the blade in place and adjust the 'mouth' to just smaller than the finished size. With everything in position, glue on the roughly shaped sides; Aerolite or Cascamite are recommended glues. Use plenty of cramps and possibly the vice as well. A router with an edge trimming cutter

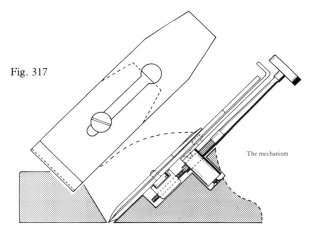

Fig. 317

The mechanism

brings down the rough sides to the base of the blocks, otherwise, they can be whittled down to shape. The front knob is routine turning; aim rather at a mushroom shape to take good downward pressure comfortably.

The cap-iron, Fig. 319B, is simply made from bright drawn mild steel, the end hammered over a round bar to produce the curve. If an old cap-iron is used, its large brass nut will need to be removed. A Record/Stanley type cap-iron can be modified to suit. The wedge, Fig. 319A, can be sawn and filed from the solid or an aluminium casting made and cleaned up, (see page 109). The two screw/knobs for wedge tension and blade adjustment, Figs 319D & 318, can be engineered from aluminium or brass, or else made up as described on page 150. The end of the wedge screw, Fig. 319D, must be finished to a smooth dome; if it is left square ended, it

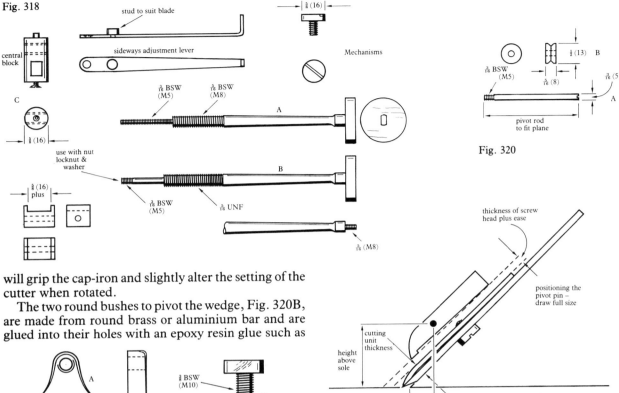

Fig. 318

central block

C

stud to suit blade

sideways adjustment lever

Mechanisms

$\frac{3}{16}$ BSW
(M5)

$\frac{5}{16}$ BSW
(M8)

A

use with nut
locknut &
washer

B

$\frac{3}{16}$ BSW
(M5)

$\frac{3}{16}$ UNF

$\frac{3}{16}$ (16)
plus

$\frac{5}{16}$ (M8)

$\frac{3}{16}$ BSW
(M5)

$\frac{1}{2}$ (13)   B

$\frac{5}{16}$ (8)

$\frac{3}{16}$ (5)

A

pivot rod
to fit plane

Fig. 320

will grip the cap-iron and slightly alter the setting of the cutter when rotated.

The two round bushes to pivot the wedge, Fig. 320B, are made from round brass or aluminium bar and are glued into their holes with an epoxy resin glue such as

A

$\frac{3}{8}$ BSW
(M10)

D

wedge

B

Fig. 319

cap-iron

blade

C

thickness of screw
head plus ease

positioning the
pivot pin –
draw full size

cutting
unit
thickness

height
above
sole

distance behind
mouth

Fig. 321

Araldite. One way of finding out their position is to glue on only one side of the plane, assemble all the metal components, and mark the centre, through the wedge with a sharp piece of $\frac{3}{16}$ in rod. The other side is then glued on and trimmed. Alternatively, work from a full-size drawing, Fig. 321. Fit the wedge pivot rod, Fig. 320A, alone directly in the wood first to check its position and movement. If it proves necessary to move the pivot, the $\frac{1}{2}$ in (12 mm) hole to be drilled for the bush will remove the unwanted hole. The wedge should fit as close as possible to the cap-iron, but still allow easy removal of the cutting unit. Exact details cannot be given since wedge, cap-iron and blade are all variables.

When all the metal components have been made, they can be fitted into place. The screw beneath the central block, Fig. 318C, is adjusted to bring the mechanism very slightly below the wood surface.

Finishing
It is now time to plane up the sole and to pare out or file

the mouth to the smallest aperture which does not clog. The jack plane, for rather rougher work, can possibly be given a slightly wider mouth. The plane can now be tried out. When satisfied with the feel and action of the plane, a sole of ebony or rosewood may be fitted. (Those who have had enough can of course get off here and leave well alone!) Remove $\frac{5}{16}$ in (8 mm) from the sole, preferably by machine planing, and glue on the new sole, slightly overlapping. This is the best method to follow for a first plane, but with more experience, plane makers will avoid this by making the main body glue-up with a larger gap, which will give an escapement as in Fig. 322. Drill a series of small holes and file out the mouth using a large warding file. A number of timber suppliers advertise rosewood and ebony; pieces sold as guitar fingerboards will make two smoothers, but they are just too narrow for a jack plane.

When thoroughly tested and all is well, the plane can be finished, either with raw linseed oil and lots of rubbing or with a polyurethane varnish – but not on the sole.

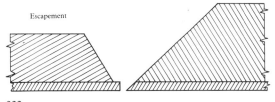

Fig. 322

Observations

If it is definitely decided to fit an ebony sole, the rear block can be laminated by adding two shaped blocks to the completely shaped handle, thus avoiding morticing. Similarly, if thick enough material is not available, both the body blocks can be made from two thinner pieces glued together. The end-grain pattern should be arranged symmetrically, Fig. 323.

The cylindrical centre block, Fig. 318C, can be left as a tight fit in case it is required to remove it later, or a $\frac{3}{16}$ in (4 mm) pin can be put through it; the very confident may decide to glue it in with an epoxy resin, for which two flats must be filed on it.

For final truing up of the sole, fit the blade in with the wedge screw at normal working tension but with the blade *well withdrawn*. Check and double check before passing the tool over the planer on a fine cut. Often these soles do not respond well to hand-planing, but will finish well on a machine. Alternatively, sand the sole true using a length of beltsanding material on a machine surface, or on a piece of plate glass.

To set the plane, the wedge screw is slightly slackened, the cut adjusted (always finishing with a clock-

wise rotation to take up any slack), then the wedge screw is re-tightened. This is not as messy as it sounds – with experience one becomes quite slick. Enormous tension will distort the sole; the screw must be just tight enough to prevent easy sideways movement of the blade with the fingers.

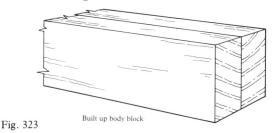

Fig. 323   Built up body block

A wooden jack-plane using Stanley-type components
Fig. 324

This makes a particularly sweet running light plane which is well suited to youngsters and for softwood work.

The body of the plane is built in the manner described from page 117. An open handle is required. Replacement handles for wooden jack planes can very occasionally be located but generally the reader will have either to carve his own handle or to fit a Record/Stanley replacement. This latter will be glued and screwed, having thoroughly cleaned the bottom of any polish.

The dimensions given are for a plane with a 2 in (50 mm) cutter. Naturally they can be modified slightly and will need to be if the $2\frac{3}{8}$ in (60 mm) cutter is chosen.

Glue up the body as described earlier, then on a circular saw or by hand, work a slot a full $\frac{3}{16}$ in (5 mm) wide, to take the adjusting crank.

Glue on the cap, which has provision made to accept the lateral adjustment lever. This will be similar to that on page 118. Cut the adjusting crank from $\frac{3}{16}$ in (5 mm) bright mild steel. Use the full size pattern.

The position of the $\frac{1}{8}$ in (3 mm) pivot pin is best

Fig. 324   Wooden jack plane using Stanley type components

Fig. 325

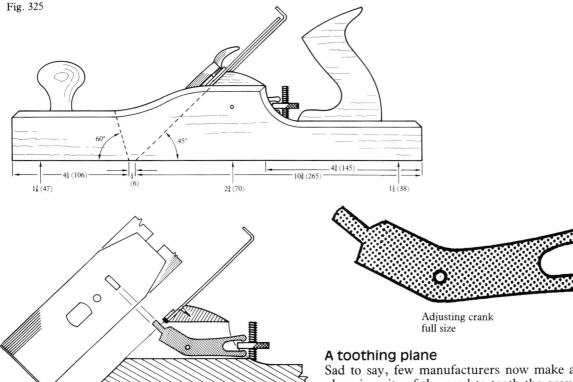

Fig. 326

determined by a full size drawing, Fig. 326. Try the assembly of crank and cutting unit to see that all is well. If so, fit a No. 10 round head woodscrew as the lever cap screw. Adjust this so that the blade can just be moved sideways with a little effort.

A piece of screwed rod can now be fitted for the adjusting wheel. If normal rod is used, $\frac{1}{4}$ BSW (M6), the adjustment will be opposite to that in normal planes, i.e. a clockwise adjustment will *decrease* the cut.

In order to conform the convention, a left hand tap and die are required to cut the threads on the rod and in the adjusting wheel. These are not much more expensive than the normal taps and dies and can be ordered by good tool dealers.

Only when the whole mechanism is working is the handle glued in. The front knob is straightforward.

This mechanism does not lend itself to the much shorter smoothing plane.

The wedge can, at a pinch, be made from hard wood with a let-in nut. A sole also of very hard wood may be added. Finish with linseed oil or polyurethane varnish, the latter not on the sole.

Adjusting crank
full size

A toothing plane

Sad to say, few manufacturers now make a toothing plane in spite of the need to tooth the ground before laying veneers and plastic laminates, so if one is needed there is the pleasure of making before that of using. The body presents no difficulty, but the toothing blade, on the other hand, is virtually unobtainable. Again, none are manufactured and second hand ones rarely come onto the market. This model has therefore been devised to take throwaway blades of different degrees of coarseness, Figs 327 & 328.

Fig. 327   Toothing plane with throw-away cutters

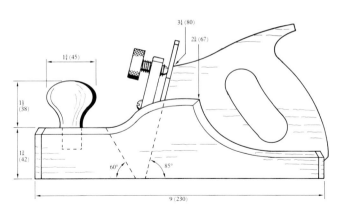

Fig. 328

The body construction begins in the manner described on page 117 onwards.

The bed is planed accurately at an angle of 85° and a $\frac{1}{8}$ in (3 mm) pilot hole is drilled for the wedge-securing screw, a No. 12×2 in, which is screwed in at this stage and then removed, to be replaced finally just before the front knob is glued in place. The front of the mouth is finished at an angle of 60°. Before the sides are glued on, a small housing is cut at the bottom of the bed to take the slight protrusion of the blade clamping screw.

Cut the sides to just over $\frac{5}{16}$ in (8 mm), gauge round them, then glue the plane together on an assembly board. Plane the sides down to thickness and finish off the curves. The shape near to the handle can easily be worked using an edge trimming router cutter. Level up

the sole and screw in the wedge retaining screw. Turn and fit the front knob but delay the gluing until later.

The wedge, Fig. 329F, may be an alloy or brass casting (the pattern for this is very simple), cut from the solid or made from dense hardwood with a sunk-in metal nut. A clamping screw with knob completes this component, G.

The cutting unit consists of a carrier plate, A, a clamping plate, B, and the actual cutter, C, which is made from a hand hacksaw blade. Naturally a high-speed blade will last longer. Several degrees of coarseness are available; broken but little used blades are the ideal source, the teeth near the handle having generally had but little use.

The required length can be snapped off in the vice and then ground to size, leaving clean edges and corners. The type and width of blade chosen will decide the exact position of the locating pins and the blade clamping screw.

The carrier plate is made from bright mild steel, sawn and filed to shape. The two small locating pins, D, can be fitted in several ways, depending on preference or resources. They can be tightly screwed in, then filed flush and to length, or given a tiny shoulder and riveted or silversoldered/brazed. If heat is used it will be necessary to clean up afterwards. Since the carrier plate is to be drilled and tapped anyway for the blade clamping screw, E, the reader will probably opt for the first alternative. The clamping plate is made from the same material and the two are gripped together and drilled with the tapping drill. Then the holes in the clamping plate are enlarged to clearance size. A large

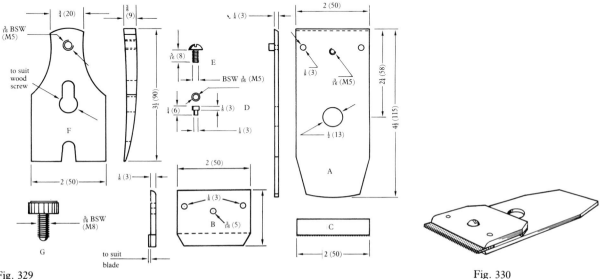

Fig. 329

Fig. 330

hole is drilled in the carrier plate to give adequate movement round the large woodscrew in the body. A thin slip of metal, about the same thickness as the hacksaw blade is soldered to the clamping plate to give a better gripping action. As there is no strain on this, soft solder is strong enough. When fitting together, cut a gap in the wedge to accommodate the head of the blade clamping screw.

It is not considered worth fitting a mechanism to a toothing plane.

All the details of the components are shown in Figs 329 & 330.

It is strongly recommended that a full size drawing be prepared from which individual details can be sorted out. Do not omit either the dome end to the clamping screw or to give width clearance of about ⅛ in (3 mm) when preparing the body blocks to size. For heavier work, of course, the whole width of the plane may be increased but for general cabinetmaking the 2 in (50 mm) cutter will be quite satisfactory.

Routing
Routing by hand
The power router has come to stay. Of that there is no doubt and it must be the ambition of most readers to own one if they do not have one already. Nevertheless, there is still a place for the hand router. Small operations and corrections can be done by hand more quickly than the time taken to sort out the spanners and cutters and to fit up that extension lead for the power router.

In the great days of hand work Stanley and other firms each made several patterns of router. Now, alas, apart from two Stanley models these have all gone and long ago the wooden 'old woman's tooth' router has been reduced to an illustration in rather obsolete textbooks. The cost of the metal router at the time of writing is well on the way towards the cost of a small power router, so it is not surprising that this tool is not all that common in the tool boxes of the present generation.

However, the great usefulness of the hand router

makes its construction well worth while, particularly as the methods are quick and easy and the components are cheap. Before considering the two models described here, it is worth examining the two distinct cutting actions used. That shown in Fig. 331A is the normal plane action, used in the traditional wooden routers. Like the moulding planes, the pitch is rather high; 60° was common, though of course it could be made lower. Fig. 331B shows the cranked cutter which came in generally with the metal routers, though on the continent this cutter was used with wooden routers in the manner later described.

Bearing in mind that a great deal of routing is done across the grain, this shearing of B cut is probably better than the more scraping cut of A. To give a more slicing action on difficult wood, (and also to get into corners on inlay work, a pointed cutter was produced, Fig. 334. Quite obviously this shape needs its lower face to have no clearance at all, but to be parallel to the base of the router.

The vertical stem of the cranked cutter made it easy to devise and fit an adjusting mechanism. However, the cranked cutter has one disadvantage. It cannot operate in a cavity much smaller than three times the cutter length because of the uncut area which must remain in the centre. Fig. 331B shows this. It is for this reason that the small wooden router has been included.

An improved router
Figs 332 & 333
Again a good dense hardwood should be chosen for the body of this tool. Beech, or a fruitwood are obvious choices. As a refinement for a de luxe model, a thin face of ebony or rosewood can be added. Multi-ply has successfully been used with a sole of plastic laminate. As this may tend to warp the body, a balancing layer needs to be applied to the top. If this is considered, an adhesive such as Aerolite with its special laminate hardener should be used rather than the common

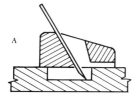
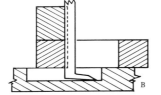

Fig. 331

Fig. 332   An improved router

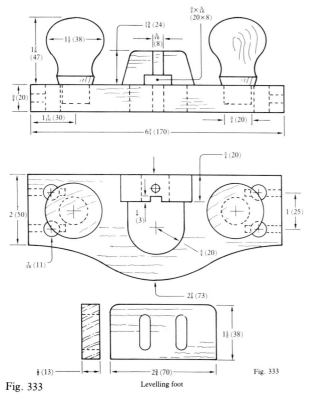

Fig. 333

Levelling foot

Fig. 333

through and jointed after the cutter block has been glued on and grooved. The body can now be sanded to its ultimate finish. Drill for the cylindrical nuts, Fig. 334 and for the handles. Drill and tap for the adjusting screw. Now turn, sand, polish and glue in the knob handles. They are shaped to individual taste.

Now for the metal parts. The four cylindrical nuts are produced from bar material and pushed into place. Steel is normal. Brass looks well on the de luxe model. They should be a tight fit. Drill a 5 mm tapping hole through both the body and the nut. Remove and tap the nuts then drill out the body at $\frac{1}{4}$ in or 6 mm, taking the drill a little way beyond the nut hole. Replace the nuts. When making the cylindrical nuts, they should be turned or filed just a little less than the body thickness, to avoid scoring the work.

The cutters, Fig. 334, are quite straightforward if they have to be made. The stem is from mild steel, notched to take the adjusting nut. The cutting end is made from ground flat stock, i.e. tool steel, secured to the stem with a small round tenon. This is riveted over then silver soldered, which is generally neater than brazing.

The clamp or drawbolt is quite simply made. File the shank round, trying it with a washer, see page 154. Then cut the thread. The square hole in it can be a bit sloppy. A wing-nut and washer apply the pressure.

The adjusting wheel needs to be nicely made and there is really no short cut for this. In brass it can be worked with hand tools in a woodturning lathe. Otherwise it means cultivating an engineering friend.

The great innovation of this router is its levelling foot, which when fitted at either end, permits the router

impact glues. Most readers will probably wish to stay with solid wood as the finish appearance is far superior.

Bore and saw out the escapement and produce the outline shape. For convenience, the body may be sawn

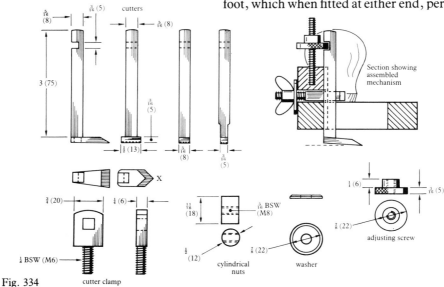

Fig. 334

cutter clamp

Fig. 335

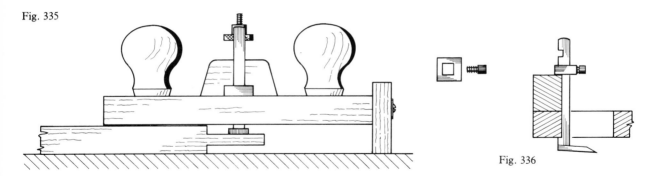

Fig. 336

to be used with one side unsupported by the work. One such application, illustrated in Fig. 335, is the thinning down of an over thick tenon. The reader will certainly discover further uses for this facility.

Place the work on a level surface and the router on top of it, with the cutter fully withdrawn. Fit the levelling foot, allowing it to drop to the surface then tighten its clamping screws.

Always adjust the cut with the blade in the housing or on the work. Unlock, increase the cut then lock again. If the tool is held in the air when unlocking, the cutter will drop by the amount of slack in the mechanism, giving an increase of cut greater than was intended.

Unlike the plough, the router cutter cannot be pre-set at a given depth, so when a number of identical housings are to be cut, time can be saved by making a depth stop which can be pre-set to limit the depth of cut. This is shown in Fig. 336.

Small wooden router
Figs 337 & 338
The tricky part of this project, the cutting of the hole, tapered at 60° and 78°, is avoided in the early stages. Prepare a suitable block of any dense, close-grained

hardwood, slightly over-size and saw through at 60°. Plane up for a good joint, then from the front section saw and cut out the main part of the escapement and in the rear section cut a shallow housing to take the cutter. If cutters are made thick enough, two shallow housings can be made to take cutters of both ½ in (12 mm) and ¼ in (6 mm).

Glue together, true up the sole and remove the shallow escapement in front of the blade. The whole of the shaping can now be done, according to taste, and the wedge made. The most suitable finish is probably a number of coats of raw linseed oil. Polyurethane varnish may be preferred by some readers. If used, this must not be applied to the sole. Plough plane cutters can most successfully be used. Cutters can be made from tool steel, sometimes sold as 'gauge plate'. The hardening and tempering process is described on page 155.

These sizes can be scaled up to make a traditional type of full sized wooden router.

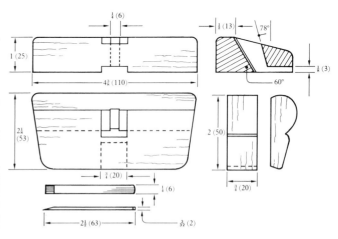

Fig. 337   A small wooden router

Fig. 338

A Metal Scratch Tool

Figs 339 & 340

In the late 19th century, the American tool company Stanley were producing a lot of wooden tool designs in metal, many of which are now collectors' pieces, such as the No. 66 Universal Two Handed Beader. The decline in demand for such tools seems to have been caused not so much by declining standards of handwork – it is as good or better than it ever was – but by the declining volume of hand work. The Beader, patented in 1886, is 11½ in long, of cast iron and nickel plated over copper. It was sold with 14 double ended cutters, two fences, (one for curved edges), and two blanks for the owner to grind to special shapes. Those who have seen and used the tool are both envious and enthusiastic, so the following design has been worked out which can be made with the minimum of metalworking equipment and the average woodworker's metalworking skills.

Small mouldings, beads, small corner rebates, narrow grooves for stringings, small routings – these are just some of the applications of the tool, which is well worth making.

The back plate, A (Figs 341 & 343) is cut to size and a shallow 15 mm central groove formed. Use a milling or shaping machine if one is available, otherwise it is a rather tedious and cautious filing job.

The depth is not critical – 1 or 1·5 mm is enough. As an alternative, four small pins can be inserted to position the blade, Fig. 343. The clamp slot is simply drilled with a number of 5 mm holes between the 6 mm end holes and then filed out. The small handle holes can then be drilled and countersunk on the flat face.

The sole-plate, B, Figs 341 & 342 is easier. The long slot is drilled, sawn and filed out, after which the mouth can be cut. File the jointing edge accurately to 80° to braze the back plate on. Hold the two pieces together for brazing or silver soldering with two simple clamps, Fig. 344A, and suitable screws, nuts and washers. Readers without brazing facilities will have to ask a garage or small engineering firm to do the job – it is

elementary when correctly clamped together. Use brazing rod of the lowest melting point available. Notice in Fig. 344B that the two parts are assembled with a marked projection and that three corners are slightly chamfered.

Clean the tool well with successively finer grades of emery cloth, and note that the front bottom edge of the sole-plate is rounded slightly, Fig. 342B. The handle tangs, C, Figs 340 & 342 are quite straightforward; they are drilled then countersunk on the outer side only. Saw the rod for the rivets to the total thickness of the two components, plus 1½ times the rivet diameter. Rivet on the handles then file all flush.

The blade clamp, D, Fig. 341, can be made in either of two ways. The whole thing can be cut from one piece, the stem filed round and then threaded, or a pre-formed screw can be fitted to a threaded hole and fixed with a touch of brazing or silver solder. This latter is much easier but as with all heat methods, some later cleaning up is required. The clamp must not be too thin and therefore weak, so it protrudes slightly through the back plate. This calls for a grooved washer, E, Fig. 341. The clamp is held either with a nicely turned and knurled knob, F, Fig. 341, or a wing-nut which does the job just as well.

The fence, G, Fig. 341, is a simple filing or milling job. Make two, for working with a fence on both sides of an edge ensures accuracy and makes it unnecessary to concentrate on avoiding a slip. The original tool was fitted with a shaped fence for working from curved edges, but it is easier to drill the fence with two holes through which round headed screws can secure specially shaped wooden facings. Fix a piece of screwed rod into the fence block, which will be locked in the required position with a washer and wing-nut.

As $\frac{5}{8} \times \frac{1}{16}$ in ground flat stock (tool steel) is increasingly difficult to find, it is best to settle for 15×1·5 mm, which a good tool dealer will stock in 18 in or 330 mm lengths.

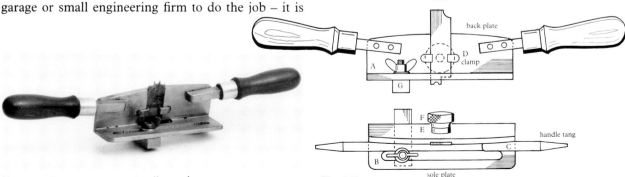

Fig. 339   A metal scratch or beading tool

Fig. 340

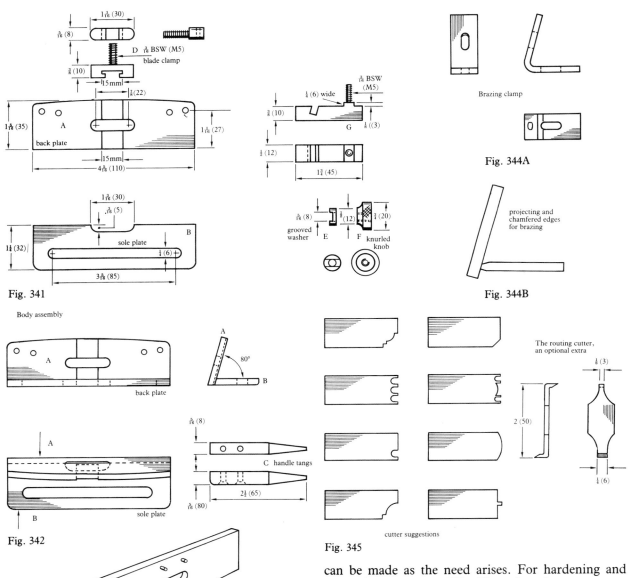

Fig. 341

Body assembly

Fig. 342

Fig. 343

Alternative to the groove for cutter

Fig. 344A

Fig. 344B

Fig. 345

cutter suggestions

Excellent cutters can be made from worn-out and broken power hacksaw blades, but avoid the 'all hard' type which are not workable. The type needed has been described on page 45.

File the double-ended router cutters to shape, heat them red then bend them over, Fig. 345. Other cutters can be made as the need arises. For hardening and tempering see page 155. Note that the cutters are shaped at a slight angle rather than square.

Lastly, the handles. Turn them to shape, fit suitable ferrules and drill a hole of about 7 mm. Heat the tips of the handle tangs to a dull red (a small propane torch is adequate) and push on each handle to almost the final position, remove it, wait for the metal to cool then tap the handle on permanently.

There may be a bad spot on the timber which will not scratch well. In that case, this can be left over-size until all the other work is complete. Then move the fence across and push the tool in the opposite direction.

Naturally this can only be done when the cutter shape is symmetrical. To reverse the tool when using an asymmetrical cutter, it must be sharpened at 90°. It will then be possible to turn the cutter over.

A Wooden Scratch Tool

Figs 346 & 347

The scratch tool illustrated (if at all) in most text books is a pathetic specimen. It neither looks nor feels attractive. Its setting is messy and imprecise while its performance is doubtful.

The virtue of this tool, apart from improved appearance and handling, is that while the blade is set approximately by screwdriver, a fine final adjustment can be made by moving the fence.

The cutter and fence are clamped by using three gutter bolts and a roofing bolt easily obtainable at hardware shops. These are M6×30 and M6×70.

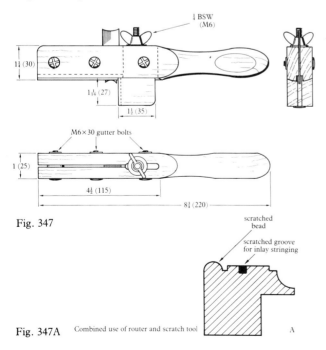

Fig. 346   Improved wooden scratch tool

Fig. 347

Fig. 347A   Combined use of router and scratch tool

Prepare the stock from hard, well seasoned material. Make very shallow borings for the gutter bolt heads then drill through at $\frac{1}{4}$ in. Assemble with three square nuts in place, scribe round the nuts and chop out cavities to receive them. Alternatively hexagon nuts can be pulled in, see page 155.

Chop or rout the $\frac{1}{4}$ in mortice for the fence bolt, then continue this as a groove on the under side. Slightly round this face.

The handle can now be turned or whittled, any excess length removed and the slot sawn. Do not make too fine a slot. To avoid distortion when tightening, a thin washer is inserted on the end screw.

The fence is made from an offcut of the same material. Make the same shallow boring for the bolt head then drill through for the shank. Preferably drill at 5 mm and tap to screw in the roofing bolt, thus ensuring that the bolt will not turn when tightened. Or simply drill a 6 mm hole. Work a tongue to fit into the groove in the stock and make a shallow groove to accept the cutter. Trim back the shoulders to match the round stock. Add the wing-nut and washer.

Cutters can be made as required, see page 126.

The scratch tool can combine with the small electric router, providing shapes which the latter cannot produce. Fig. 347A shows a picture moulding worked by a combination of router and scratch tool.

Cutters may be slightly angled, but if filed to shape dead square, can be used to cut in both directions. The crisper the wood, the better it will scratch. As a rule, softwoods perform poorly.

A Veneering Hammer

Figs 348 & 349

The veneering hammer, though an essential tool for hand veneering, cannot be bought, and usually articles on veneering are not very informative. This model should suit most woodworkers, at least to begin with.

Make the handle from any good hard wood. Ash is

Fig. 348   Veneering hammer in ash
Working edge made from hard plastic

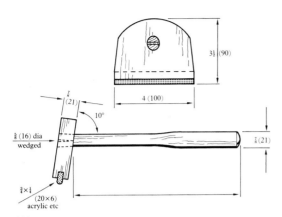

Fig. 349

ideal for the handle though most straight-grained timbers are suitable. Turn, plane, whittle or work it with rounders.

Traditionally the working edge is of brass, which can be expensive and hard to find, except in large cities. A good alternative is acrylic sheet, about $\frac{3}{16}$ in (4 mm) thick; this can be clear or coloured. Small offcuts can usually be obtained from firms making plastic signs. These can be found in the classified telephone directories. Fit the strip tightly into the groove in the working edge, and glue, remembering to roughen the gluing surface. Small pins or screws can be added as an extra safeguard. When secure, round over the working face with a file, then successively finer grades of abrasive paper, to give a really good finish.

Make the handle to fit tightly into the hole and fix with a hardwood wedge. File or pare the hole into a slight ellipse for this purpose. If turning the handle a small shoulder may be added. Form the angled hole by tilting the drilling machine table or, if using a simpler drill stand, drilling onto a wedge-shaped block.

The sizes given are only suggestions. Personal preference comes in, particularly over the handle, which some workers prefer as short as 6 in (150 mm).

An Inlay Thicknesser

Figs 350 & 351

When buying inlay stringing, choice is generally limited to boxwood or black (dyed), in $\frac{1}{16}$ or $\frac{1}{8}$ in square sections. Sycamore, holly, rosewood, walnut, padouk and so on are not produced by manufacturers. Orders take time to arrive and minimum quantities are often demanded.

This tool will instantly produce stringings of the chosen species in any required size. Very fine size adjustment is possible so it is much easier to produce

stringings for a previously made groove than to produce a scratch tool cutter to suit a particular stringing.

Two models are described. One is based on an alloy casting, Fig. 350A. The other is fabricated from aluminium alloy or steel bar and strip, Fig. 350B.

The working face and the feet of the casting are filed or machined true. A small step is worked across the bottom of the face to accept the slight cutting hook.

The fabricated model is brought to the same stage. The bed, from bar material, is angled on its underside, Fig. 352A. The sides are sawn from sheet or strip and suitably drilled and countersunk, Fig. 352B. The bed is screwed to the sides and any slight projection is filed flush.

Holes for the adjusting screws are drilled, Figs 351A & 351B. Either borrow parts from a Record spokeshave or buy them as spare parts. Record use threads of 1BA for their adjusting screws and nuts, though if the adjusting nuts are to be made, Fig. 352C, any suitable thread may be used.

At this stage it is convenient to make the wood baseboard, Fig. 350 or 351, either rebating, for gripping in the vice, or building up from two pieces.

Temporarily fix the casting or fabrication of the baseboard and critically mark the centre for the wedge screw. Dimensions are suggested but make sure that when the cutter is set for $\frac{3}{16}$ in material, the wedge will

Fig. 350a   Inlay thicknesser from a simple aluminium casting

Fig. 350b   Inlay thicknesser. Fabricated construction

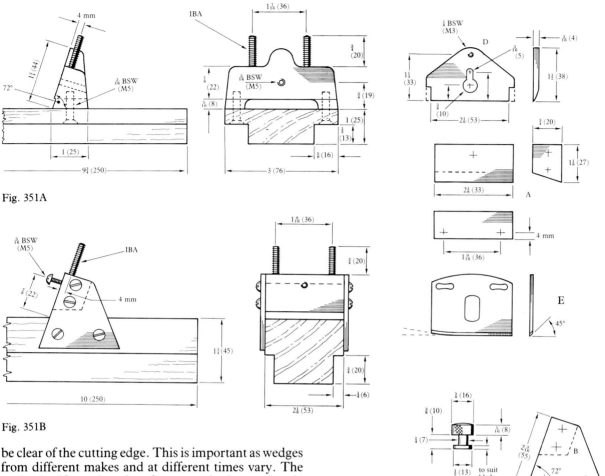

Fig. 351A

Fig. 351B

Fig. 352

be clear of the cutting edge. This is important as wedges from different makes and at different times vary. The wedge itself may be taken from a spokeshave or made from sheet steel. If the latter, omit the two notches of the Record wedge which serve no purpose here.

A $\frac{3}{16}$ BSW (or M5) round head screw secures the wedge to the bed. The blade clamping thumb screw, as manufactured, is $\frac{1}{8}$ BSW but any similar thread will do. Round the end of this screw, otherwise it may displace the blade when tightened. The adjusting nuts should have the flange corners softened and be a comfortable fit in the cutter slots. As with a plane, the final nut adjustment must be clockwise to avoid slip-back. The finished tool can now be permanently screwed to the baseboard.

The standard blade should be re-ground to 45°. Additionally, it needs to be ground away for ease of entry, as shown in Fig. 252E. It is then sharpened in the manner of the scraper plane, that is, hone keenly then burnish the edge, slowly increasing the angle, up to about 75°, Fig. 354, producing the finest hook edge.

The blade is inserted in the tool with the bevel *away* from the bed.

To use

Make a sawing board to produce stock which will be slightly over-size. That shown in Fig. 353, for a small bandsaw, can also be used with a tenon saw. Most circular saws however, are too coarse, though thin sharp blades can be found.

Set the blade so that the stringing can just pass through at the entry side. It is then advisable to grip the end with pliers. Pull through, at the same time both sliding the stringing across to the main section of the blade and also holding it flat to the baseboard. Obviously, the first few inches have not been cut, so repeat the process with the other end leading. Do this to all the

129

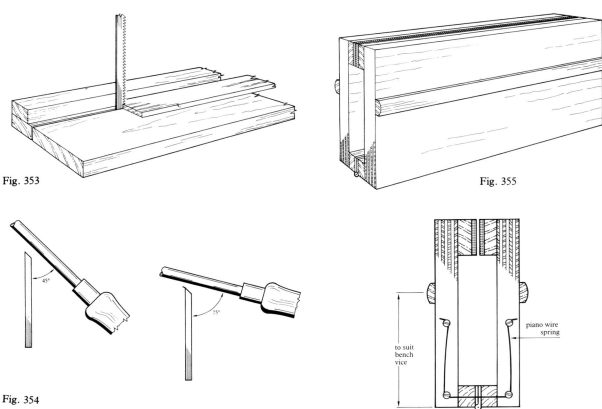

Fig. 353

Fig. 355

Fig. 354

Fig. 356

material prepared before minutely increasing the cut and repeating. Remember that there should be one good, i.e. planed surface before starting and also that two fine cuts will produce a better finish than one heavy cut. Thickness the width accurately to fill the groove, but leave the stringing standing slightly proud, to be scraped level after gluing.

A Saw Sharpening Vice

The saw vice, though essential, is, for the amateur, expensive for the limited use which is made of it. Fortunately one can be simply made. The model illustrated will satisfy most workshop needs. Fig. 355.

The vice consists basically of two hinged plywood jaws with spacing strips top and bottom to accept the thickness of a saw handle. The jaws can be about 12 in (300 mm) long, or the length of the vice jaws. If a much longer vice is planned to sharpen handsaws at one gripping, then extra G cramps will need to be added at the ends. Two rounded strips in the outside take the pressure of the bench vice jaws. The inside capacity of the saw vice should be such that the widest handsaw

will fit in. It may be preferably to make a second, smaller vice simply for tenon saws.

The jaws are lined with leather or rubber (pieces from an old car inner tube are quite suitable) to reduce the unpleasant noise often associated with saw sharpening.

It may be necessary to cut away part of the jaw strips of the saw vice in order to accept the handles of smaller saws.

It is more convenient if an opening spring is fitted, Fig. 356. This is made from piano wire, often obtained from model shops.

Improved Shooting Boards
Fig. 357

A well made shooting board is a joy to use, producing accuracy with little skill or effort.

The standard shooting board suffers from two inherent defects. It is possible to cant the plane over, resulting in an unsquare edge or end. This further cuts

Fig. 357   Improved shooting board
Method of use, showing workpiece and thrust block

away the end stop, with the result that the work is unsupported, so end grain spelches (breaks out).

The innovations of this board are the top rail, which guarantees a square cut, and the loose thrust blocks, which can be advanced to take up wear and so give perfect support to the work, Fig. 358.

90° Board

Start by making the baseboard from medium density fibreboard (MDF), multi-ply or blockboard. If this has a vice batten fixed, this will be a convenient method of holding during construction.

Prepare two rubbing strips from acrylic sheet, (see page 128). Drill, countersink and screw one to the baseboard.

Prepare the end blocks to size, rout the slot and notch the ends. From the fixed rubbing strip, square the housings to accept the end blocks. Remove the strip and rout to a depth of $\frac{1}{8}$ in (3 mm). Now glue and screw in place both the rubbing strip and the two end blocks. Check at once, with a try square that the end blocks are square to the working edge of the rubbing strip.

Now prepare the work-face and screw in place. The purpose of this is to lift up the workpiece well into the cutting area of the blade.

Produce the top rail to size and secure the rubbing strip to it. The true edge of this should project very slightly. Drill over-size holes at each end and screw in place.

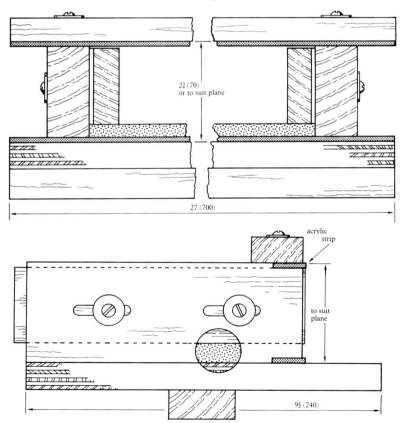

$2\frac{3}{4}$ (70) or to suit plane

27 (700)

acrylic strip

to suit plane

$9\frac{1}{2}$ (240)

Fig. 358

131

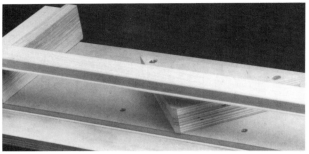

Fig. 359   Improved shooting board. Showing mitre shooting block

Saw off a piece from a small plastic geometry set-square and use this to test that when the plane is held in the working position, it is truly square to the workface. Adjust the top rail then screw firmly.

The two thrust blocks are produced to size with a small bevel worked on the trailing edge to prevent spelching. They are screwed in position then planed until the plane will cut no more. They can subsequently be advanced to take up any wear.

For mitred work, produce a 45° block, which must be built up from plywood. (Any shrinkage would alter the angle). This can be screwed in place as and when required. It will be convenient to drill a hole in the top rail for a screwdriver, Fig. 359.

45° Board
Fig. 360
In general the construction is similar to that of the 90° board. The common plastic laminate, such as Formica, is probably more suitable than acrylic sheet, Fig. 361.

Make the baseboard, screw on the vice batten then glue on a laminate strip. Work a $\frac{1}{4}$ in (6 mm) groove along this with a router or circular saw. The end blocks must be built up from layers of plywood, again to avoid shrinkage and the reduction of the angle. Work the slots, notch the ends then cut the 45° angles. The blocks are glued and screwed in place, accurately square to the groove, (i.e. square to the edge of the baseboard).

Fig. 360   Mitre shooting board – detail

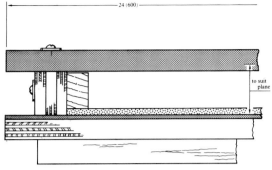

Fig. 361

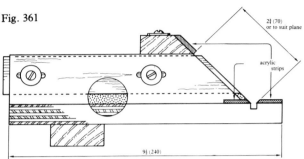

The work-face is next made and fitted.

Prepare the top rail, angle the working face, glue on the plastic laminate then trim up the edges. Drill over-size holes for fixing. Check, using a small set-square, that the plane in position makes an angle of 45° to the workface. Then screw the top rail permanently. Thrust blocks are added then planed until the plane will cut no more.

It is recommended that a special blade be sharpened exactly square and kept exclusively for shooting board work.

These shooting boards are not made double-ended for the convenient of left-handers, though this is in fact so. Mouldings, such as Fig. 362, must be planed into the moulding, as A. Working in the direction B will cause splitting out, hence to shoot both ends of a moulded component, a double-ended board is required.

Fig. 362

A Tool for Veneer Strips

This tool was devised when faced with a number of students, all requiring crossbanding at the same time. It proved successful so was given a permanent place in the workshop.

The drawing, Fig. 363A, is fairly self explanatory but a short description may avoid confusion. The base-board can be about $12 \times 3 \times \frac{3}{4}$ in ($300 \times 75 \times 20$ mm). It has the usual vice batten underneath. There is a renewable hardboard strip for cutting into, with a small packing square of the same material at each end. The cutting bar is of bright drawn mild steel which must have square edges, not rounded; this is screwed firmly to the baseboard through the packing pieces. Between the bar and the packing there is a thin washer to give clearance when the veneer is fed in. Initially a 20×3 mm and a 25×3 mm cutting bar were used. Other sizes are of course available.

A thin bladed knife is required for the cutting. It should be ground on one side only, Fig. 363B. Feed in the veneer until about $\frac{1}{8}$ in (3 mm) projects, then, pressing firmly on the centre of the bar, cut along it with the flat side of the knife against it. The banding thus produced has two accurate square edges. In the 20 mm size, this makes suitable edge banding for 19 mm multi-ply to which a corner stringing may later be added.

Success in making crossbanding led on to the making of chessboard veneers. The device for this, Fig. 364, is generally similar but has the following variations. The cutting bar is a piece of 50×3 mm bright drawn mild steel. Check that its edges are good. Reject it if it is roughly formed, for any inaccuracies in filing it true will be considerably multiplied by the time the squares are assembled. The total length should be about 450 mm, to give comfortably more than 400 mm between the bolts. The hardboard cutting board should have larger holes to take the coil springs which keep the cutting bar open. The bar itself should be slightly bent, to make sure of a good grip in the centre when the wing-nuts are tightened: this can be arranged by nipping the ends in a sash cramp to produce a bow.

To make the veneer squares, ensure that both veneers chosen are of the same thickness as a difference in thickness discovered after laying will cause a lot of trouble. For safety, cut five long-grain strips of dark and light veneer as long as possible and tape four of each together with gummed paper tape, not plastic tape, alternating them. Place this assembly in the device, projecting the very minimum and check for squareness at the cutting bar with a large set square (not a try square). Cut both sides and release the strip. Repeat, making eight strips. Assemble and tape together, Fig. 365.

After laying chess board veneers, by careful brushing or use of a vacuum cleaner or air line, make sure that the sanding dust from the dark squares does not fill the pores of the light wood.

Readers with access to a milling machine, (or a milling machine operator!) will find the template, Fig. 366, useful in that accurate squares can be cut from the

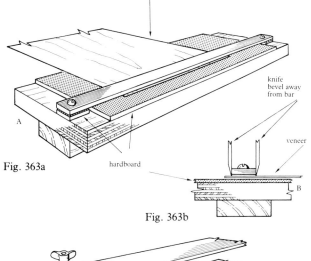

Veneer

knife
bevel away
from bar

veneer

A

hardboard

Fig. 363a

Fig. 363b

B

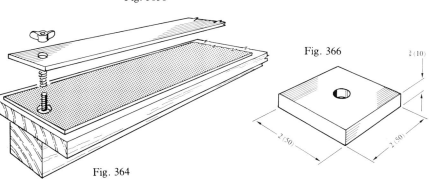

Fig. 364

Fig. 366

$\frac{3}{8}$ (10)

2 (50)

2 (50)

Fig. 365

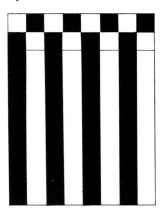

smallest veneer offcuts. The centre hole is merely for the holding down bolt for machining. Accurate filing of this piece is immensely difficult whereas the milling machine guarantees both a vertical cut and accurate right angles. Any inaccuracy here, reproduced sixty four times will ruin the assembly. Simply cramp the template and the veneer offcut on a hardboard scrap and cut round with the knife.

Mitring Tools for Dovetails

The corners of dovetail joints are frequently mitred to permit the working of a groove, rebate or moulding. None of the standard mitre blocks or boxes is of any help in this case. The special mitre block of Fig. 367 produces an accurately sawn mitre. The paring block, Fig. 368, will eliminate any error created when paring back to a line, freehand.

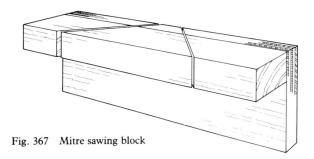

Fig. 367   Mitre sawing block

Fig. 368a   Mitre paring block

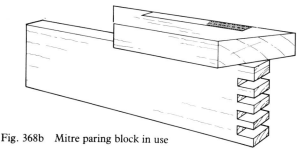

Fig. 368b   Mitre paring block in use

For the block, choose a piece of dense, well seasoned hardwood. Insufficiently seasoned material will shrink and so alter the angles of the sawcuts. For the cheek, use multi-ply of $\frac{3}{8}$ in (10 mm) or $\frac{1}{2}$ in (12 mm).

Glue on the cheek, making sure that it makes an accurate right angle. Every trace of glue must be cleaned from the corners.

Mark out and knife the mitres, then make the sawcuts with the thin tenon saw which will be used with the device. Never use any other saw, as the sawcuts could be widened by this. Bearing in mind the small amount of use which this tool will have, it will stay accurate for a long time.

The paring guide is used on mitres which through caution are sawn a little over-size. Again, very seasoned timber must be used to avoid shrinkage. In any case, the 45° angle needs to be checked from time to time. The cheek again can be plywood.

Preferably cramp the guide to the workpiece, or grip both in the vice. When paring, use the widest available chisel.

Two Large Squares

A try square
Fig. 369

In old cabinet making workshops, hanging somewhere on the wall, there was generally a large mahogany or oak try square, used mainly for marking out large panels. Sadly, over the years these have warped off, so any remaining are generally untrue. With the enormous increase in the use of sheet material, there is an even greater need for this tool.

Plywood gives the tool great stability and modern adhesives allow an easy built-up construction. Sizes are not important. A suggestion is for arms of about 36 and 20 in, (900 and 500 mm) using $\frac{1}{4}$ or $\frac{5}{16}$ in (6 or 8 mm) plywood. Good quality birch plywood is recommended in preference to some of the splintery imported material.

Build up the stock first, notching the short centre section to provide a mortice for the peg. Plane the edges straight, square and parallel, then square the ends. Prepare the blade, straight, or parallel and with the end shaped, (traditional) and the hanging hole bored.

Glue the blade in place, cramp well, then instantly check for a true right angle by applying the 3;4;5 rule of Pythagoras. Mark a length of three units on the stock and four units up the blade. If there is a true right angle, the distance between the two marks will be five units. for example, if a unit of 5 in is chosen, the measurements will be 15, 20 and 25 ins.

Make, shape and glue in the peg.

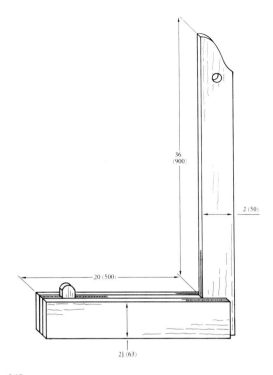

Fig. 369

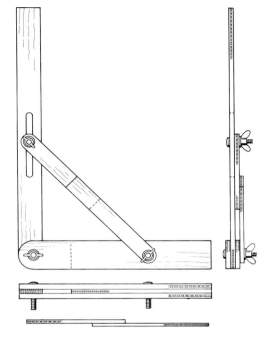

Fig. 370

Give several coats of clear polyurethane varnish. Remember that this tool is for pencil marking only. Use with a marking knife will quickly render the square untrue. This is not the ideal tool with which to check the squareness of carcases. A diagonal lath is more reliable.

A large fitting square
Fig. 370
Many readers will have encountered the difficulty of fitting tables, shelves, worktops and the like into square corners of rooms which turn out to be anything but square. How is this odd angle to be set out on widths greater than the span of a sliding bevel? This large adjustable square solves the problem. It can be similar in dimensions to the large try square described above.

Glue and clean up the stock. Mark and cut the semi-circular end and drill the two $\frac{1}{4}$ in (6 mm) holes. Chop these square on both sides to accept the square under-head of short coach bolts.

Make the blade and work a slot for the under-head of the coach bolt.

The brace is glued together from two sections in order to make up for the difference of level between the blade and stock. It may be assembled on either side of the stock, to suit the job in hand.

Set the tool by pressing hard into the corner of the room and tightening the wing-nuts. It then becomes a normal, large try square. It must not be used with a marking knife.

Miscellaneous

Steam Bending

This equipment, suitable for most small scale bending, was developed primarily for the bending of components for traditional country chairs. It consists of the steam generator and the steam-box.

The common textbook example, a gallon can, heated over a fire or gas ring, supplying steam via a thin rubber pipe, is not really a practical proposition. A ready made electric generator, shown in Fig. 371, can be a small domestic laundry boiler, or better still, an old caterer's tea urn. Failing either of these, a two or three gallon container can be fitted with a kettle element. While paint and food containers will serve, an aluminium vessel, which will not rust, is an improvement. A 3 kilowatt element is necessary; anything less will not generate sufficient steam.

The lid is replaced by one of plywood, either external or marine grade. An inner lip, or blocks keep the lid in position. A felt strip may be fitted to reduce the escape of steam. Two strips are glued to the top of the lid to locate the steam-box. There is a central hole of about 4 in (100 mm).

The steam-box, Fig. 372, is also best made from 'boilproof' plywood. It is glued and screwed together (non ferrous screws). The bottom has a matching hole

and two blocks which will definitely locate the box on the lid. The two are not fixed together. A rebated lid is built up from two thicknesses. The ends are removable to accommodate long components. When required these ends slide in between glued on guide strips. They must be quite a loose fit to allow for later painting.

A few triangular fillets are glued to the bottom, their purpose being to keep the work clear of any condensation and to allow a complete circulation of steam.

The box and generator lid should be well painted, i.e. primer, undercoat and two gloss coats. Allowance must be made for this when planning the lid and ends. The lid is held in place by several strips of car inner tube, screwed at one end and with a 'buttonhole' cut at the other.

Method

Partially fill the water container and bring it to the boil. Try a depth of 6–8 in (150–200 mm). Check the water level from time to time, though generally this will be enough for one steaming. Small components like arms, rails and back splats are loaded in the obvious way. Back legs and larger bends are loaded with the area of bend central. If they project from the box, the end is stuffed with newspaper.

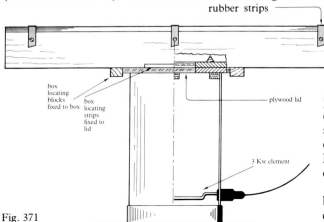

rubber strips

box locating blocks fixed to box

box locating strips fixed to lid

plywood lid

3 Kw element

Fig. 371

Some generators produce more steam than others so judgement of time will mainly be gained from experience. Turned chair legs of $1\frac{3}{8}$ in (35 mm) and the smaller components of chairs can be bent after one hour of steaming. If a lot of steam is being generated, a small hole can be bored at each end of the lid for escape, with a cork when this is not required.

Do not undertake steaming in a small workshop because of the rusting it will cause. Use an extension cable to an outdoor site.

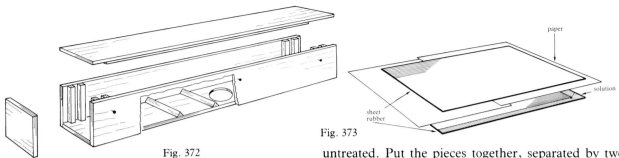

Fig. 372

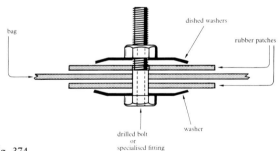

paper

solution

sheet rubber

Fig. 373

The Vacuum Bag Press for veneering and laminating

The vacuum bag press is a method for laying veneers and making laminations by means of atmospheric pressure, which is approximately fourteen pounds per square inch. Though commercially available, this is quite an expensive piece of equipment. It can however be put together reasonably cheaply and with no special skills.

Before embarking on the actual construction it is wise to obtain the compressor. A small portable machine is required, such as is used for tyre inflation or paint spraying. It must operate by piston not fan and can have an integral motor or be mounted on a board with say a $\frac{1}{4}$ hp motor. These are often obtainable second hand from firms advertising air tools in the local press. Otherwise try the yellow pages. It must be possible to transfer the hose from the output to the input of the compressor. The air pressure gauge can be replaced by a vacuum gauge at no great cost, though it is quite possible to work without a gauge. An air filter somewhere in the line can be useful but again many users work successfully without this by making sure that only clean material is put into the bag.

Airline hose and the necessary fittings are available from local garage tool and equipment dealers. A talk with them will reveal what is in stock and suitable for the individual requirements.

The bag itself is constructed from black sheet rubber, $\frac{1}{8}$ in is sufficient for the 'owner driver'. For a communal workshop $\frac{1}{4}$ in might be better. Size is of course dictated by personal requirements. For a start 4 ft×3 ft is suggested. A larger or smaller bag can be added later. Local agricultural engineers sometimes stock this, though for what purpose I have not found out.

Purchase two pieces of 4 ft from a 3 ft roll and the smallest tin of standard rubber solution. Assemble on a large table or a sheet of chipboard. Apply the solution to three sides of each and allow to dry. A short side is left

untreated. Put the pieces together, separated by two pieces of paper which overlap in the middle, Fig. 373. Weight down or cramp one half exactly in position and slide the paper from the other half. Press the joints firmly together then hammer, using a wood block, or run over heavily with a paperhanger's seam roller. When secure, slide out the other paper and repeat.

The hose can be joined to the bag in one of two ways. The mechanical method is illustrated in Fig. 374. Rubber patches inside and out are fixed with solution and the hole put through the lot. Suitable metal fittings can be obtained or adapted. Saucer shaped washers are more effective than flat ones. Alternatively a short length of rubber hose can be attached with one of the 'super glues'. Check carefully that it is recommended for use with rubber. Drill through the sheet after fixing. A tapered coupling adaptor permits the main hose to be disconnected at will.

bag

dished washers

rubber patches

drilled bolt or specialised fitting

washer

Fig. 374

Fittings required

A stud fitting to connect 8 mm nylon tubing to the compressor or similar to accept rubber airline hose. The same for the other end; a female adaptor to join to the coupler (fitted to the bag). A screw-down type of stop tap. Where an air filter is fitted, two further stud fittings are needed. Much will depend on the particular system stocked by the garage supplier, hence his advice will be appreciated.

The bag can be closed by two wood battens and a number of G cramps. To avoid tying up so many G cramps a closing cramp can be made, Fig. 375, using a number of bolts with nuts or wing-nuts.

A grooved baseboard is needed which is about 6 in (150 mm) less than the bag's length and width. $\frac{3}{4}$ in (29 mm) blockboard is suitable. It is divided into about 3 in (75 mm) squares by grooves routed out at $\frac{1}{4} \times \frac{1}{4}$ in (6×6 mm). The corners of the board should be comfortably rounded. Fig. 376.

A square or round spacing washer is made to go under the air outlet to prevent the bag from closing up here in use. Again the corners should be well rounded. Fig. 377.

An assortment of hardboard sheets covered with Fablon or similar will come in handy. Glue will not stick to them.

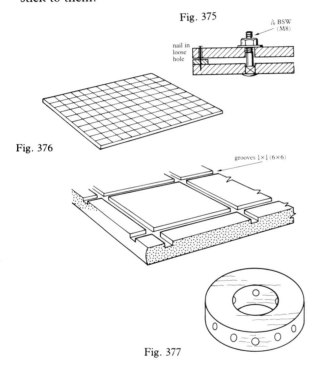

Fig. 375

Fig. 376

Fig. 377

Adhesives

Scotch glue is impracticable, it chills too quickly.

PVA begins to set before preparations are complete and pressure obtained. This prevents surplus glue squeezing out or the proper bedding down of the veneer so on balance is not always successful. It needs great operating speed.

Cascamite, a synthetic resin glue, has proved to be the most successful but if thickly applied will ooze through the pores giving a glazed finish almost impossible to remove.

Veneering a ply panel

Lay the grooved board on a sheet of polythene which is of the board width and twice the board length. Onto the board place one hardboard sheet, Fablon side up.

Glue both sides of the panel, lay the veneers on both sides and fix with four tabs of masking tape. A very quick rub over with a rubber roller may help to stabilize the veneer. Remember that the glue should be spread very thinly either with a serrated plastic spreader or better still, with a rubber roller. Place this sandwich centrally on the hardboard sheet, put the second hardboard on top then pull the polythene sheet over the lot. Fig. 378.

The entire assembly is slid into the bag press and the spacer positioned below the airpipe. The mouth of the bag is closed and the compressor switched on. Extraction continues until a vacuum of about 14 pounds per square inch is reached or until the bag feels very tight and the shape of the panel and the grooved board can be clearly seen. The note of the compressor will have been heard to change as this stage approaches. Close the stop tap, switch off and wait for the recommended time.

When several bags are in use it must be arranged that each bag has its own stop tap.

Sharp edges are dangerous so all corners must be rounded. Angled fillets are pinned round thicker shapes. Larger laminations will require a considerable amount of this preparation to avoid damage to the bag. Fig. 379.

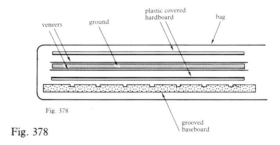

Fig. 378

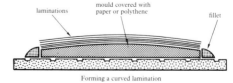

Fig. 379

It is important at all stages to take every care to prevent exuded glue from coming into contact with the bag.

Should the bag not hold the vacuum, close the mouth

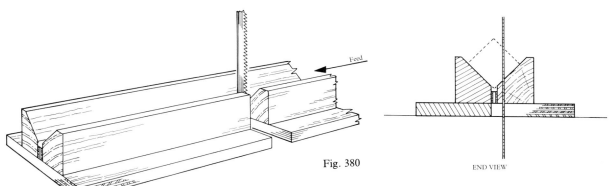

Fig. 380

END VIEW

and inflate it very slightly and with little pressure. Moisten all the seams with a strong solution of washing up liquid and search for bubbles. When dry insert more rubber solution. There is no strain on the seams as the nature of the vacuum is to pull them together.

A Cradle for the Bandsaw

Fig. 380
This will prove handy for several purposes. It will cut squares diagonally, producing fillets and glue-blocks. Octagonal components can be accurately prepared for planing and also for use with rounders (rotary planes). Although spindle turners seldom plane their material to octagons first, as some writers still recommend, when a number of identical spindles are to be turned, quickly sawing them all to octagons can save a lot of time.

The construction is as described previously for cradles. A good sawdust groove is essential. The overall length, and the width of the baseboard, must be such as will make cramping to the saw table convenient. Sizes generally will depend on the particular machine and the work contemplated.

The notch is cut out, including the centre packing, to suit the width of blade to be used. Keep it to the minimum.

The saw must not be set outside the cradle's width for big work. This is dangerous as the work is liable to rotate out of the cradle. For big work, prepare a bigger cradle. Use always with push-sticks.

A similar arrangement can be used for a circular saw. If a really big notch is cut out, the work is inadequately supported. Instead, cramp the cradle and wind up the saw, cutting a slot. This slot is easily widened subsequently, but a bridge of wood remains to support the work.

Veneering – Alternative Methods

Veneering with glue film
The occasional or small scale veneerer, not wishing to become involved with gluepot, hammer laying, presses and cauls, may find this method to his taste. He may even become converted.

At first the question will be 'What is glue film?' It is a thermo plastic adhesive film, sold as a paper backed roll, which will bond the veneer to its ground by the heat of a normal domestic iron. Photographers will find it reminiscent of the dry mounting tissue with which photographic prints were secured to their mounts. It is available in rolls of 36 in width. The method of use is both simple and straightforward.

1 Cut a piece from the roll, marginally larger than the ground. Place it in position with the glue against the ground and the paper uppermost. During this time an ordinary domestic electric iron has been switched on to warm up, set to 'rayon', its lowest setting.

2 Smooth over with the iron and allow to cool.

3 Peel off the backing sheet and keep it intact.

4 Position the veneer, if necessary holding it lightly in place with a few strips of gummed paper.

5 Lay on the discarded backing sheet and slowly iron over the veneer. Check that the iron is at its lowest heat. Go well over the surface a number of times. Dwell on each area for about three seconds to be sure of a good melt. There is little danger of destroying the adhesive but overheating can scorch the veneer, drying out too much moisture and causing cracks. Work outwards from the centre and make sure that the edges are not neglected.

6 Obviously the ground is going to retain heat for some time. This keeps the glue tacky, during which time the veneer may lift in places, particularly near the edges. A rubber covered roller, say six inches wide, can be worked over the surface until cool. Additionally there is the old fashioned non-electric 'sad iron', still to be found in junk shops. This both presses and chills at the same time and can be kept cool between uses by standing it on a concrete or tiled floor. Another alternative is an iron plane with its cutter well withdrawn.

7 In jointed work make sure that the joints are a good fit and held well together with gummed paper or professional veneering tape. In this case, always iron towards the joints.

8 If the joints are made by knife, directly on the ground, a second heating allows the removal of the waste piece trapped underneath and also the subsequent smoothing down.

The method's advantages are obvious. No smell, no boiling over, no sticky hands, no water and wet rags. glue film will equally easily secure fabrics, leathercloth, baize and linings. It is also a very clean method of securing the backing canvas to moderately-sized tambour doors. 'Iron-on' edging veneer can easily be made by ironing glue film onto a piece of veneer and later cutting into strips. Edges of chipboard require two thicknesses of glue film, one on the veneer and one on the edge.

There is a problem in that glue film can seldom be bought over the counter though slowly more stores are stocking it. It is not cheap either, though it must be borne in mind that there is no waste; the smallest offcuts can be used. It is obtainable, generally by post, from good veneer dealers. Catalogues give a shelf life of three to four years, probably as a precaution, but it has been found that well stored seven or eight-year-old stock still works perfectly.

The joint is waterproof and heat resistant, being able to withstand temperatures of up to 100°F. It is not affected by damp or condensation.

Finally note that only gummed papertape should be used. Plastic tapes melt under the heat of the iron and are very difficult to remove.

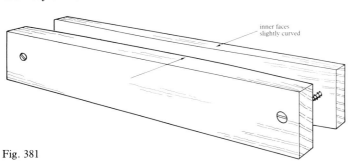
inner faces slightly curved

Fig. 381

Veneering with PVA

This method works well with a number of PVA (white) glues too, though not necessarily with all, so a trial is needed. It involves making use of the adhesive's thermoplastic qualities.

1 Join the veneer if necessary, see page 141. The joints must be firmly pulled and held together with veneering tape or gummed paper. Do not use plastic tape or masking tape. Cut the veneer slightly oversize then tape up the ends to reduce splitting.

2 Now prepare a container of glue size, consisting of one part PVA to five parts water. Stored in a plastic pot with a snap or screw-on lid, this will keep well. The size is brushed onto the back of the veneer and also the ground. Do not over wet or the veneer will buckle badly. Allow to dry overnight. Next day, sand very lightly to remove the nibs (small pimples). Clean the brush at once with warm water and detergent.

3 Coat the veneer and ground with the adhesive, this time a mixture of five parts PVA to one part water. PVA should always be decanted from its metal container to prevent staining from rust. Strangely some manufacturers still supply in metal cans. Again allow to dry overnight and lightly sand smooth the following day.

4 Place the veneer in position on the ground and hold it there with a few strips of gummed tape, meanwhile heating up a domestic iron to the setting marked 'wool'. Then iron on the veneer. For a single piece, iron outwards from the centre; for a jointed piece, iron as much as possible towards the joint. Ironing away from the joint may cause it to open. Do not neglect the edges. Iron always through a piece of clean paper; drawing or wrapping paper is suitable. Avoid printed paper as the ink may be transferred to the veneer.

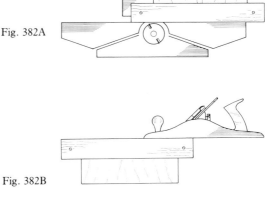

Fig. 382A

Fig. 382B

5 Chill the glue as quickly as possible, see page 000.

6 When the glue has set, test for good contact by tapping lightly with the finger nails. Any place sounding hollow can be ironed over and chilled again. Then trim off the surplus veneer, moisten the tape with warm water and peel off. When all is dry, gently sand and polish.

Experienced workers should note that this is not a method for beginners only. For all purposes it is a very successful way of laying veneers of moderate size.

Jointing veneers

This is not a very profound idea but is nevertheless useful to know of when veneers are being laid by veneer press, vacuum bag press, cauls or Glufilm, i.e. when the two pieces are taped together before adhesion.

Two long strips are prepared, say 3×1 in (75×25 mm), cramped together and drilled with pilot holes for No. 12 woodscrews (about $\frac{1}{8}$ in or 3 mm). On separation, the holes in one are enlarged to $\frac{1}{4}$ in or 6 mm) and deeply countersunk, Fig. 381.

The two inside faces are planed to give a slight curve in length only.

The two pieces are screwed tightly together with the two veneers firmly gripped between them and standing up slightly.

This protrusion is removed with a sharp block plane, then two possibilities are presented for making the joint.

Either pass the assembly over the planer until the entire surface has been cut, Fig. 382A, or, grip in the vice and carefully plane with a finely set sharp jack plane, Fig. 382B.

Many joints will be made before the strips become too narrow and are discarded. It is worth keeping several pairs of different lengths. If much veneer jointing is contemplated, it is worth replacing the woodscrews with more convenient coach bolts, washers and wing-nuts, the heads being well counterbored.

Making Small Curved Laminations

This method of lamination derives from a musical instrument making technique. The model illustrated was built for the easy making of the curved tops for small boxes. The sizes are subject to considerable variation, but obviously there is a limit, so when really large laminations are required, other methods must be used. Fig. 383.

As Fig. 384, shows two blocks are prepared, slightly longer and wider than the finished sizes required. They should be of ample thickness. If too thin, they will bend

Fig. 383   Device to make small curved laminations

Curved laminations. Component details

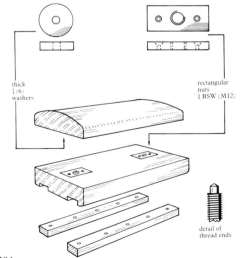

Fig. 384

or snap under pressure. Layers of multi-ply would be very strong but good quality hardwood is quite satisfactory and certainly works better. The two pieces are cramped together (with register marks on them) and two small pilot holes, say $\frac{1}{8}$ in (3 mm), are drilled through the plain block and just into the shaped one.

On these centres two 1 in holes are bored into the shaped block, about $\frac{1}{4}$ in deep. Into these are set two very thick $\frac{1}{4}$ in washers, specially made. They should be a tight enough fit, but two small screws may secure a loose one. Drill through these a further $\frac{1}{4}$ in into the wood.

Now for the fixed block. Enlarge the pilot holes to $\frac{1}{2}$ in. The two rectangular nuts are now required. They are threaded $\frac{1}{2}$ in Whitworth, which is a strong, quick acting thread but a metric 12 mm is quite satisfactory. With a piece of screwed rod to locate them, the two nuts are scribed and cavities cut to receive them. Four $\frac{1}{2}\times6$ screws secure them. On the reverse side of the block two housings are ploughed or routed and the corners only slightly rounded. Readers with limited facilities can let in two square or hexagon nuts, but this is inferior.

The shaped block is now planed accurately to the required curve, there being virtually no spring-back. The corners are generously rounded.

The woodwork can now be varnished. The shaped block requires a number of coats to bring it to a good finish, which will discourage any surplus glue from sticking.

The making of the screws from threaded rod is obvious. While short cuts are possible at the handle end, in no way should the stubby pointed spigots be omitted.

The two hardwood strips should be a tight fit with the

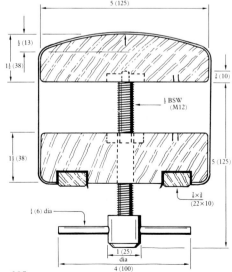

Fig. 385 END VIEW

fabric round them. They are secured with five 1×8 woodscrews.

The fabric chosen should be a strong canvas. It should be cut as an accurate rectangle and fixed very precisely to the block. A thin coating of PVA adhesive prevents the edges fraying. Mark the centres at each end on both the canvas and the shaped block. Assemble as in Fig. 385.

Recommended Method of Working

Make a hardboard pattern from which to cut the veneer laminates. Veneer is commonly 0·6 mm thick so five layers make 3 mm or approximately $\frac{1}{8}$ in. Seven laminations, including the glue layers, approach $\frac{3}{16}$ in. As in plywood, successive layers have the grain at right-angles to each other, hence an odd number of laminations is necessary. The top lamination may be quartered. A little more care will be needed and the four quarters should be very firmly held together with strong tape.

Cover the shaped block with clean paper, not newsprint, taping it onto the underside. Mark the centre line on the top lamination then glue together. A synthetic resin glue, such as Aerolite or Cascamite is to be preferred to the PVA glues as the latter harden too quickly and may not allow the layers the necessary movement to take up the curve. Lay the stack on the shaped block, line up the centre marks and fix at the centres with plastic tape. Cover with clean paper.

Insert this assembly into the canvas, noticing the register of the two blocks and locating the screw spigots. Take up the slack, checking the centre marks on the canvas. Cramp a small batten along the centre line, then tighten the screws. The batten can then be removed. Some judgement is required to get enough pressure without tearing out the canvas. A feel over the canvas and inspection at the ends will provide this. Generally speaking the canvas is quite robust. The 'owner driver' should find no difficulty. In a school or communal workshop supervision will be essential.

A variety of curved blocks can be fitted to one device.

Chessboards by Hand Methods

Accurate strips of veneer or thin hardwood can be produced using a jack or smoothing plane by the use of this simple jig, Figs, 386 & 387. Assuming that the squares are to be 2 in (50 mm), prepare two identical hardwood strips of $20\times2\times$th in ($500\times50\times$th mm). The thickness, th, is such that $2\times$th equals the width of the plane sole. Add a tiny amount for ease. The added thickness of the veneer or veneers gives a comfortable working clearance. Ideally the two blocks, held

Fig. 386   Chessboard jig for hand planing

together with two $\frac{3}{8}$ in (10 mm) steel dowels are put through a thicknesser or circular saw to guarantee that they are identical. A ply edge is glued to each, giving an upstand of about $\frac{1}{4}$ in (6 mm). Drill holes for $\frac{1}{2}$ in (12 mm) clamping screws. One block has an easy clearance hole, the other is tapped for the thread.

Cut strips as long as the jig will take, four black and five white. A width of, say, $2\frac{1}{4}$ in (55 mm) will do. Grip those between the blocks, making sure that each piece overlaps on both sides. Sharpen the plane and set both cap iron and mouth very fine. Plane both sides of the strips until the plane will cut no more. Although the cut has been set very fine, a few shavings will have been removed from the blocks, but a tiny running strip will soon be built up on each side.

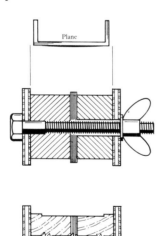

Fig. 387   END VIEW

The strips are then taped together, or if solid wood, glued together, in alternate colours. This assembly is now held in the device, checking that the joins are exactly square to the blocks and the top edge planed. The bottom edge is marked with a pencil and cut off with a little to spare. This is repeated eight times, giving eight strips, each with one true edge and one merely cut. These are stacked together, preferably in fours, in the jig, which is stood on a planed strip of wood, so that all the true edges are at the bottom and level. Tighten

up. The top edges are now planed true, working towards the centre to prevent the corner breaking out. Plane as before, until the cut stops. Repeat with the other four strips. Naturally when solid wood is being used it must be planed one thickness at a time.

The strips are now ready for assembling.

The Bespoke Picture Frame

That special watercolour, photograph or drawing deserves something better than the run of the mill ramin moulding or over-decorated plastic faced framing, nailed together at the corners. In any case, for some subjects, no suitable moulding exists. For example, a good watercolour behind a thick double mount, plus glass, plus hardboard backing will not fit into most commercial mouldings. Mounted embroideries and collages present the same problem.

Fortunately the small power router makes the production of individual mouldings relatively simple. English hardwoods in a natural finish, oak, ash, chestnut and sycamore are all successful. The mahoganies too can be used for pictures of the right general colourings.

First measure the combined thickness of the various parts then draw out just the rebate to full size, Fig. 388.

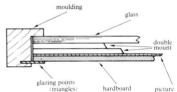

Fig. 388

The router can produce grooves, rebates, flats, quarter rounds and quarter hollows. The scratch tool can produce half rounds, fine grooves and reeds. Using both tools an immense range of mouldings can be build up. Most of the routing can be done on a routing table, but far superior, is the Bosch POF 52 router mounted in a drill stand. Used in this way the whole operation can be clearly seen. Additionally, a $\frac{1}{2}$ or $\frac{5}{8}$ in cutter can be used as a miniature thicknesser.

A few combinations are illustrated, Fig. 389. The reader will be able to devise many more.

A typical routine could be to first produce sufficient stock to the required rectangular section. If necessary, the overhead router can complete this stage, Fig. 390.

The rebates are quite straightforward. The waste is removed with a rebate cutter, taking several gentle cuts. Some of the waste could first be taken out with a circular saw. A slotting cutter in the router, say $\frac{1}{16}$ in, will cut a shallow decorative groove. The scratch tool can now be brought in to work the corner bead. The level of the face

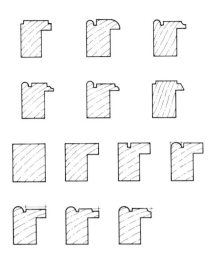

Fig. 389

Fig. 391   Mitre block for disc sander

Fig. 390   Working a small decorative rebate with the overhead router

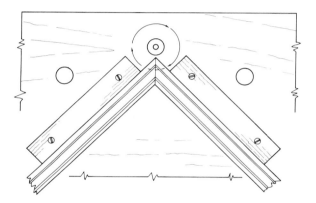

Fig. 392

can be very slightly lowered with a rebate cutter, which can then cut another small rebate. A cove or a rounding cutter can make the final cut.

Cut the mouldings close to the finished length then clean up with glasspaper previously glued to small wood blocks. Use flat blocks for the flat and convex areas and pieces of suitable dowelling for the concave shapes. Mark the picture size plus $\frac{1}{16}$ in on the inside of the rebates and saw off, at 45°, slightly over-size. Now trim accurately to the marks using either a disc sander or a mitre shooting board, (see page 132).

It is important that the block used on either of these should be built up from plywood layers. A solid wood block will eventually shrink, causing the 90° to increase, Fig. 391.

Glue up the frame. In the absence of a commercial cramp, suitable arrangements were described on pages 31 and 32. Clean off the surplus glue and leave to harden overnight. The frame is very fragile at this stage so handle it gently. The corners are now slotted. Two slots will generally be enough.

A $\frac{1}{16}$ in slotting cutter on an arbor is fitted to the router, Figs, 392 & 393. A special wooden table, illustrated, is fitted for an overhead router. Something similar can be arranged for a router table. Larger frames can be slotted with a small radial arm saw, set horizontally.

A length of material for the slips is sawn roughly to size then thicknessed to a nice fit, either using the overhead router or by hand planing. The slips are sawn off square and glued in place, Fig. 394. If triangular slips are made and a tight fit necessitates a tap with the hammer, the short grain corner will often break off, so glue in big and saw off later. When thoroughly dry, saw off, plane flush and finish by further sanding, Fig. 395.

Two thin coats of matt polyurethane varnish are a good finish for the English hardwoods. Such a frame can then be kept clean, unlike the unfinished wood frames which eventually become grimy.

A number of economical mount cutters are now

Fig. 393   Slotting a frame corner showing jig and slotting cutter

Fig. 394   Inserting the strengthening slip into the mitred corner

Fig. 395   The finished corner of a slim ash picture frame

available from shops supplying artists' materials. They make accurate 45° cuts, no special skills being required. Watercolours and pastels in particular are best behind a cut out mount. At the present time the fashion is to use a double mount. This needs to be borne in mind when calculating the rebate depth.

Obtain the glass, picture weight, (2 mm), by taking the frame to the glazier, thus avoiding measuring mistakes. Reflection free, etched glass is available.

Consider carefully before ordering since this does not suit all subjects. The backing is hardboard, no longer the traditional cardboard which bowed and warped in time. Ideally, particularly for small pictures, 2 mm hardboard should be used. Unfortunately this is rare and not stocked by many firms because of the high cost and the amount they are obliged to purchase. So, $\frac{1}{8}$ in (3 mm) has generally to be used. Make sure of a good fit. Should the rebate depth be insufficient, the hardboard edge can be thinned down by hand planing.

Clean and polish the glass, dust over the picture then assemble, face down, with the backing in place.

Small wedge shaped glazing sprigs were formerly used, but they make a lumpy finished job. Small panel pins, now generally used, are not a lot better. Professional glaziers now use little sheet steel equilateral triangles of about 10 mm sides, shot into place with a tool not unlike a staple gun. Unfortunately this is quite an expensive tool for the occasional framer. However, there is an alternative. From a friendly glazier obtain a block of these triangles and separate them with a sharp knife.

These can be pressed into place using a pair of water pump pliers, Fig. 396. The imperfect tips of the jaws should be filed flat and square. Use a strip of metal to prevent damage to the outside of the frame. During this process it may help to press down firmly onto the

Fig. 396   Squeezing in the steel triangulars with waterpipe pliers

triangle with a small screwdriver to ensure a really tight flat fit in the frame.

The whole assembly is kept dust free with gummed tape. Obtain a roll of 2 in wide parcel tape. Cut the strips over-long. Wet one with a sponge, not by licking, wait a few moments for the glue to become tacky, then lay it in place. Press down well, using a paperhanger's hard rubber seam roller. Add the remaining strips. When all are dry, trim round with a cutting gauge set to about $\frac{1}{16}$ in.

Fit suitably sized screw eyes with split rings. Drill or bore for these, since if just forced into hard wood the screw eyes tend either to break off or distort.

Hang by twisted brass picture wire. Secure the ends very thoroughly as sloppy twisting tends to unwind when the weight is applied.

Finally glue to the hardboard a label showing title, artist, date acquired and any other interesting details.

After the Glue-up

Difficulties are seldom encountered when it comes to putting on glue; problems do arise, however, when it comes to taking it off. Glue which has exuded and been left overnight can be extremely difficult to remove and the surface can easily be damaged by such attempts. Of course the best way to remove glue is not to let it get there in the first place. Several methods of prevention can be used. Glue which overspills onto a surface which is later to be planed or skimmed over does not matter so can be left. Glue on a finished surface is the problem.

A wax finish is one solution. Take for example a box or a carcase. Protect the joints during polishing with plastic tape, cramp the job up dry for the usual last minute check. At this stage rub a little extra wax into the corners but do not polish off. After overnight hardening the glue flakes off easily, perhaps just needing the corner of a sharp chisel to start it off.

Other polishes unfortunately give adhesion to the glue so further protection is needed. Before assembly position plastic tape right up to the corners of both parts of the joint. This is better than masking tape whose wrinkled surface sometimes permits glue to creep under it. When the glue has hardened, glue and tape can be peeled off together.

In cases where this is not applicable the glue must be washed off. Bearing in mind that synthetic glue manufacturers give an assembly time of about ten minutes, and that Scotch glue chills very rapidly, speed is of the essence. Time will be spent anyway in positioning the cramps and blocks, measuring diagonals and checking for twist, so all requirements must be to hand before starting. Get equipped with the following; a plastic washbowl of hot water with a mere touch of detergent added; a wet rag; one or two absorbent dry rags (all of cotton, not synthetics); several wooden 'chisels' with good sharp edges and some old newspapers. Some brushes suitable for the job in hand would be an oldish kitchen wash-up brush, rectangular, not round, an old stubby paintbrush and an old toothbrush.

As soon as the glue-up is complete, scrape off the excess glue with the wooden chisel, wiping it frequently on the newspaper. This takes off the thick. One of the brushes, probably the wash-up brush, well wetted, will scrub into the corners, removing the last traces there. Finish with the wrung-out wet rag then dry thoroughly.

If the inside surfaces have been treated with, say, polyurethane varnish, this is the end of the task. If, on the other hand, the surface is untreated, then inevitably the grain will have been raised. The quicker the work is dried off, the less this will be, but in any case, the surface, when completely dry, not before, will need rubbing over with flour grade glasspaper.

The two essentials then are, speed and preparation. Do not run around looking for rags as the glue is hardening. If the job is done quickly, and a helper is often useful, there is no need to use bench chisels, which often damage the work.

A final warning. Throw away the rags. A rag used a second time may contain lumps of hardened glue, which can inflict deep scratches on the surface. Similarly wash out well any brushes which have been used. This is a serious operation; give it as much care as was given to cutting the joints.

In a communal workshop, as soon as the glue-up is completed, it is wise to fix a note or chalk on the job the 'cramps off' time. This should prevent cramps being removed too soon and will also release cramps for further use at the earliest opportunity.

Edge Planing by Hand

After the war, for a decade if not more, workshops in British schools were devoid of any machines. Eventually there appeared a small circular saw for the use of the teacher and the technician. Planers arrived relatively recently but still not for pupil use.

In those early days, teachers were faced with the problem that young pupils with ability in the basic joints and capable of making simple furniture, were seldom able to plane the edge joints needed for table tops and panels – quite an advanced skill. Teachers came up with a variety of similar aids to this end. These appear from time to time in the woodworking press, though not always fully described.

The device which follows, Fig. 397, may still be of

Fig. 397   The square-edger preparing a panel joint

Fig. 398   Section of fence

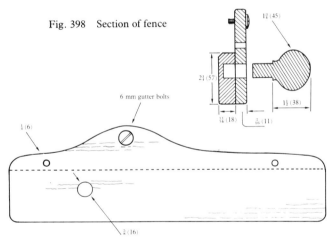

Fig. 399   The fence

use to readers lacking either the skill or a planer and also to parents of aspiring woodworkers, now sadly denied the craft skills at school. The model illustrated is for the 2 in jack plane, which is quite wide enough. It will adapt to the larger $2\frac{3}{8}$ in plane.

Good dry stable hardwood is required. Beech has been used here. Thickness a piece to $\frac{7}{16}$ in (11 mm) then lay the plane on and draw round. Before removing it, draw a parallel line $2\frac{1}{4}$ in (57 mm) below the sole face. Cut out and shape this piece, giving a little extra at both ends where the sides of the plane are rather shallow, then blending in to the main shape. Prepare the fence block to $2\frac{1}{4} \times \frac{11}{16}$ in (57×18 mm) then glue the two pieces together. Clean up flush, round the corners and soften all the edges. Plane a small dust chamfer. Fig. 399.

Now cramp the plane in place and carefully mark where the screw holes are to be. These are 6 mm holes to take 20×6 mm gutter bolts, which are now more easily obtained than Imperial sizes. Drill through the wood to make a dimple on the side of the plane. Remove the wood components and drill through with a 5 mm drill. Tap the holes with M6 taps. Both taper and plug taps will be needed. If not available locally, a garage will often tap your holes. Thoroughly clean and sand the wooden fence then finish with linseed oil.

Assemble the fence tightly onto the plane. The holes may need a little adjustment with a round file if they do not match perfectly with the plane. The gutter bolts too will need to be shortened a little. Turn and fit a substantial fore-knob.

Using the tool

1   The side of the plane may not be truly square to the sole. You cannot do anything about this, but anyway it does not matter.

2   The finished fence may not be square to the sole. This does not matter much.

3   The cutting edge may not be parallel to the sole. This also does not matter much. Just do your best, by eye, using the lateral lever.

What does matter though is that alternate faces of the boards are placed against the fence. That is, the true face of one board and the non-true face of the other. In this way, all inaccuracies are cancelled out, as for example if one board was planed to 89° and the other to 91°, ensuring a flat joint, Fig. 400.

Plane the joint hollow, avoiding an inch at each end, until the plane refuses to cut any more. Now plane through and stop when the first full length shaving is obtained. Repeat on the second board.

Set up in the vice and test the joint as follows. Do a

straight-edge test for flatness, Fig. 401. If satisfied, put the two boards together, gently push one corner with the fingertip. If the board pivots, then that is the high spot. If the board falls off then the joint is either correct or hollow. Inspection into the light will reveal which, Fig. 402. The traditional 'rubbed joint' is only possible with hot Scotch glue. All modern adhesives require to be cramped.

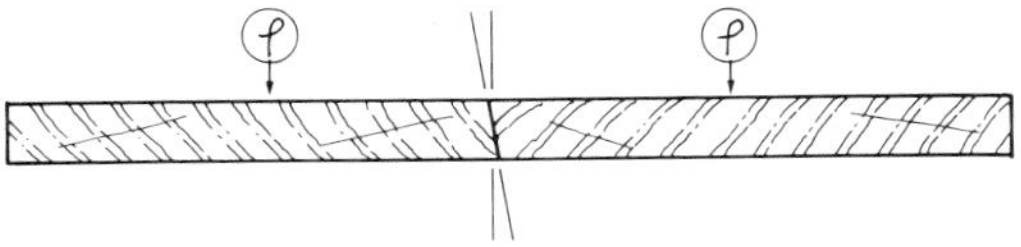

Fig. 400

Fig. 401

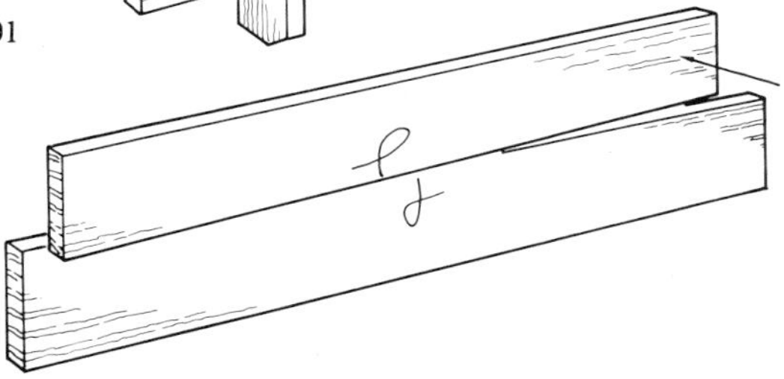

Fig. 402

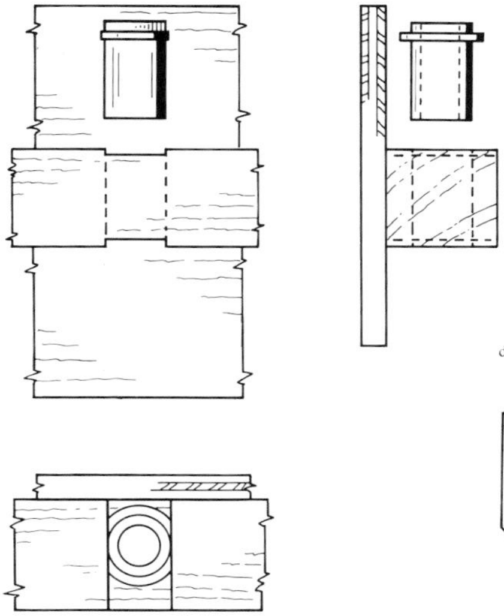

Fig. 403

Obviously all the wear is on one section of the cutting edge. If this is objected to, a second, auxiliary fence may be screwed to the basic fence as required to spread the wear. For perfection in jointing, it is recommended that a special plane cutter be kept which is ground and sharpened absolutely straight across, with no trace of curve.

Bushed Dowel Jigs
Fig. 403

When any repetitive dowelling is planned, the making of a jig is to be recommended. It saves time in the long run and guarantees accuracy. Wooden jigs, of course, suffer from wear. The more they are used, the less accurate they become, so it is well worth while fitting steel bushes to the holes to prevent this. Dowelling bushes can either be obtained from a good engineering supplier or as spare parts for a rather elaborate and expensive dowelling jig by Record. Metric and Imperial sizes are made so a small stock should be maintained of the commonly used sizes. The Record bushes fit into a 12 mm hole. To eject them a simple tool can be made. From a piece of round metal a little larger than the dowel size, turn down a short end to easily fit the bush. This is then used as a punch.

Making the jig
Fig. 404

Make the block long and wide enough for the joint in hand with faces truly square. Clearly mark the true face, which is the datum face. Set a gauge to half the timber thickness and gauge on the block the centre line for the holes. Mark the exact hole centres and drill the holes using a wood cutting 'lip and spur' drill, not a twist drill which will not start precisely. If possible use a drilling machine or an electric drill in a drill stand. Mark and cut the shallow housings which prevent the bushes from turning.

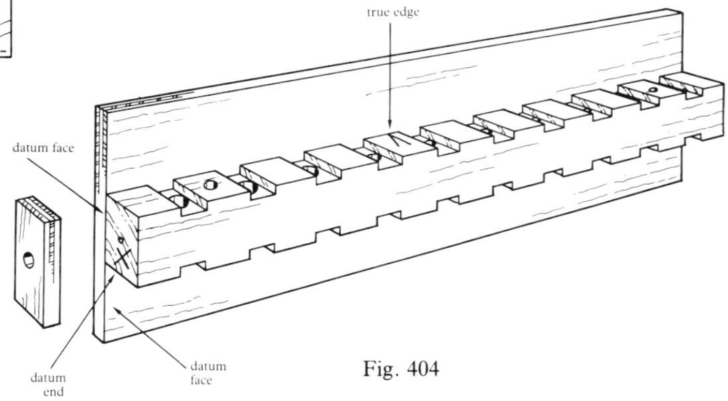

true edge

datum face

datum end

datum face

Fig. 404

Screw on the plywood fence, which is also a datum face. A small plywood end stop is a very useful, though optional, addition.

Making a shelving or carcase joint

Cramp the jig on one shelf end, Fig. 405, with the datum face against the true face of the job and the end stop, or marked end, to the true edge. Do this to one end of each shelf, then reverse the bushes and drill the other ends.

Remove the fence and fit the jig to the side components. Locate on the marked position of the shelf, lining up the datum face with the upper shelf marking. Screw in place and drill. The bushes will be reversed for the second side component, Fig. 406.

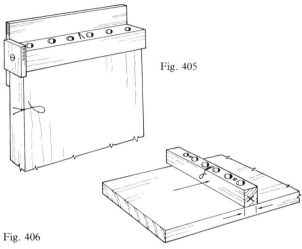

Fig. 405

Fig. 406

Dowel joints for flat frames or stool constructions will work much the same way though of course, the jigs will be much smaller.

With the jig, either a woodboring 'lip and spur' drill or the common twist drill may be used either in an electric drill or a hand-drill. Depth stops are frequently sold with the lip and spur drills. Otherwise a drilled wood block will serve as a depth stop. It is important on, say, a carcase end to drill the deepest possible hole yet not come through.

A dowel groover

Manufactured pre-cut dowels are multi-grooved. Individually prepared dowels can easily be grooved with the simple tool shown in Fig. 407, which will cut either one or two grooves.

Adjust the woodscrews to give the desired depth of groove then simply tap the dowels (or length of dowelling) through the appropriate hole.

Trying to work without grooves is a false economy since the surplus glue is unable to escape. This can lead to thin wood bursting under pressure as the job is cramped up or to an oozing of glue through the more porous woods.

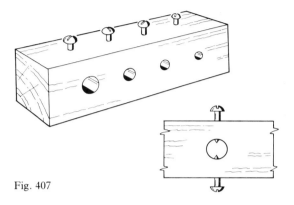

Fig. 407

A dowel cutter

When dowels are required in quantity, particularly when they are to be fitted to holes drilled accurately to depth with some form of stop, the tool shown in Fig. 408 will quickly saw them accurately to length. Simply feed in, flush with the far end, then saw off. An improved model, Fig. 409, allows different lengths to be sawn. Feed in, saw off, remove the pin and push out. Repeat. Naturally a tool will be needed for each size of dowel. Dowels are available in both Imperial and Metric sizes. Note that $\frac{5}{16}$ in and 8 mm are virtually indistinguishable.

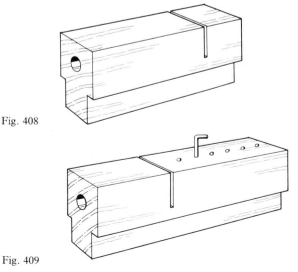

Fig. 408

Fig. 409

Dowel marker pins

A Victorian accessory, the dowel marker pin, Fig. 410, has made a welcome re-appearance after an absence of many years. This enables dowel joints to be made quickly and accurately with the very minimum of marking out. The pins are made in both Imperial and Metric sizes.

A typical joint, for a flat frame, is shown in Fig. 411. The joint must first be identified (i.e. A-A), so that the correct pairs eventually go together. The position of the

Fig. 410   Dowel marker pins

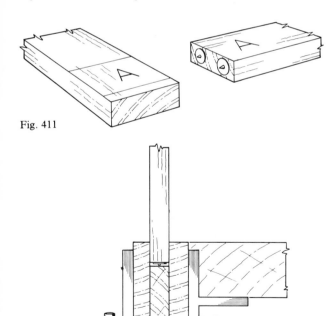

Fig. 411

Fig. 412

joint must be marked. Dowel holes are drilled in either piece, in any reasonable position. No marking is necessary. The pins are then inserted and the two parts brought together and tapped to give clear marks. While the joint is being tapped up, it can be held firmly on a flat board, true face down. Alternatively, in this case, Fig. 412, one piece is held on the bars of the bench vice with the other placed above it. The vice is closed, finger tight only, and the joint tapped up.

To join long boards, insert the two end pins only, lightly cramp as shown in Fig. 413, (or use the drawer slip cramp on page 23) and tap up. Put in these dowels and the remainder of the marker pins. Correct any warp by cramping on a pair of battens, then tap firmly. The components are then separated and the final holes bored.

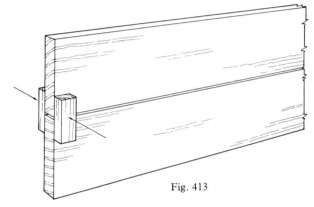

Fig. 413

Making Knobs

Many individually-made aids, tools and devices, such as gauges and planes require locking or adjusting knobs. On a well made and carefully finished article nothing looks better than a nicely knurled brass knob. However, most readers will not have the facilities or friends to produce these. Fortunately knobs are not particularly difficult to make. Two distinct forms are possible; to make in wood or in a synthetic material.

For wooden knobs choose a dense, hard wood such as ebony, rosewood or some of the fruitwoods. Choose by the suitability of individual pieces rather than by a particular species. Knobs tend to be turned, though they can of course be bench-made. Cut out a block, over-size, drill and tap it centrally then clean up the inside face. On the end of the selected metal screw, file two considerable flats, Fig. 414. Thoroughly degrease. Coat the end of the thread well with an epoxy resin adhesive such as Araldite and assemble. Pack any gaps well with adhesive, leaving it slightly proud. Give ample time for the adhesive to harden thoroughly, even several days. Possible shapes are shown in Fig. 415.

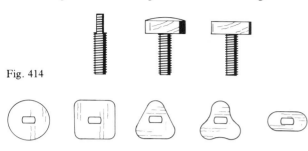

Fig. 414

Fig. 415

The turning can be done in the chuck of a wood or a metal lathe. If the former, keep the metal screw below the surface and turn down almost to it. In a metal lathe, finish by taking a fine cut across both wood and metal. Using the power of the lathe, a durable finish can quickly be built up with linseed oil.

Synthetic knobs can be made from a number of materials. Satisfactory ones have been made from synthetic resin glues such as Aerolite and Cascamite. Give ample time, i.e. several days, perhaps near a radiator, for the chemical action to become complete. Motorcar body filler is another and quicker possibility. By far the most successful materials are fibreglass resin or the casting resin sold in model shops. This can be coloured. Care must be taken to avoid bubbles as far as possible. A successful mould can be made by boring or routing a hole in a wood block, Fig. 416. A smaller hole is drilled through and tapped to take the chosen screw. Either file flats on the screw, as described or use a headed screw with large flats filled on the head, Fig. 417. The portion of the screw in the wood should be well greased to prevent unwanted adhesion. When the casting is well hardened, split the block to release the knob.

A more sophisticated and re-usable mould can be made by using rigid plastic water pipe in which slides a well fitting turned wood block, threaded to take the screw, Fig. 418. Several blocks can be made to take different screws. The tube and block are oiled or waxed to permit easy release of the finished castings. The block can be adjusted to give different thicknesses.

Internally threaded knobs can be produced in much the same way and using the same mould, Fig. 419. A nut, preferably a square one, is positioned suitably on a well greased screw. In all cases where the casting is to be carried out by a second person, it is advisable to fit a lock-nut below the wood block, thus preventing accidental movement of the screw.

These synthetics turn best at a fairly high speed and best of all in a metalworking lathe, using a trailing cut. In a wood lathe, scrape, using a tool with a steep angle, as for metal turning. Polish with successively finer grades of glasspaper and finally 'wet and dry' paper.

A large number of shapes is possible and readers will no doubt wish to create some of their own. A few have already been suggested. Flats can be accurately planed or filed on turned knobs using the simple jig shown in Fig. 420. The knob is held firm by a washer and nut on the back. The knob is successively turned to the appropriate guide marks for the next cut.

A re-usable wooden mould is illustrated in Fig. 421. This must always be very well waxed or greased.

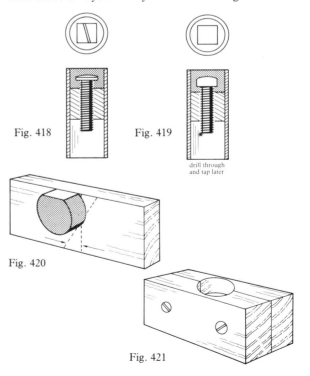

Fig. 418

Fig. 419

drill through and tap later

Fig. 420

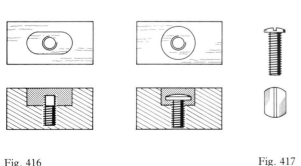

Fig. 416

Fig. 417

Fig. 421

Photographing Small Objects

This does not mean still life. Why photograph small and often unattractive objects, items such as small cabinets, turnery, treen, sculptures and tools anyway? Such pictures may be required for articles or as slides for talks and lectures. Correspondence with fellow enthusiasts calls for this work. The next best thing to collecting antiques is to collect photographs of them. Finally, there is the value of good photographs for insurance purposes and in case of burglary. What is required is not an artistic creation – merely a first class record shot which can be obtained quickly and at will by relatively inexperienced photographers.

To facilitate this type of work, a set-up is required which can be quickly assembled and dismantled and for which exposure conditions are constant and can easily be repeated, Fig. 422.

Make a studio by joining together with a calico hinge two pieces of hardboard 48×24 in, i.e., a quarter of a sheet. A thin string at each corner holds the pieces at an angle of about 100°. On this is hung the background paper, held in place with large wire paper clips. The best background paper is just off-white, for example cream or buff. Very light objects need a darker paper, particularly when black and white pictures are wanted. Gray carpet underlay paper is cheap and easy to obtain. This is better for colour than for monochrome. Wrap-

ping paper from a wide roll is another possibility. Black is occasionally needed. Very small objects are easily arranged by using suitable wallpaper. When specimens are being made specifically for photography, the colour of the wood should be carefully considered first. Oiling always enriches the colour of wood and brings out the grain.

There are three lighting possibilities. Daylight, out of doors on an overcast day is excellent – but few days in the year are suitable. Wind is always a hazard outdoors. Flash is harsh and if mounted directly on the camera gives a cardboard cut-out effect. If placed on one side, the shadows are dense and unpredictable. Also reflections cannot be judged. With bounced flash it is difficult to estimate the exposure or to foresee the actual effect. By far the best system for the moderate amateur is to bounce a photoflood lamp off the ceiling, measuring the exposure either on the subject if big enough or on a Kodak 'grey card'. Such exposures will be fairly constant if the set-up is accurately reproduced.

Colour presents no special problem. A filter such as the 80B is required which will match the film and the lamp. A good dealer will advise here. Alternatively a film should be chosen which is balanced for artificial light.

A firm tripod is essential used with a long cable release. To achieve adequate depth of focus, apertures of f16 and even f22 will be required. Camera shake can

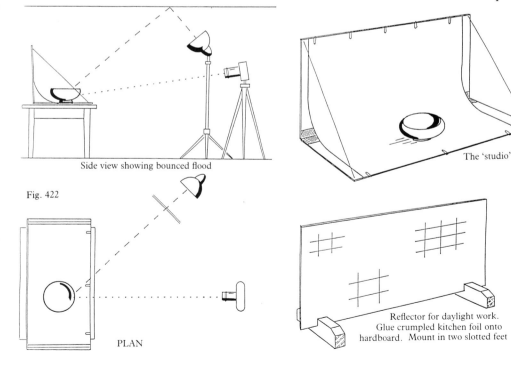

Side view showing bounced flood

Fig. 422

The 'studio'

PLAN

Reflector for daylight work.
Glue crumpled kitchen foil onto
hardboard. Mount in two slotted feet

Fig. 422

be further reduced by using the delayed action shutter release. The slower films will give better resolution of fine detail.

In black and white work, aim for good strong negatives which will yield a print of greater than normal contrast on a normal grade of paper. This is essential if it is needed for reproduction. Glossy surface is also preferred.

In some cases, the inclusion of an inch or centimetre scale may be an advantage. One inked on thin, square section wood-strip is less obtrusive than merely including a ruler.

For colour work where there is a high ceiling, use two of the larger photoflood lamps positioned close together.

Gap-filling Methods

One does not have to work long on the woodwork of a house before discovering gaps which need to be filled, which are too big for woodfillers: gaps between fitments and walls; gaps between skirtings, plinths, and the floor. The making of these filler strips is not difficult, but measuring for and marking them is. Here are two methods to overcome the problem and which provide a good, accurate fit.

Prepare the wedge shown in Fig. 423 and calibrate it in, say, cms. Mark a series of stations along the gap and number them. Insert the wedge at each station and record the reading on it. Prepare an adequate strip for the filler, calibrate and number it to match markings on the gap. Now from the record, take a caliper measurement, Fig. 424, for each station in turn then plane the strip down to this size. Alternatively, set a marking gauge to the wedge calibration and gauge a short mark on the filler strip. This will be quicker but not quite so accurate.

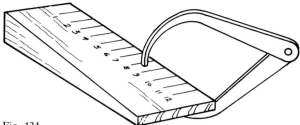

Fig. 424

Another way to deal with gaps is not to have them in the first place. This means accurately scribing the component in question to fit the uneven wall or floor. If the workpiece can be held in place, as for instance a work-top or a skirting board, a matching line can easily be scribed by using a large washer, Fig. 425. It may be more convenient to turn a plywood disc, as the insert in Fig. 425, particularly when the gap is large. The small centre hole is used; the two larger holes being for the screws attaching the disc to the wood faceplate. When work is to be painted, a ball-point pen will give a clearer line than pencil. When fitting a piece into an alcove, obviously it will be too big until the final cuts have been made. In this case it will be worth scribing a hardboard or plywood template, as shown dotted. When close to size, an alcove shelf may be wedged in at an angle for scribing.

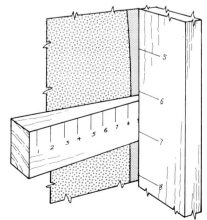

Fig. 423

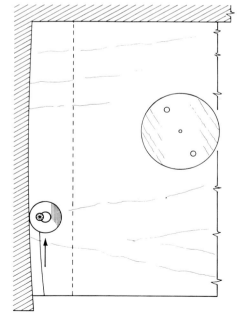

Fig. 425

SECTION 10 Appendices

Appendix 1   Cramp Handles

Turned handles can easily and accurately be planed flat on two faces to give an improved grip.

Turn the handle initially a little thicker than otherwise. Drill in the lathe to the tapping size, page 155, then tap with the taper tap only, to its full depth. Or use the improvised tap described on page 155.

Grip the handle in the vice very firmly. Ignore any bruising, which will be removed by the planing. Screw in the threaded rod. Two lock-nuts and a spanner make this easy. Continue until the screw reaches the bottom of the drilled hole.

Drill a small block of waste wood, near the edge with a clearance hole and secure the screwed rod with two nuts. Lower this assembly into the bench vice until the handle sits on the bench top. With the plane guided by the block, as Fig. 426, plane one flat. Reverse the handle and repeat.

Appendix 2   Filing Spigots on Round Bar

For this operation two steel washers are required. One is the size of the bar itself and the other is the size of the intended spigot.

Grip the bar vertically in the vice and slip the larger washer over it. The bar should protrude the length of the spigot. File round, using a safe-edge file, constantly trying the second washer for size. Not only will the spigot be to size but a good square shoulder is produced suitable for riveting. Fig. 427.

Appendix 3   Easing a Hole

In order to give ease for moving components, a hole sometimes needs to be minutely enlarged: far less than the next size of drill would produce.

To accomplish this, take a short offcut of the moving component or rod and very lightly hammer round the edges, Fig. 428, producing a very slight mushroom head. Put this in the drill or drilling machine and re-bore, giving the required free movement.

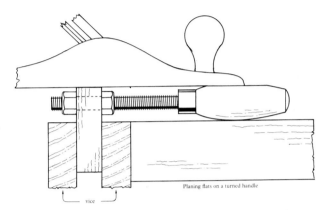

Planing flats on a turned handle

vice

Fig. 426

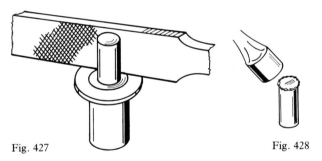

Fig. 427   Fig. 428

Appendix 4   Threads and Nuts in Wood

Cutting threads

A tap of limited life, for cutting threads in wood, can easily be made from a short piece of screwed rod, Fig. 429.

Saw off, say, 3 in (75 mm) and file four tapered flats which, at the end, more than remove the thread. Add two lock-nuts. Screw into a correctly drilled hole with a spanner. After use, clean the tool with a wire brush. When several holes are to be tapped, it is worth drilling a short length of steel strip and fixing this between the two nuts making a tommy bar.

When using manufactured taps, use only the first or

Fig. 429   An improvised tap for wood

taper tap. Screw this in until the end protrudes only slightly. The same applies to the above. Thus the thread in the hole is incompletely cut, giving a strong grip on the screwed rod when it is forced in using two lock-nuts.

Convenient tapping sizes for wood

BSW	in	mm		M	mm
$\frac{1}{4}$	$\frac{3}{16}$	5		6	5
$\frac{5}{16}$	$\frac{1}{4}$	6·5		8	6·5
$\frac{3}{8}$	$\frac{5}{16}$	8		10	8.5
$\frac{1}{2}$	$\frac{3}{8}$	10.5		12	10

Sinking in nuts
Fig. 430
Bore a hole just deeper than the nut thickness and of the same diameter as the distance across the flats, i.e. the spanner size. Then bore through using a drill of the screw diameter. Press the nut into its hole by means of a piece of screwed rod and a large washer with a second nut. This method ensures that when a screw is inserted it is perpendicular to the wood surface. This is not necessarily the case when the nut is hammered in or crushed in with a G cramp.

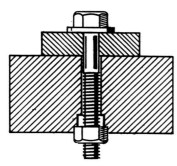

Fig. 429

Appendix 5   Metalwork

Hardening and Tempering
The bulk of steel generally available is mild steel, which cannot be hardened and therefore will not hold an edge. For cutting tools something better is required. This is sold under various terms; tool steel, silver steel, ground flat stock or gauge plate. When bought this is soft enough to saw and file a cutter to shape. To harden this is heated to a very bright red. For small items a propane torch is adequate, the work being supported on fire-bricks, arranged to concentrate the heat.

When really red, the tool is quenched in a can of water or, probably better, of oil. It is now glass hard, brittle and quite unsuitable for use. The hardness needs to be tempered, i.e. modified, to a state of hardness suitable for its purpose. It must be hard enough to keep an edge yet able to be sharpened. Too brittle an edge will chip on the very hard woods.

To do this, first clean up one face with emery cloth until it is bright again and free from scale. When gently heated, colour changes will be observed, starting at pale yellow and ending at a rich purple. When the required colour reaches the cutting edge the tool is again quenched to prevent further progress. On small pieces the changes are too rapid to handle so they are placed on a much larger piece of steel, which slows the process down. If the colour is missed, the entire process can be started again from the beginning. The darker is the colour, the less is the hardness.

An approximate guide to colour selection is as follows.

Pale yellow	—	Scribers
Pale straw	—	Hammer faces
Middle straw	—	Brace bits, machine cutters
Dark straw	—	Twist drills, punches, wood-turning tools, plane irons, chisels, gouges, knives, scratch tool cutters.
Blue	—	Screwdrivers

Should a tool in practice lose its edge too quickly, re-temper to the next lighter colour.

Silver soldering and brazing
This must not be confused with the more common lead or soft soldering which has nothing like the strength. More heat is needed and totally different materials. Silver solder and brazing rod are bought in long thin strips which can easily be snipped into small pieces. Different melting points are available but for the work required by the woodworker choose the lowest melting point available. The special flux is also different. This comes as a powder to be mixed in small quantities with water to the consistency of cream.

The essence of silver soldering is scrupulous cleanliness. The joint must be bright and totally free from dirt, scale and grease. It must also be of a good fit since this solder cannot be flooded in to fill gaps. The joint must be firmly held together by rivetting, cramping or with binding wire. The joint area is painted with the flux which is then allowed to dry. Small snips of solder, about ⅛ in (3 mm) square are similarly coated and applied to the job. Heat is applied. A propane torch is sufficient for the work described here. Suddenly the solder will melt and run. It can sometimes be helped on its way with a tickler, which is a pointed piece of thick wire, not galvanized. This will have been heated and dipped into the flux powder. If a touch more flux fails to complete the run of the solder, there is some dirt. Let the work cool, clean well and start again.

When cold, remove the scale with an old file, then clean and polish with successively finer grades of emery cloth.

Appendix 6   Fixing Pressure Feet on Cramps
Fig. 431
These feet must be free to remain stationary as the screw turns. They may be square or round.

File or turn a spigot on the screw end, counterbore it slightly, then countersink. Drill the foot to accept the

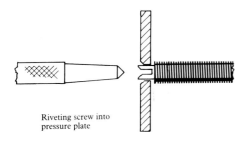

Riveting screw into pressure plate

Fig. 431

spigot as a loose fit. Countersink well. Now assemble and, with a large centre punch, swell out the spigot sufficiently to keep the foot in place. While doing this, the screw can be gripped in the vice using a nut with a sawcut in one side.

Appendix 7   Drawing a Spiral
Fig. 432
This shape is useful when making holding devices using cams.

Draw suitable concentric circles and 12 equi-spaced radii. Plot, as shown, moving out one circle at each radius. For finer adjustment, draw closer circles.

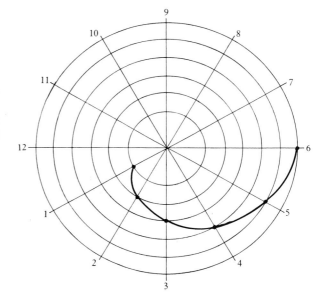

Fig. 432

Appendix 8   Scale drawings of fully adjustable jack plane and smoothing plane (see pages 116–119)

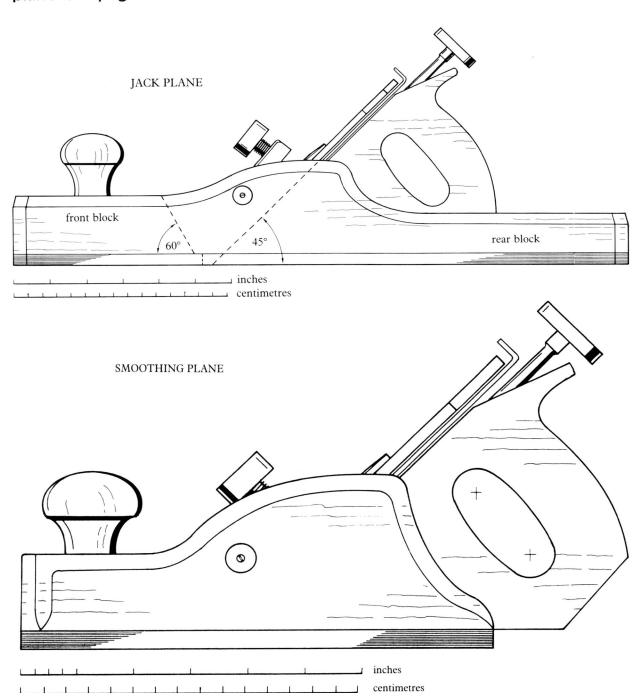

JACK PLANE

front block

60°

45°

rear block

inches

centimetres

SMOOTHING PLANE

inches

centimetres

Glossary of Equivalent British and American Terms

BRITISH	AMERICAN
Araldite	Epoxy resin
Battens	Wood flooring
Countersink screw	Flathead screw
Cramp	Clamp
Communal workshop	Community workshop
DIY shops	Crafts and hobby shops
Drilling machine	Drill press when referring to upright drilling machine
Felt marker	Soft-tipped marker
Fix	Attach
G-cramp	C-clamp
Glasspaper	Sandpaper
Housing joint	Dado joint
Laundry boiler	Dryer
Motor-car	Automobile
Panel pin	Brad
Plough	Plow
Plough plane	Plow plane
Polythene	Polyethylene
Rebate	Rabbet
Sawbench	Table saw
Stoutheart	Manufactured plywood with very thick center
Surface planer	Jointer
Tenon saw	Backsaw
Thicknesser	Surfacer
Timber	Lumber if cut; timber if standing
Vice	Vise

Index